Joyce's *Ulysses* as National Epic

The Florida James Joyce Series

Copyright 2002 by Andras Ungar. This work is licensed under a modified Creative Commons Attribution-Noncommercial-No Derivative Works 3.0 Unported License. To view a copy of this license, visit *http://creativecommons.org/licenses/by-nc-nd/3.0/*. You are free to electronically copy, distribute, and transmit this work if you attribute authorship. *However, all printing rights are reserved by the University Press of Florida (http://www.upf.com). Please contact UPF for information about how to obtain copies of the work for print distribution.* You must attribute the work in the manner specified by the author or licensor (but not in any way that suggests that they endorse you or your use of the work). For any reuse or distribution, you must make clear to others the license terms of this work. Any of the above conditions can be waived if you get permission from the University Press of Florida. Nothing in this license impairs or restricts the author's moral rights.

Florida A&M University, Tallahassee
Florida Atlantic University, Boca Raton
Florida Gulf Coast University, Ft. Myers
Florida International University, Miami
Florida State University, Tallahassee
University of Central Florida, Orlando
University of Florida, Gainesville
University of North Florida, Jacksonville
University of South Florida, Tampa
University of West Florida, Pensacola

Joyce's *Ulysses* as National Epic

Epic Mimesis and the Political History
of the Nation State

Andras Ungar

University Press of Florida
Gainesville · Tallahassee · Tampa · Boca Raton
Pensacola · Orlando · Miami · Jacksonville · Ft. Myers

Copyright 2002 by Andras Ungar

All rights reserved

07 06 05 04 03 02   6 5 4 3 2 1

Library of Congress Cataloging-in-Publication Data
Ungar, Andras, 1947–
Joyce's Ulysses as national epic : epic mimesis and the political history
of the nation state / Andras Ungar.
p. c.m. (The Florida James Joyce series)
Includes bibliographical references and index.
ISBN: 978-1-61610-140-4
1. Joyce, James, 1882–1941. Ulysses. 2. Nationalism and literature—
Ireland—History—20th century. 3. Politics and literature—Ireland—
History—20th century. 4. National characteristics, Irish, in literature.
5. Epic literature—History and criticism. 6. Fables—History and criticism.
7. Ireland—in literature. 8. Mimesis in literature. I. Title. II. Series.
PR6019.O9 U753 2002
823'.912—dc 21   2001054025

The University Press of Florida is the scholarly publishing agency
for the State University System of Florida, comprising Florida A&M
University, Florida Atlantic University, Florida Gulf Coast University,
Florida International University, Florida State University, University
of Central Florida, University of Florida, University of North Florida,
University of South Florida, and University of West Florida.

University Press of Florida
15 Northwest 15th Street
Gainesville, FL 32611-2079
http://www.upf.com

Contents

Foreword by Zack Bowen   vii

Acknowledgments   ix

Abbreviations   xi

Introduction. The Epic Fable: A Negotiation with History and Nationhood   1

1. The Argument of the Fable: An Overview   24

2. The Ascent of Stephen Dedalus from Messianic Ambition to Epic Discourse   35

3. Joyce and the Fate of Arthur Griffith's *Resurrection of Hungary* in *Ulysses*   49

4. Closure and Millicent Bloom   67

5. Epic Mimesis and the Syntax of *Ulysses*   80

6. Other Alternatives: Nationhood and Forgetfulness   94

Notes   109

Bibliography   129

Index   147

Foreword

Andras Ungar's *Joyce's* Ulysses *as National Epic* embodies some of the most original and plausible ideas behind the methodology, structure, and sources of *Ulysses* to come along in more than a decade. Ungar stresses the importance of epic parallels in the novel in translating them into a familial fable of Irish sovereignty in keeping with the epic's traditional interpretation as an allegory of nationhood. Manifest in his book is the exceptional idea of *Ulysses* as a real Irish nationalistic epic in its most ancient and politically figurative form, ultimately drawing on Arthur Griffith's version of Sinn Fein for a promise of Ireland's future emergence as a sovereign country.

Ungar begins by redefining/clarifying the intent and purposes of the epic in regard to the various nationalistic epics of antiquity: the *Aeneid*'s relationship to the foundation of the Roman Empire and its future destiny and the celebration of Portugal and its empire in *The Lusiads*, both turning the epic into a fable of national consciousness. "By making its own fable the essential frame of the articulation of this horizon, for the conjunction between the quest for an appropriate epic voice and national self-awareness, *Ulysses* connects its Dublin scenes and conversations to the grand lexicon of legitimacy in the West. The result is a celebration of the epic as a formative power in everyday life."

Joyceans have been struggling for a long time to provide a sufficient answer to the problem of Joyce's intent beyond the mere comic value of parody in connecting his novel to Homer's great ur-epic. Ungar's solution is that Joyce is going far beyond his stated goals for *Dubliners* in exposing Ireland's hemophilia/GPI, when in *Ulysses* he pursues a path toward eventual salvation laid out in Griffith's *Resurrection of Hungary*. While we have already made a good deal of the political implications of Griffith's pamphlet in Joyce's work, no one I know of until Ungar traced its connection to the events following the turn of the century and the evolution/

decline of the Hapsburg Empire in terms of Joyce's presence in Trieste in the middle of the historical upheaval in which the politics of Hungary's "resurrection" were taking place. Applied to the idea of Joyce's celebration of the epic fable as a formative power in everyday life and creation, Joyce's scene of 1904 Ireland, at a crossroads of its own nationalistic destiny, expropriates the significance of Sinn Fein for its own political fable of national destiny, weaving the whole into the domestic drama of the Blooms' extended household.

While the history of the Sinn Fein party and the politics of the 1922 treaty are generally well known to Joyceans, the details of the relationships of the crowns of St. Leopold and St. Stephen in the Hapsburg/Hungarian context of late-nineteenth- and early-twentieth-century Europe, particularly disputed territories like Trieste, may come as news, as they are linked to the Joycean vision of the Nova Hibernia of the future. Throughout, Ungar's close reading of segments of *Ulysses* produces new interpretations founded in nearly every case not on speculation but on solid historical grounds and common sense.

Zack Bowen
Series Editor

Acknowledgments

Many people have contributed to the shaping of this text. I'd like to thank my readers at the University Press of Florida: Zack Bowen for his patience and suggestions; Dominic Manganiello for his encouragement; Enda Duffy for his careful survey of the whole argument and detailed commentary.

I remain grateful to Joseph Ronsley, then of McGill University, for patience in his encounters with several *ur*-versions of the argument. I profited from conversations with Marika Finlay, Bob Myles, Richard Cooper, Robert Holton, and Robert Bennet, at the time all at McGill, for strands of this composition. At Concordia University, where I completed several degrees and have now taught for many more years than I was a student, I have learned a great deal from G. David Sheps' interest in modern literature, Eyvind Ronquist's work on Dante, Laszlo Gefin's analysis of Pound, and Fred Krantz's studies in *menschheit*. I'd like to thank Ramesh Rambaran at the Webster Library for his help and consideration and my students both in the English Department and at the Liberal Arts College for helping to keep alive the ideas that went into this work.

I can't begin to detail my debt to my family. This book owes a great deal to my late father, who never heard of Joyce. A refugee from Stalinist Hungary, fatally ill soon after his arrival in Canada, he was determined to understand the politics and historical events that had destroyed his first family and had forced him to emigrate with the very young children of his second family. I owe my interest in history and language to the daily duty of having to translate for him at an age when I could hardly manage English or the news. My father had a terrific appreciation of how practical things worked. In Joyce, I was attracted to the intellectual horizon of an émigré, a poet with infinitely complicated talents who was committed to elaborate conversations with acquaintances, poets, historians, and politicians, living and dead, and who thrived on the practical difficulties of providing a coherent historical account. Bela Ungar would have wanted to know how Joyce's story worked.

I'd like to thank Viola Schwartz-Ungar, Suzanne Ungar, Giselle Foti, and especially Kathryn Gill for just being around and for forbearance, humor, and support throughout the long composition of this book.

Some of the material here has appeared in print previously as "Among the Hapsburgs: Arthur Griffith, Stephen Dedalus and the Myth of Bloom," *Twentieth Century Literature* 35.4 (winter 1989): 480–501; "Joyce's Hungarian in Ulysses," *James Joyce Quarterly*, 27 (1990): 648–50; and "Ulysses in Ulysses: What the Nolan Said," in *A Small Nation's Contribution to the World: Essays on Anglo-Irish Literature and Language*, ed. Donald E. Morse (Gerrards Cross, Buckinghamshire, England: Colin Smythe, 1993).

Abbreviations

The following abbreviations in parentheses appear in the text.

Simple parentheses without any letters refer to chapter and line in *Ulysses*, for example (1.11). I used the 1986 Gabler edition.

(D) *Dubliners*. London: Jonathan Cape, 1967.

(FW) *Finnegans Wake*. London: Faber, 1982.

(G&S) Don Gifford with Robert J. Seidman. *Ulysses Annotated: Notes for James Joyce's Ulysses*. Rev. and exp. ed. Berkeley: University of California Press, 1988.

(P) *A Portrait of the Artist as a Young Man*. London: Penguin, 1976.

Introduction

The Epic Fable: A Negotiation with History and Nationhood

Ulysses' distinctive contribution to historiography is as comprehensive as its systematic elaboration of the expressive possibilities of different styles. With apparently atavistic nonchalance, *Ulysses* recovers the claims of the epic to represent historical events and the communal "we," a premise of coherent narrative representation both for historians concerned with collective agency in the past and for nationalists concerned with future communal self-definition. *Ulysses* construes the epic, which since the Enlightenment had been deemed inherently not "suited," in Hayden White's phrase, "to the representation of historical events," as a distinct discursive opportunity for historiography, distinct from, but in close dialogue with, the present-mindedness that treats history as representative of current concerns and comes to the fore with twentieth-century historiography.[1]

Ulysses, in other words, earns the invidious label "time-book," though not at all in the privative sense that Wyndham Lewis intended.[2] Joyce's extraordinarily reflective attention to his craft did not lapse when the detail prefigured specifically historical arguments. Indeed, it is when we note the absence of a privileged role for a deliberative middle style as the medium appropriate for historiographic representation that we form a first notion of the extent of the discursive domain that Ulysses has reserved for innovation.

Ulysses implicitly argues that epic precedent constitutes the cohesion required in the representation of historical agency. The epic fable negotiates a continuous self-reflective dynamic relation between the action of the characters and the historical constraints on the formation and expression of a national communal identity.

In effect, *Ulysses'* shaping of the epic as historiography belongs with the late-nineteenth-century shift in historical study from concentration on political history toward various forms of interdisciplinarity. Innovative German historians—Lamprecht, Schmoller, Hintze—opted for historical narrative sustained by borrowings from social sciences. "New Historians" in the United States—Charles Beard, James H. Robinson, Vernon Parrington, Perry Miller, Frederick Jackson Turner—prepared studies around the influence of the economy, ideas, religion, and the frontier. The *Annales* historians in France shifted the focus to geography, economics, and anthropology, replacing the linear view of time with a nonprogressive, relative, and multilayered understanding.[3] *Ulysses*, in an analogous move, borrows and adapts a pattern of expectation from the tradition of the epic, a loan and adaptation which it is the prime concern of this book to specify and describe, and which subtends a highly self-critical allegory of contemporary political developments.

The move is radically new and surprisingly conservative. *Ulysses* has withdrawn from "the de-rhetoricisation of historical thinking," from the project of methodological restraint deemed by White the acme of modern historical writing.[4] The radically heterodox medium for historical reflection in the wake of this withdrawal hosts every kind of extravagance. Incidents that would traditionally have been "conceived to be the stuff of religious belief and ritual (miracles, magical events, godly events)" compete with material apt for "farce, satire, and calumny."[5] Simultaneously, however, *Ulysses* annexes this disruption of historiographic convention to a sustained meditation on contemporary Ireland's awareness of having arrived at a turning point in its history and to the concern with the political history of the nation-state, the raison d'être of nineteenth-century history.[6]

Ulysses construes the writing of history on the model of the epic's traditional concern with the establishment of legitimacy. At issue is the modality of the communal "we," the requirement, equally, for the transmission of a distinctive narrative and for national vision. In approximating this communal focus, *Ulysses* resumes the perennial conversation with the epic tradition.

This recourse to the epic as a touchstone for historical argument is rich with precedent. At the turn of the twentieth century, discussions of the link between history and literature were commonplace. Dilthey, Croce, Collingwood, all called explicitly on imaginative vision to serve as a tool of investigation; Pound and Eliot had "investigations of history" frame the workings of imagination.[7] Much earlier, in *The Aeneid*, Virgil had imprinted epic scenes with politically motivated interpretations of Roman history. *The Aeneid* has Jupiter praise empire, Anchises foresee the rule of the Caesars, and Aeneas's shield prefigure imperial triumphs.[8] In overstepping the boundary between literature and history without the extravagant signposts of its later styles, *Ulysses* relies on this heterogeneous context as precedent.

Ulysses elaborates the fable of Stephen Dedalus's encounter with Leopold Bloom and their efforts at continuity as the embodiment or, in G. M. Hopkins's phrase, the "bodying forth" of a historical self-understanding possible for Ireland in the wake of these concerns.[9] This approach to historical representation nevertheless departs from the treatment of historical change in Joyce's earlier work. *Dubliners* had presented history as the absent cause of national paralysis. *A Portrait of the Artist as a Young Man* had dramatized the hope that a "Great Man" would create an alternative to the deformed legacy of the Irish past. *Ulysses* treats the making of history, the prospect of a distinctively contemporary Irish historical horizon, as a fait accompli. In representing this self-understanding, it adds incrementally to the vision. The self-awareness enables a conversation about the parameters of historical experience that is much more substantial and far-ranging than the poetics of the earlier works had permitted.

The readiest analogue for the resumption of this conversation with the epic tradition is Virgil's return to Troy in his apologia for Rome. The fable of *Ulysses* exploits the coincidence between its own publication and the proclamation of the first sovereign Irish state in seven hundred years as the occasion for a comparable disquisition. The coincidence serves as a warrant for making the historical prospect and destiny of Ireland a principal theme, an epic warrant prefigured by *The Aeneid*'s vision of a future Rome and by *The Lusiads*'s celebration of Portugal and its empire. By making its own fable the essential frame of the articulation of this horizon, for the conjunction between the quest for an appropriate epic voice and national self-awareness, *Ulysses* connects its Dublin scenes and conversations to the grand lexicon of legitimacy in the West.

This is tantamount to a celebration of the epic as a formative power in everyday life. This holistic, material celebration of epic comprehensiveness cannot be confused either with the idealizing abstraction of the classical past evident in Tennyson's passéism[10] or with the modernist dilution of a specific, and inherently epic, function as in Hugh Kenner's characterization of *The Odyssey* as "Western man's pioneer novel."[11] Instead, the fable of *Ulysses*, as contemporary as archaic, constitutes a site, reflective and proleptic and functional. It concentrates the action responsible for the shaping of the polity in a synthetic overview of the comprehensiveness of communal destiny and creativity on the model of *The Aeneid* and *The Lusiads*. Through the sustained reflection on the epic task, the fable links the self-awareness of the Irish polity and the imperatives of positivist historiographic documentation to the rhetorical force of the powerful topos of "natality, the corner stone," in Hannah Arendt's phrase, "of the human condition."[12]

The result is an exploratory historiography open to universalist claims and also able to accommodate explicitly the otherness, the deadness, that shapes the characters of *Dubliners* and the ironic postponement of formative achievement that Stephen Dedalus contends with in *Portrait* and encounters again in the *Telemachiad* chapters. The fit between the ironic liminality of community in these earlier writings and the generous exfoliation of communal bonds in *Ulysses* suggests a triadic sequence and *Ulysses* as mastering contradictions in a quasi-Hegelian synthesis of earlier naively passive, quasi-objective, and vaingloriously self-determined subjective moments. In such a progression *Dubliners*, *Portrait*, and *Ulysses* function as symbolic shorthand for, respectively, a history-burdened actuality, a messianic subjectivity, and national self-definition.

This is a stronger statement of the case than I would argue. James Longenbach described the distinctive twentieth-century stance in historiography as the "rejection of the presuppositions about the nature of historical knowledge that make the construction of any sort of teleological or even linear event possible."[13] *Ulysses* conforms to this rejection. Its resuscitation of the epic, in historiography an obsolete mode of discourse, brackets teleology in a new way. Instead of a submerged Hegelian logos, the recourse to the epic tradition opens the prospect of an open-ended meditation on historical continuity, present-minded but resistant to foreshortening the prospect to accord with current definitions. While acutely attentive to implications of tradition, *Ulysses'* resumption of the conversation ensures that the significance of a historic moment will be recognized as finally sui generis.

It made it easier to turn to the epic for such a synthetic representation of historical change that events in Ireland were arguing for a dramatic climax which, at least in the short run, suggested that Irish history would have to foreground the traditional value of communal self-determination. Ireland was about to achieve a measure of political sovereignty for the first time in seven hundred years. In formal scope, if not in metaphysical sweep, such a redefinition of the political context allowed for a potential resolution of the deadlock and isolation featured in the earlier works. In refusing the self-limitation of *Dubliners* and the mistaken solace of an aesthetically self-subsisting and historically ideal artist figure of *Portrait*, able, in Ezra Pound's mistaken appreciation, to describe "things as they are, not only for Dublin, but for every city," the resort to the epic genre holds out the promise of a broad synoptic understanding.[14]

The element complicating such a design is the modern phenomenon of nationality. Tom Nairn has recently speculated that the recurrent problem in modern thought might well be the intractability of this inevitable aspect of social experience to adequate symbolization. "The true subject of modern philosophy is nationalism, not industrialization," he writes, "the nation, not the steam engine and the computer."[15] Whatever one concludes about this ranking of the phenomenon, it is patent that, in addition to historical accounts, the formulae for its regulation include the constitutions of states, unitary and federal, and philosophical anthropologies with investments in political equality or political disequilibrium. An adequate account of nationality, while paradigmatic for rational collective agency, figures among the recurrent issues of political life.

The need for a programmatic approach to the political status of Ireland as part Britain was a hotly debated topic in contemporary Irish politics. The index of the mounting radicalism of debate is the rising significance of Sinn Fein. In the parliamentary elections subsequent to the collapse of the 1916 Easter Rebellion, Sinn Fein captured 73 of 106 Irish seats. Through 1919, Sinn Fein constituted itself, albeit illegally, as an independent parliament in Dublin. There was war between Sinn Fein and the British through 1920, climaxing on "Bloody Sunday," November 21, 1920, in Dublin. The British Parliament passed the Government of Ireland Act in 1920, granting Ireland, without Ulster, quasi-dominion status. The Dáil ratified the treaty, proclaiming the Irish Free State on December 6, 1922, with Arthur Griffith, the founder of Sinn Fein, the chair of the Executive Council.

Ulysses translates this preeminence into the epic design. In this perspective, the salient point is Sinn Fein's climactic role. For Joyce, at least in 1906, the choice, he informed his brother, Stanislaus, was "Sinn Fein or Imperialism," the ascendancy of Griffith's party or the continued British rule of Ireland.[16]

The recognition of this point does not detract from Emer Nolan's observation that *Ulysses* foregoes the opportunity to endorse either of the "two traditions" that are generally accepted "in Irish nationalist history: the extremist and radical 'physical force' tradition and the reasonable, constitutional one."[17] Nor does the recognition of the importance of Griffith's Sinn Fein imply that Joyce subscribed to, or overlooked, the less salubrious aspects of Griffith's program: his pro-imperialism, anti-Semitism, and racism.[18]

Ulysses expropriates the significance of Sinn Fein for its own fable. The engagement is analogous to the commitment Nolan identifies as a "narrational complex," a site of dramatic energy motivating the communities of speech and the public world of *Ulysses*, which, in Nolan's reading, hosts a choric allegiance by the work to nationalist values.[19] I will argue that *Ulysses* sidesteps the need to underwrite such an amorphous response. Instead, the epic design of the work formulates a comprehensive reflection on the historical conjunction that in 1904 signaled the prospect of future Irish political independence from Britain.

Ulysses contextualizes the prospects of Irish nationhood within its compositional frame. The central encounter of Stephen Dedalus and Leopold Bloom engages epic precedent in a suggestive twofold response. The practice sanctioned by Virgil and by Camões of providing the polity with a vision of its genesis and essential features guides both aspects of the design. However, the pattern is fluid. The freedom of the formal deployment resembles topological investigations of the archaic that "work backwards into the past from physical and rhetorical *topoi* made fragmentary by breaks in tradition."[20] *Ulysses* postulates this kind of fragmentariness and forgetfulness in its recovery of communal allegiances within secular urban experience.

The appeal is to a readership that appreciates the necessarily tentative application of such a pattern. As an ideal of representation, it is skeptical of closure and open to novelty. David Weir describes the confluence as a recovery of identity-in-opposition, a dialectical relationship pervading an individual's interior and exteriorized experience, involving the constant negotiation of these inner and outer worlds. The final outcome is always deferred.[21]

The reader is required to remain critically alert, proof against the beguilement of closure. As the challenging succession of discrete styles in the second half of *Ulysses* makes evident, the fable of *Ulysses* returns the reader to a preindividualized, pre-Socratic order of experience. To situate the fable, we respond to aspects of the world taking shape in front of our eyes. Rather than fixed design derived from established identities, the fable straddles competing affinities in an open-ended appeal to allegiance and interpretation.

The twofold engagement with epic precedent with which I am concerned twins the immediate political horizon of the polity with the perspective of a distant future. The engagement is analogous to the phenomenon of parallax. Instead of simultaneity or stylistic heterogeneity, the approach hinges on diverse modes of involvement with the life cycle of the polity, on perspectives that, after due allowances have been made, are mutually comprehensible if still challenging.

One aspect of the design appeals to a perspective possible for the generation alive in 1922, who, familiar with contemporary events, would have recognized *Ulysses'* freedom with the historical record and might have drawn conclusions from the changes. The premise of such a step is the rather hubristic proposition that the proclamation of the Irish Free State and the publication of *Ulysses* were phenomena of, at the least, comparable significance for the future of Ireland. The extravagantly hubristic trespass on the discursive preeminence of political history requires a conscious commitment from the reader: the deliberate adhesion, the loan of empathy to the extension of the narrative design.

Hegel distinguished sharply between two kinds of historiography: the testimony of "family memorials, patriarchal traditions . . . [with] an interest confined to the family and the clan . . . [that] is not subject to serious remembrance" and discourse devoted to the State, an entity that does not only "present subject matter . . . adapted to the prose of History, but involves the production of such history in the very progress of its own being."[22] *Ulysses* brackets this distinction and proceeds to unravel Irish political history through the family concerns of its dramatis personae.

A central aspect of this focus is the coincidence between *Ulysses'* eventual publication and the return of Irish sovereignty. In a sustained gesture, *Ulysses* appropriates the argument current in 1904 concerning the future of Ireland, which readers in 1922 would have judged to have been the political development most prescient about the establishment of Irish sovereignty eighteen years later. The developing relationship of Stephen and Bloom performs this reading of recent Irish history. The performance requires that readers recontextualize aspects of Irish national self-definition through the fable of *Ulysses*. Through this claim on the most comprehensive vision of Ireland available in 1904, the recently publicized program of Arthur Griffith's Sinn Fein, *Ulysses* asks to be construed as vitally implicated, quite literally, as I seek to show in chapters 4 and 5, in the material genesis of the future Ireland. In this sense, *Ulysses* monumentalizes its own fable.

A view so removed from the everyday reverses the archaic temporal horizon of toponymic inquiry through the appeal to the understanding of distant, unknown, future generations. For these possible descendants, who would not even be Irish in a style recognizable to Joyce's contemporaries, *Ulysses'* treatment of the foundation of the Irish polity would have the aura of epic foundational moments: Virgil's paen to imperial Rome in *The Aeneid*, the Pentateuch's commemoration of Israel's covenant with Yahweh, or the celebration of Portuguese national identity in *The Lusiads*. Thanks to the distance, national identity in this perspective, impossible for the generation alive in 1922, has self-evident coherence. Irish continuity through time would be sufficient occasion for its retroactive celebration. The account might aspire to the coherence of legend and myth without worries about empirical documentation and historical method.

In this book, I will be describing the strategy that constitutes *Ulysses'* mediation of these two perspectives on nation formation. As far as I am aware, the role of the epic fable as a historical argument mediating between present and future has not received any critical attention.

There are very good reasons for the oversight. The large and recurring discursive gaps in the text obviously seem to challenge the rhetorical focus of the kind of achievement ascribed to Aeneas, Moses, and Vasco da Gama. The "epic hero" is passive in *Ulysses*, and the "epic action" is inconclusive. The treatment of Irish nationalists is mockingly irreverent. *Ulysses* does not focus on a radically formative intervention in the world, on the serious—that is, nonparodic—actions which the epic should celebrate.

Even more fundamental is the circumstance that the epic genre itself seems intrinsically foreign to, in fact, a kind of antagonist of, the modern age. Thus, Theodore Adorno describes "contemporary novels that count [as] those in which an unleashed subjectivity turns into its opposite" and then tags these "negative epics," noting that they "delight in dissonance and release . . . [in] a state of affairs in which the individual liquidates himself." The hallmark of the dissonance is a breakdown of the ability to tell "whether the goal of a historical tendency . . . is a regression to barbarism or the realization of humanity."[23] Similarly, for Franco Moretti the modern epic, a category that includes *Faust, Leaves of Grass, Moby-Dick, Ulysses*, and *A Hundred Years of Solitude*, cannot register what Hegel described as "a living attitude of mind."²⁴ In its stead, we have a residual polyphony that testifies to the abandonment of individual effort to order the world, to the "discrepancy between the totalizing will of the epic and the subdivided reality of the modern world."²⁵ Polyphony and indeterminacy facilitate the conception of events in terms of agencies such as "feminine narcissistic discourse" and "phallocentric male discourse."²⁶

The scale of abstraction diminishes the value of deliberate human agency. The bias argues against the likelihood of a coherent engagement with the historical complexity of nationality and nation building. The epic, the editors of a recent anthology argue, has "typically claimed to narrate the recovery of an originary identity of a group by linguistic ties (the Homeric epic), tribal bonds (the African poem "Sun-jata"), religion (the Pentateuch), nationality (Camões's *Lusiads*), or empire (Virgil's *Aeneid*)."²⁷ A genre characterized so monumentally, it seems, cannot have anything in common with the discipline of empirical historical research.

I will be arguing that the fable of *Ulysses* engages the thematic horizon of nationality and nation building, with due attention to historical evidence and genre constraints, a performance that has lacked attention because of contemporary prejudice against the likelihood of the epic in the twentieth century seriously undertaking such a task. *Ulysses* accords the epic a functional relevance. The fable of *Ulysses* manipulates the terms of this engagement and elaborates a comprehensive reflection on national identity on the scale of *The Aeneid*'s orchestration of the Roman past. In this sense, the fable's sustained perspective on Ireland's historical destiny is an epic achievement.

By the term *fable*, I refer to a formally relatively underspecified segment of narrative. It includes the basic story materials, corresponding to *fabula*, to *histoire*, and to *story* in works on narrative by, respectively, Propp, Barthes, and Chatman.²⁸ The fable of *Ulysses* involves Stephen Dedalus and Leopold Bloom, their hopes of continuity, and the checks on these hopes. It is especially concerned with the drama of Stephen's need to imagine himself afresh on his return to Dublin and with Bloom's desire for an heir, mirrored in his recollections of his father, Rudolf; in his memories of his son, Rudy; in his attraction to Stephen; in his speculations about Stephen's future; and in his hopes for his absent daughter, Milly. Through these materials, the fable attempts a continuity that is eventually dispersed in a process Robert Spoo has described as a "pragmatic, anti-essentialist immersion in history and textuality, an immersion so complete that narrative meaning in any conventional sense may be impossible."[29] I will be describing the epic fable as this minimal narrative unit attempts this continuity in the environment of *Ulysses*.

This diachronic remnant is entirely distinct from the Homeric parallel. Frederic Jameson is quite right to insist that the parallel with *The Odyssey* is "not itself the interpretation" of the narrative. However, his suggestion that it is *The Odyssey* parallel "qua organizational framework [that] . . . remains to be interpreted" skews inquiry into the epic performance needlessly toward Homer.[30] Interpretation is not to be confined in this way. Joyce's practice, David Weir has observed, "always seems to run slightly ahead of his aesthetic; that is, the technical means to a particular effect always go beyond aesthetic effect alone and create effects in addition to the original aims of the aesthetic."[31] The action of the fable has this unpredictability. The fable, like plot in Peter Brooks's definition, functions as a "principle of interconnectedness and intention that we cannot do without in moving through the discrete elements" of the narrative.[32] However, the action of the fable, an approximation of a synthesis limited by the criterion of "identity-in-difference," entails an open-ended commitment, a boundless—dare I say "epic"—horizon, which subsumes earlier instances such as Homer without restriction to such models.

To what extent can this "principle of interconnectedness" in this open-ended prospect be specified in the abstract? The fable draws on the life of contemporary Dublin. It presupposes that an eponymous master code to the communal experience of modern Ireland may be uncovered in the fates of the characters. Individual traits serve as indexes to historical choices. The narrated action is a cipher to collective destiny. It corresponds to something like Eric Auerbach's notion of legend as a tale comprised of syncopated references to "a great number of contradictory motives . . . [to a] hesitant and ambiguous groping on the part of [social] groups."[33] The fable of *Ulysses* indicates a simplified summary overview of Dublin life, eliding many cross-purposes, which, thanks to historical hindsight and the epic sanction of national self-definition as a commemorative occasion, includes skeletal traces of the future.

The overview concerns a turning point in the history of Irish nationality and communal destiny. The imminence of Irish independence focuses a comprehensive vision of the polity, a mode of closure as comprehensive as Herder's foundational notion of the Volk, a totality, a Volkgeist, the "metaphysical entity" responsible for "a particular language, art, culture, set of great men, religion, and collection of customs."[34]

We approximate the comprehensiveness of this focus by concentrating on a specifically epic aura, the phenomenon of "pastness." In *Ulysses*, this is tantamount to a reconsideration of the traditional epic topos of national renewal. The fable renders the fait accompli as a compact with destiny, the quotidian as motivated by a horizon of potential significance that saps it of arbitrariness.

Such foreshadowing of significance through the fable can perhaps most readily be situated on the model of the French literary tense, the *prétérit*. Barthes describes the treatment of time in the *prétérit*, a purely literary tense, and therefore outside of daily experience, in the following way:

> Obsolete in spoken French, the *prétérit*, which is the cornerstone of Narration, always signifies the presence of Art; it is a part of a ritual of Letters. Its function is no longer that of a tense. The part it plays is to reduce reality to a point of time, and to abstract from the depth of a multiplicity of experiences, a pure verbal act, freed from existential roots of knowledge, and directed toward a logical link with other acts, other processes, a general movement of the world.[35]

The foreshortening of the cause-effect operative in the *prétérit* suggests an elemental narrative nexus, a kind of virtual context for events, a readiness for an order of significance distinct from commonplace multiplicity. *Ulysses* elaborates its claim to epic lineage in a medium able to sustain a comprehensive reflection on the making of the Irish polity and nationality, on contemporary moves toward state formation and on the future of Ireland, at a virtual remove from the ordinary and the accidental comparable to this elemental narrative nexus.

From this stance, this epic function maintains a dialogue with the preoccupations of cultural nationalists for whom "the nation is the primordial expression of individuality and the creative force of nature."[36] Motifs congruent with the theme of nation-making get foregrounded in this exchange. Myths that affirm the unity and continuity of national experience are prominent. From other national histories, Lawrence M. Friedman cites as instances the story of William Tell and the apple, Alexander Nevsky's victory over the Teutonic knights, the mission of Joan of Arc, and the Jewish exile in Babylon.[37]

In form, this function sidesteps the invidious distinction between "the past" and "historiography," the dichotomy responsible for the opposition, according to Keith Jenkins, of the "modern" and the "postmodern" in historical writing. For Jenkins, the terms distinguish between the object of historical study "speaking itself" and a self-consciously constructivist view of the object as constituted by contemporary concerns re-created from "traces" of past events that do not in themselves express any kind of narrative pattern.[38] Through its link with the epic tradition, *Ulysses* stakes a claim to a more inclusive discursive domain, one that annexes to the act of composition the concerns with the status of the historical record as fait accompli and with the writing of history as constitutive, per se, of history.

The epic telos avoids the alternatives Jenkins poses through the assumption that the making of history is its raison d'être. In "speaking itself," the epic performance enacts the standard that situates its audience's claim to legitimacy. *Ulysses'* performance is comprehensive and dramatic in this inclusive manner.

The representation spans extremes. Robert Spoo has drawn attention to the "opening paragraphs of the 'Oxen of the Sun,'" the chapter which in microcosm presents the stylistic variety and concern with birth and renewal in *Ulysses*. He notes that "Oxen of the Sun" mounts a "siege [against] the sentence as a unit of meaning" interfering with even a minimalist teleology.[39] In contrast to this, the fable tends toward holistic affirmation. It invokes completion without ever achieving more than an approximate representation of what this totality would be like. We are again reminded of Auerbach's description of legend as "a smoothing down and harmonizing of events, . . . a simplification of motives, . . . a static definition of characters which avoids conflict and development."[40] The epic approach to the significance of the Stephen-Bloom encounter positions it on the verge of enclosure within an always larger domain of significance, on the verge of always having been inevitable.

How does the reader set limits to this epic function in the text? *Ulysses*, as one would expect, has great fun with its candidacy for the role of modern Irish epic, experimenting with the shape of the awaited achievement, muddying the waters for any schematization. The "Scylla and Charybdis" chapter gives us the literati assembled in the National Library acknowledging that national self-awareness has need of just such a crown jewel.

> Our national epic has yet to be written, Dr. Sigerson says. Moore is the man for it. A knight of the rueful countenance here in Dublin. With a saffron kilt? O'Neill Russell? O, yes, he must speak the grand old tongue. And his Dulceana? James Stephens is doing some clever sketches. We are becoming important it seems. (9.310–13)

They are insensible to the radical alternative to earlier ideals of Ireland embodied in Bloom. Joyce seems never to have tired of drawing attention to the change required of Ireland's much too formulaic self-definition.

The massive inflation of Stephen's and Bloom's claims to significance for the story of modern Ireland is a response to this need. In forming its fable as the articulation of Ireland's national destiny, *Ulysses* performs in a compositional horizon conducive to the proliferation of the largest, most inflated, pseudo-historical entities. This is the domain of creatures such as "the Aryan," "the Gaul," "the Saxon," and "the Celt." National feeling, Benedict Anderson has written, balances between a "secular, time-clocked temporality and the epic sense of nations, appearing to loom out of an immemorial past and glide into a limitless future."[41] Stephen and Bloom inherit this magnification.

Joyce reclaims and populates the domain by according the present a potency comparable to that of his predecessors in the epic. The fable of *Ulysses* expands the prospect of nation formation that had been associated with Stephen Dedalus since he announced the metaphorical "forging" of the nation's conscience in *Portrait*. The telos of the process is not parody but a point of view still more inclusive, a voice that accomplishes a critical reflection on Ireland's contemporary effort at self-definition and proposes an alternative to it through the naming and relationships of the principal figures.

In this mode, the fable of Stephen and Bloom enacts the drama of nation formation and hope. The telos of the fable maintains the characters in a movement of atavistic regression to quasi-allegorical significance. With epic pattern separate from their awareness, the invidious effects of the subject-object dichotomy that Adorno judged to be inevitable and the dispersal through commodification that Moretti emphasized do not disrupt the elaboration. Consciousness tends to individualize characters. The epic role de-centers this individuality, preempting differentiation through sensibility.

Georg Lukacs had imagined a "world of deeds" with self-evident meaning where a difference between "interiority and adventure" is simply inconceivable.

> When the world is internally homogenous, men do not differ qualitatively from one another; there are of course heroes and villains, pious men and criminals, but even the greatest hero is only a head

taller than the mass of his fellows, and the wise man's dignified words are heard even by the most foolish. The autonomous life of interiority is possible and necessary only when the distinctions between men have made an unbridgeable chasm ... when the world of deeds separates itself and because of this independence, becomes hollow and incapable of absorbing the true meaning of deeds in itself.[42]

The iteration of basic narrative components foreshadows an engagement productive of all-encompassing significance.

Ulysses sustains this breadth of reference in its consideration of Irish national identity. The fable of Stephen and Bloom weighs the raison d'être of the formative moment of the national polity, as though it were a moment prior to hierarchical order and conceptual refinement. Hegel theorized that the epic aimed to express "the occurrence of an action ... in the whole breadth of its circumstances and relations."[43] With the establishment of the State, something of this autonomy, something of this ability to see the experience as a whole gets turned over to and "objectified in laws and the state apparatus."[44] *Portrait* had treated with irony Stephen Dedalus's imagining his self-realization as one with Ireland's belated individualization when he vowed that he would "forge the conscience of [his] race in the smithy of [his] soul" (253). In *Ulysses*, ironic reflection at Stephen's expense is subordinate to an unfettered effort to do justice to the prospect of Irish national sovereignty.

Turning away from the *Kunstlerroman* trajectory and ironies of *Portrait*, the fable of *Ulysses* incorporates the Irish effort at national definition in a horizon validated by the fable itself. As in the prétérit where, according to Barthes, "the narrator reduces the exploded reality to a slim and pure logos, without density, without volume, without spread whose sole function is to unite as rapidly as possible a cause and an effect," the new orientation channels response to character and events differently.[45] In counterpoint to the polysemic expansion of the text, the fable of *Ulysses* reiterates the identities of Stephen and Leopold, compounded of historical allusion but also self-subsisting, as forms of virtual closure. In this way, the fable of *Ulysses* retrieves the creative force that Hegel had deemed to have been alienated with the foundation of the State, the event that Hegel valued as the original "subject matter ... *adapted* [italics mine] to the prose of History," a social entity that "involves the production of such history in the very progress of its own being."[46]

The design of this claim on our attention deserves to be called epic despite the opprobrium the form has inherited from Bakhtin's invidious comparison of the epic, innately authoritarian and monologic, with the novel. Only the epic, Frederick T. Griffiths and Stanley J. Rabinowitz observe, can "offer for glory or reproach to array *All That Precedes* [italics mine] as a foil for the current dispensation."[47] The achievement of *Ulysses* in this optic is to have reappropriated a primordial freedom to delineate the parameters of communal existence and to have elaborated these parameters as material on every vital point resonant with the horizon of infinity.

We can trace this ideal comprehensiveness in Joyce's earliest fascination with Ibsen. In the essay *Drama and Life*, he interpreted the legacy of the "breaking-up of tradition, which is the work of the modern era" as a call for the artist to integrate the disorder anew, to "express his fable in terms of his characters."[48] With Ibsen's example before him, he imagined an aesthetic order in which "drama would naturally take up its position at head of all artistic institutions."[49] Drama would have this primordial role because Joyce envisioned it as a representational nexus, immediate, appearing "spontaneously out of life and ... coeval with it." Drama always had a national focus. "Every race," Joyce observed, "has made its own myths and it is in there that early drama often finds an outlet."[50] The synoptic view postulated by the achievement points to the artist's having come to terms with communal identity.

From the perspective of the creative artist, the integration of nationality was a challenge. For a lecture to a university audience in Trieste in 1907, Joyce wrote:

> Nationality (if it really is not a convenient fiction like so many others to which the scalpels of present-day scientists have given the coup de grace) must find its reason for being rooted in something that surpasses and transcends and informs changing things like blood and the human word. The mystic theologian who assumed the pseudonym of Dionysus, the pseudo-Areopagite, says somewhere, "God has disposed the limits of nations according to his angels," and this is probably not a purely mystical concept. Do we not see that in Ireland the Danes, the Firbolgs, the Milesians from Spain, the Norman invaders, and the Anglo-Saxon settlers have united to form a new entity, one might say under the influence of a local deity?[51]

The epic dimension of *Ulysses* anthropomorphizes this creative insight.

The fable, like the appeal of national feeling, treats the characters as "at one level of their existence lifted out, abstracted from the binding relations of the flesh." It articulates the abstraction as syntactical order disentangled from personal awareness, while affirming the value of "disembodied relations of time and place."[52] Insofar as it is self-consciously an epic, it undertakes the task with the synthetic reach of a form that had undertaken such comprehensive work repeatedly in Greece, in Rome, and in Florence and thus invites comparison with earlier articulations of communal identity. The distinctive epic form facilitates discussions of national identity, which the amorphous, reactive nature of the phenomenon tends, as Benedict Anderson has recently argued, to frustrate.[53]

It is the possibility of this distinctive, holistic grasp that comes to the fore with Stephen's reappearance in *Ulysses* after his avowal of historic personal significance in *Portrait*. "Conscience recognizes," Gary J. Handwerke notes, "that the subject and the suprapersonal are so inextricably mixed that their reconciliation must be the primary task of consciousness."[54] *Ulysses* addresses the issue by annexing the fable of Stephen Dedalus, Leopold Bloom, and their hopes of continuity to "the shadow of a future immensity," which C. S. Lewis's study of Virgil's *Aeneid* had termed the epic genre's "Great Subject."[55]

Can we read *Ulysses* as though this issue has been merely postponed? What happens if the challenge of such a synoptic understanding is slighted?

Nationalism, Anthony D. Smith writes, through "its ability to unite the dead, the living and the yet unborn in a single community of fate, and through its vision of the judgement of posterity, provides humanity with a secular version of immortality through absorption into the nation."[56] This might bespeak an ideal communal transparency, but it is a formula for the "absurd never-to-be-forgotten Johnny circling the statue of King Billy in *The Dead*" and for the Dubliners who "themselves [circle] endlessly . . . unable to break free from the gravitational pull of the past."[57] Joyce seems to have been convinced that conscience subordinate to national myth meant such an unwitting sacrifice of freedom.

The telos of this consideration in *Ulysses* is an extraordinary celebration of formative force. Whereas for Virgil the "immensity" is the greatness of Rome, "the future of Aeneas's race, the present of the poem's audience," *Ulysses* transposes Stephen's and Leopold's hopes of fulfillment as commentary on an emergent Irish national identity.[58] The epic design assumes a warrant to join "the nation-wide multiform reverie," the common dream which W. B. Yeats deemed to "distinguish [the nation] from a crowd of chance comers."[59] Like the "Angel" in Ranier Maria Rilke's poetry, "the demiurge who provides the creative moment with its impersonal and inconceivable warrant," *Ulysses* uses the occasion to affirm an identity inconceivable through the lens of ideology.[60] A gesture at the limit Jacques Lacan imagined as the symbolic order, the formative moment invokes the sublime as the basis of epic values, the prospect of an infinitely expanding horizon, a never-compromised beginning, the prospect of limitless increase without the awe and self-surrender.

Ulysses' treatment of national identity balances this open-ended intergenerational compact with an appreciation of the relationship as a daily negotiation, a contract having to be amended, to borrow a phrase from Auden's poem "In Memory of W. B. Yeats," in the "guts of the living." National allegiance is contracted almost unconsciously. "Nations from a political point of view," Margaret Canovan writes, "are particularly attractive because they can attract so much support with so little by way of organization, doctrine and continuous mobilization."[61] National allegiance generates "a collective power, the capacity to create an 'us' that can be mobilized and represented, and for which a surprising number of people are prepared to make sacrifices."[62] *Ulysses* balances its account of the sublime as the basis of epic value and nationality with detailed reflections on how this commitment is accepted and forgotten, represented and lived.

This approach to Joyce's treatment of national identity differs, in method and substance, from existing studies of the treatment of nationality in *Ulysses* through the focus on Irish national statehood and the epic as a compositional directive. To locate Joyce's position, studies of Joyce's relationship to nationalism tend to claim him as a sympathizer, an unwitting one at least, with political positions we do not know him to have seriously considered and to present his work as motivated by loyalties to which he, evidently, preferred exile. For Dominic Manganiello and Richard Ellmann, the salient aspect of Joyce's thinking on nationality is an ethos that promised an alternative to radical, physical-force nationalist extremism.[63] Emer Nolan calls attention to the violence of Joyce's imagination, argues that complex commitments of the fiction resist paraphrase, and finds the closest approximation of a coherent politics to be an "unflinching localism," reminiscent of the constituency of D. P. Moran, who wrote *The Philosophy of Irish Ireland*.[64] Enda Duffy detects a radical commitment to revolutionary disruption in the dissonances of the fiction and, in its encoding of Irish political events, the force of an "IRA bomb."[65] Seamus Deane believes that Joyce, at the minimum, has to be credited with an awareness of a link between practical Irish national politics and his own writing. Unfortunately, the conclusion Deane draws from this relationship is as vague as the notion of the creative imagination itself.

> In revealing the essentially fictive nature of political imagining, Joyce did not repudiate Irish nationalism. Instead he understood it as a potent example of a rhetoric which imagined as true structures that did not and were never to exist outside language. Thus, a model, it served him as it served Yeats and others. It enabled them to apprehend the nature of fiction, the process whereby the imagination is brought to bear upon the reality which it creates.[66]

The formative link that I propose between the epic and historiography lends itself to a narrower, more precise measure of Joyce's response to Irish nationalism.

It has a similar effect on how we view Joyce's treatment of history. Epic as a compositional imperative suggests thresholds of response different from the Nietzschean stance that Spoo identifies with Stephen Dedalus and deems to have been generalized as stylistic experimentation in the text.

> As *Ulysses* progresses, there is a noticeable movement toward imagination realizing the possibilities ousted by the choice of a single historical day as the naturalistic base. *Ulysses*, like Bloom himself, comes to terms with its limitations. In this way the text engages in rectifying its own received images and becomes self-historicising, [with] the later episodes providing a kind of implicit historiographic commentary on the earlier ones. The basic motifs—betrayal, adultery, fatherhood, sonship, homelessness—are in place early in the book... the later episodes tend toward restatement and recombination of these themes.[67]

Spoo proposes a suggestive parallel between "the persistent historiographic concerns of *Ulysses*" and Stephen's concerns. To a far greater extent than I am willing to grant, he views Stephen's "intellectual attitudes" as a litmus which although "seemingly remote from the styles of the later episodes continue to shape the text's contestatory stance toward history long after he has receded as a character."[68] He interprets the tension as the need for liberation from what Nietzsche called "the malady of history, [from] ... the cultural obsession with the past and with the explanatory power of historiography, which ... was destroying intellectual and moral health in the nineteenth century," and therefore needlessly simplifies its significance.[69] Time and again we certainly do meet with Stephen's "romantic and preterist" desire to burst through the stifling discourses of history. These are indeed transformed in "the ironic counter discourses of *Ulysses*, [and] their winking assaults on Cyclopean reductions of the past to 'a tale like any other too often heard.'"[70] There is, however, a whole dimension to *Ulysses*' response to this perspective aside from the iteration of the liberationist ethic.

"A portrait," Joyce noted in the early study for his *Kunstlerroman*, "is not an identificative paper but rather the curve of an emotion."[71] The epic fable of *Ulysses* is also a complex engagement with its context, not just a recurrent sign for the ethos appropriate to historical change. In having become self-historicizing, *Ulysses* proposes a fresh context for delineating the historical record. It locates the fortunes of Irish national renewal in the conjunction of its characterization of Stephen Dedalus and its incorporation of the historical argument, precisely on account of its contemporary relevance, of Arthur Griffith's *The Resurrection of Hungary: A Parallel for Ireland* (1904).

To appreciate the nature and scope of the argument, it is useful to review the reception of Griffith's book in Ireland and in *Ulysses*. The publication of Griffith's book was seen, in retrospect, as a milestone in Irish politics.[72] Originally a series of articles in the *United Irishman*, it was deemed the most important event in Irish politics since the death of Parnell. T. M. Kettle, for example, though himself a member of the Parliamentary Party, called Griffith's book "the largest idea contributed to Irish politics for a generation."[73] Padraic Pearse, with his very different agenda, declared:

> We do not know that there has been published in Ireland in our time any book in English more important than "The Resurrection of Hungary.". . . [It] marks an epoch, because it crystallizes into a national policy the doctrines which during the past ten years have been preached in Ireland by the apostles of the Irish Ireland movement.[74]

Provocatively enough, popular Dublin rumor, in the person of John Wyse Nolan, maintains the ideas are all Bloom's (12.1573–74). Official opinion speaking, through Martin Cunningham, for the Castle concurs: Bloom is a "perverted jew . . . from a place in Hungary . . . [who] drew up all the plans according to the Hungarian system [for Sinn Fein]" (12.1635–36).

Griffith argued for a political agenda for Ireland modeled on the Hungarian nationalists' success in the Hapsburg Empire. Of itself, the parallel between Ireland's situation in Britain and Hungary's within the Austrian Empire—two restive national entities within the boundaries of two European Great Powers—was commonplace. Unionists and anti-Unionists made equal use of it. In his poem in honor of the martyrs of the 1848 revolution, "How Ferenc Renyi Kept Silent," Yeats toasted Hungary as the "nation of the bleeding breast" with "Libations, from the Hungary of the West."[75] Unionists in 1886 stigmatized Lord Salisbury's comparison of Irish Home Rule with the powers of the Hungarian diet as a foretaste of betrayal.[76] And, indeed, some months later, Gladstone instanced the "solidity and safety" of Austria's sharing of power with Hungary to support his ill-fated Home Rule Bill.[77]

The strength of Griffith's argument was that it did not stop at admiration. On his agenda, the lesson to be learned lay in tactics. Ireland was to free itself from the domination of England by emulating the campaign that the Hungarian leader Ferenc Deák initiated against Vienna after the national defeat in 1849:

> Sixty years ago, and more, Ireland was Hungary's exemplar. Ireland's heroic and long-enduring resistance to the destruction of her independent nationality were themes the writers of Hungary dwelt upon to enkindle and make resolute the Magyar people. The poet-precursors of Free Hungary . . . drank in Celtic inspiration, and the journalists of Young Hungary taught their people that Ireland had baffled a tyranny as great as that which threatened death to Hungary. Times have changed and Hungary is now Ireland's great exemplar.[78]

He advocated a boycott of the parliamentary maneuvering at Westminster. Elected members were to refuse to take their seats. Just such a boycott of the Imperial Diet by Hungarian nationalists had resulted in a Hapsburg capitulation to Hungarian demands after Austria's defeat by Prussia in 1866.[79] The aim of Irish nationalists should be . . . "the placing of the relations of Great Britain and Ireland on exactly the same footing as the relations now existing between Austria and Hungary."[80] Ireland might share a king with England, but the monarch would be crowned king of Ireland and be responsible to an Irish parliament. Through passive resistance, Griffith wanted Ireland to insist on the recognition of sovereignty that the Irish Volunteers had wrung from Britain in 1783.[81] The Act of Union of 1800 was to be treated as illegal throughout Ireland. There was to be no violence. The key success was moral resolve.

The proposal had immediate, and noisy, practical consequences. When the policy was announced at the third annual convention of the Cumann in October 1902, John O'Leary opposed it, claiming that the policy of abstention demanded too much "moral courage," in fact, an unworldly heroism, "of the people."[82] The initiative split Sinn Fein, with Bulmer Hobson, a nationalist leader in the North, arguing that the Hungarian policy meant a break with the Fenian tradition and acceptance of less than total national independence.[83]

The recognition of Bloom as the supposed originator of the idea is hardly, in other words, an admiring gesture. John Wyse Nolan, Martin Cunningham, Lenehan, Jack Power, and the fiery Citizen do not know what to make of Bloom. "One of those mixed middlings he is," the Citizen concludes. "[Once] a month with headache like a totty with her courses. Do you know what I am telling you? It'd be an act of God to take hold of a fellow like that and throw him in the bloody sea" (12.1658–62). Bloom as the inspiration of Sinn Fein? The hypothesis derives from the impression of Bloom as somehow monstrously foreign to Dublin.

Moreover, Joyce took deliberate steps to highlight the connection. For one thing, he backdates the controversy over Sinn Fein to 1904 in order to involve Bloom. *The Resurrection of Hungary* was, indeed, published in 1904, but as James Fairhall points out, "Sinn Fein was founded in 1905, peaked in significance in 1908, waned almost from notice altogether between 1910–13, only to rise again thanks to popular anger at the executions following Easter 1916."[84] Griffith, "the coming man" in Molly's meditations (18.385–86), did not have local prominence, nor did the Sinn Fein connection, not in 1904. Only after the outbreak of World War I and the renewed nationalist agitation did the 1904 proposals retroactively acquire portent.

But this historical sleight of hand is only one indication of the attention to the matter in *Ulysses*. Far more significant is the role in *Ulysses* of the terms of Griffith's central argument. The fable recasts Griffith's argument so that the drama of Stephen and Leopold can be read as comment on, and alternative to, Griffith's vision of how Ireland is to achieve self-definition.

The Hungarian national leader Deák, Griffith's model of a staunch nationalist leader, had waged the campaign for national equality as the recognition of the constitutional prerogatives due the crown of St. Stephen. The crown of St. Stephen, commemorating Stephen, Hungary's patron saint and the first Christian ruler of the Magyar nation, made royal rule legitimate in the eastern half of the Hapsburg realm—in Hungary, Croatia, Transylvania, and most of Slovakia.[85] To mark imperial centralization, the

Hapsburg emperor Francis Joseph refused coronation with the crown of St. Stephen after the abortive nationalist rising in 1848. Had the ruler accepted coronation according to the ceremonial of St. Stephen, he would also have had to recognize Hungarian national autonomy and the traditional political liberties of the nation. From 1848 to 1867, such a compromise seemed unnecessary to the Hapsburgs. For Deák and the Hungarian nationalists, the monarch's refusal of the coronation ritual meant the nonrecognition of the nation.

In the Austrian half of the realm, Hapsburg rule was legitimized by the sanction of St. Leopold (ca. 1073–1136), "distinguished for his charity and self-abnegation" (G&S, 591). Austria had "never grown into a circumscribed nation" as Hungary had, but the popular connection between the Saint as patron and the polity was well established.

Joyce could not help but have been familiar with such lore.[86] By 1915, the second year of his writing *Ulysses* and the year when Italy's declaration of war on the side of the Allies forced him from Trieste into his second exile, Joyce had spent eleven years, a third of his life, under Austrian rule.

Moreover by distorting the historical record and fitting the rudiments of Griffith's argument to the fable of *Ulysses*, he achieved more than a prominent propagandistic effect. The temporal distortion melds 1904 and the drama of Stephen and Leopold in *Ulysses* with a political landscape of imminent Irish independence. *The Aeneid* had offered a comparable distortion in the famous instance in book 6, when kingship, reflecting the recent Caesarian triumph in Rome, is linked to the entire history of Rome, legitimating the preeminence of Julius Caesar and Augustus through early heroes, including Aeneas and Romulus.[87] Roman history is massively distorted. Aeneas's distant descendants, Julius Caesar and Augustus, are inserted among the kings of Rome so that the republican section, which chronologically intervenes, comes later and separately in the text.[88] At stake was "the official self-image of the Augustan regime as the restored republic, with the *princeps* just another magistrate and at most *primus inter pares*" and "a second, unofficial attitude," the view of "many in the inner councils of power and expressed most fully in the literature," which "saw the rule of one man as a permanent necessity" and the ruler as a candidate for godhead "as well as a king."[89] The implication of *The Aeneid* is, Fairhall cogently notes, "that the whole of Roman history can be interpreted in royal terms."[90]

What are we to make of the comparable effect in *Ulysses*? What is at stake here?

At the minimum, the nationalist project offers an "escape from triviality" in K. R. Minogue's phrase.[91] At the maximum, the nationalist project inherits the entire vacuum left by collapsing hierarchies of value in modern history. The displacement of religion by science and the spread of the printed word left the nation the legatee of "a sense of immortality ... with which otherwise anonymous individuals can identify."[92] Aside from this extraordinary mission, the concept of the nation has no clearly defined profile and thus constitutes a rare compositional opportunity.[93] In "Eumaeus," Stephen addresses Bloom with a bombastic parody of this empowerment. "You suspect [Stephen says to Bloom] that I may be important because I belong to the *faubourg Saint Patrice* called Ireland for short .... But I suspect ... that Ireland must be important because it belongs to me" (16.1160–62, 64–65). National egoism is potentially unconstrained. To Arthur Power, Joyce declared that all "great writers" are "national first and only through the intensity of their nationalism" become international.[94]

For *Ulysses*, the elaboration of this motif is anything but formulaic. As Joyce reconfigures the syntax of Irish self-affirmation, he reformulates our expectations of reading and the terms in which we imagine public events.

1

The Argument of the Fable

An Overview

This chapter previews the rhythm of the complex engagement with the contemporary foundation of Ireland. The drama unfolds with no backshadowing, with no familiar markers to underscore the inevitability of the outcome. The back-shadowing of events, described by E. P. Thompson as "the enormous condescension of posterity," imports a reverential attitude.[1] *Ulysses* stages its reflection on Ireland's self-constitution as a distinct polity on "a screen . . . poised between the historian and the living complexity" *(un écran, nécessaire pour agir . . . qui s'interpose entre l'historien et la complexité vivante)* in Phillipe Ariès's characterization of politics as a screen required for communal self-representations and action.[2] Without the characters' awareness of a possibly emblematic role, without the touch of historical grandeur Yeats marveled at in "Easter, 1916," the touch whereby "motley" is changed to a "terrible beauty," the fable activates the impress of contemporary political events as communal drama.

In distancing itself from the living complexity of the concrete and the personal, the performance "gains in generality" and in this way comes to "resemble the institutions which had preceded and would follow it" *(une part de généralité qui la rapproches de toutes les autres institutions qui l'ont précédée ou lui succéderont)*.[3] In "Easter, 1916," Yeats had invited the audience to treat the absence of foreknowledge, its inability to perceive an apocalyptic change at a historical turning point, as an occasion for wonder. The failure to meet the imaginative challenge was proof of the sublime. The fable of *Ulysses* sorts the manifold in order to facilitate a comparably synthetic grasp of daily issues, but it is not an opening to a reverential silence that connects the performance with earlier monuments of communal definition. The horizon of the manifold teems with suggestive sequences, possible arrivals and points of departure. The fable of *Ulysses* magnifies the middle distance to epic scale.

Instead of awe at the gap between the commonplace and the promotion of heroic as the gateway to a different kind of self-identity, the epic dimension of *Ulysses* hosts a comprehensive reflection on the contemporary renewal of the polity. This epic dimension of *Ulysses* is not a schema of correspondences. It is a predilection for holistic elaboration, which draws inspiration from a premise something like Giambattista Vico's axiom that whenever the human mind "is lost in ignorance, man makes himself the measure of all things."[4] The reconstitution of the totality bears the marks of this self-alienation and forgetfulness.

From the evidence of metaphor, Vico concluded that "man becomes all things" regardless of whether humans have managed to achieve a correct understanding of anything. Truth and error belong together inescapably. The argument of "rational metaphysics" is that the human "becomes all things by understanding them" (*homo intelligendo fit omnia*). The testimony of metaphors latent in language shows that a person also "becomes all things by *not* [sic] understanding them" (*homo non intelligendo fit omni*).

> It is noteworthy that in all languages the greater part of the expressions relating to inanimate things are formed by metaphor from the human body and its parts and from the human senses and passions. Thus, head for top or beginning; the brow and shoulders of a hill; the eyes of needles and of potatoes; mouth for any opening; the lip of a cup or pitcher; the teeth of a rake, a saw, a comb; the beard of wheat; the tongue of a shoe; the gorge of a river; a neck of land; an arm of the sea . . . the belly of a sail . . . the flesh of fruit . . . heaven or the sea smiles; the wind whistles; the waves murmur. . . .[5]

There is no neutral middle ground. In the absence of rational understanding, "man makes the things out of himself and becomes them by transforming himself into them."[6] The human is fated to self-representation. The project, compounded of understanding and nescience, is always in the round. It takes up the whole horizon.

The epic dimension of the fable works with a comparably broad assumption concerning the communal constitution of Ireland. Starting with irony at Stephen Dedalus's expense, the fable crafts roles for the characters emblematic of Ireland's self-awareness, but not themselves conscious of the role, as the polity approached independence. The account is dramatically different from the tales of nation formation belonging to any of the parties committed to the struggle for Irish national independence in part because historical inquiry in *Ulysses* wields Blakean temporal horizons. The magnification of the middle distance accommodates the minutiae of poetic scansion and apocalyptic premonitions concerning the polity, an aesthetic order which sustains labyrinths of reflection and resonates in the final instance to the incalculable consequences of the welcome by faithful adulterous Penelope.

This appropriation of Irish historiography by the epic fable of *Ulysses* is the theme of the five chapters of this book. Chapter 2 treats the integration of the *Kunstlerroman* perspective with the emerging pattern of the epic fable. The argument is most immediately accessible if we approach it as a legacy of Stephen Dedalus's ambition to "forge the conscience of [his] race." Stephen's appearance in *Ulysses* is tantamount to a renunciation of this goal. It is evident, writes Herbert N. Schneidau, that cultures and individuals do not "reinvent themselves by an act of will—though some remarkable self-delusions of such grandeur have been produced—given the ineluctable modality of the way language circulates."[7] Still, the prospect of such an achievement in *Portrait* leaves a legacy, a vehicle to develop the theme further when Stephen turns up again in "Telemachus."

The immediate consequence is a reversal of perspective deriving from the change in genre. Because Stephen is not depicted as having recovered "an outer dictum as inner," as a self-motivated, freely integrated productive self-consciousness, Joyce finds himself sharing the terrain of sustained implicit ironic commentary that Flaubert pioneered with *Madame Bovary*.[8] The disjunction in *Ulysses* between the consciousness of the central character and work results in a much more complex performance than in *Portrait*. As in *Madame Bovary*, the new text propounds a rhythm distinct from the character's awareness as commentary on the awareness.

In *Ulysses*, Stephen "is not a writer at all," Seamus Deane has observed. "He is an intellectual, concerned to define himself."[9] The truth he had wanted to impose on his contemporaries through his writing remains private, inward, unvoiced. Were Stephen, with what we learn of his personal resources, to find the inspiration to live up to his goal, *Ulysses* would be a portrait of a prolegomenon to epic achievement. G. J. B. Watson offers an admirable, but mistaken, summary of where following this subjective bias in the interpretation tends:

> From one angle, the development of the epic tradition might be described as a series of re-definitions or refinements of the notion of

heroism, or the heroic. From primary to secondary epic, from bloodthirsty Achilles to pious Aeneas, from the virtues of military prowess to the "better fortitude" of heroic patience celebrated by Milton, from Milton's focusing of the arena of intense moral choice to Wordsworth's sublime ego finding that "we have all of us one human heart," there is a steady internalizing of heroism and heroics, so that Milton's Adam, Wordsworth and Joyce's Bloom could say with Hamlet (a character important to *Ulysses*) "I have that within which passes show."[10]

The passivity of Hamlet is not an adequate analogue for the epic scope of *Ulysses*.

Instead, *Ulysses* subordinates Stephen to the epic medium. He becomes part of the fait accompli. We are expected to see Stephen from the outside. The task is parodied in Stephen's effort to imagine his situation through a detective novel.

Yes, used to carry punched tickets to prove an alibi if they arrested you for murder somewhere. Justice. On the night of the seventeenth February the prisoner was seen by two witnesses. Other fellow did it: other me. Hat, tie, overcoat, nose. *Lui, c'est moi*. (3.179–80)

The italicized allusion is to the character Lui in Diderot's *Rameau's Nephew*, whom the narrator Moi, despite his best efforts, cannot see in the round but only as a preposterous, deliberately carnivalesque gesture.[11] At issue is what J. M. Bernstein called "the spectatorial relation between the ironist, or reader, and the text."[12] In Diderot's dialogue, Lui exits from the scene, crowing, "Good-bye Mr. Philosopher. Isn't it true that I am always the same?"[13] Because of his disappointed formative ambition, Stephen is no more able to imagine his role in *Ulysses* than Moi could imagine Lui. The heterogeneity of the text is too much for him.

Frederick Meinecke noted that "the nation drank the blood of free personalities."[14] *Ulysses* registers such an achievement. Whereas Stephen had proposed to make his self-fashioning the touchstone of national experience, *Ulysses* depicts him as already an effect of a different kind of totalization. The reorientation of Stephen's presentation is as drastic as Joyce's decision "to rewrite *Stephen Hero* as *A Portrait* in five chapters," a drastic compositional intervention of which Joyce recognized the necessity right after the birth of his daughter, Lucia. The epic design of *Ulysses* registers a comparably fundamental change in compositional imperative and, like the newly revised "*A Portrait of the Artist as a Young Man* [which] is in fact the gestation of a soul," climaxes, as I will show in chapter 5, in the celebration of birth.[15]

In order to present this reorientation in perspective according to the telos of epic design, chapter 1 traces the appearance of the distinct rhythm in the characterization of Stephen in "Nestor" through allusions to Milton's *Lycidas*, and in "Proteus," through allusions to Lessing's *Laocoön, or On the Limits of Painting and Poetry*. References to the two works constitute a kind of *via negativa* to the distinctive achievement of *Ulysses*. Stephen is rendered as an epic character rather than a progenitor through his performance of *Lycidas*, which for Milton belonged to a progression of genres crowned by his mastery of the epic in *Paradise Lost*, and through the commentary of Lessing's analysis of Homer's achievement in "Proteus." The characterization confines Stephen to ecphrastic surfaces. The result is that instead of song, in "Ithaca" the twanging accompaniment of a Jew's harp will mark his passing from view.

Chapter 3 examines the transposition of the Griffith materials in *Ulysses*. The epic, Michael Seidel writes, teaches a culture or a people a version of its own history by testing "the ethos of the forming events it records."[16] The chapter looks at the approaches to closure crafted from the lexicon of the parallel in *Ulysses*.

The focus is on the syntax of the Stephen and Leopold encounter. The identities that Stephen and Leopold assume reflect the liminal quality of their participation in the syntax of an ideology that proposes that the principal actors in history are collectivities. At its most abstract, the allegiance to such a collective identity appears as a trace that hangs in "the solitude [of] individual novel—or newspaper—readers" who sense that such texts "are being read simultaneously by other individual readers, in [the] community in anonymity which is the hallmark of modern nations."[17] At its most compelling, the allegiance "is imagined as welling up from the depths of all our subjectivities: our truest self, according to the principle of nationality is the same as our nation and our nation indistinguishable from our truest self."[18] The chapter examines the staging of the fable as a historical account of the gap between these two very different calls to allegiance.

Karl Marx wrote that, in the state, "man is the imaginary member of an imaginary sovereignty, divested of his real individual life, and infused with an unreal universality."[19] Griffith proposed a relationship among these "imaginary sovereignties," Ireland/Britain and Hungary/Austria. To these imperfect approximations, *Ulysses* opposes Stephen (the liberator, St. Stephen) and Bloom (St. Leopold, the Austro-Hungarian or perhaps Hungarian Jew), both figures showing the strain of the "unreal universality" required by the comparison. Their encounter, the implications of Bloom's effort to imagine continuity spanning his Hapsburg origins, his Irish present and future prospects incorporate Griffith's prescription for Irish self-understanding as a reflection on historiography.

Chapter 3 is not concerned with the self-evident point that a quasi-allegorical equivalence—first, between the different nations that figure in Griffith's argument and then between the two individuals, Stephen and Leopold, and the roles of these nations—is absurdly inadequate to deal with empirical instances. *Ulysses* certainly does show us these abstractions afoot in Dublin and shows the imperfect fit of abstraction and historical particulars. However, the quasi-allegorical equivalence gets tested because it refers to an apparently inescapable dimension of national experience. Abstract citizenship as the foundation of the nation-state is an effort at awareness of the historical process and an effort to situate the particular as universal.

However imperfect the heroes' sense of their own consequence in this drama, the argument builds from the medley of traits ascribed to Stephen; Leopold; his grandfather, Lipoti; Bloom's father, Rudolf; and his infant son, Rudy. For Bloom, allegiance to family tradition is a struggle to keep intact and translate a minimal pattern of mutual recognition in changing historical circumstances. The conjunction with the legacy of *Portrait* and with *The Resurrection of Hungary* accords a tentative formative universality to these efforts at continuity. The abstractions of nationhood and of historical generalization come "down to earth," and the dramatis personae of *Ulysses* offer intimate footnotes to the abstraction. "A man's life of any worth," wrote John Keats, "is a continual allegory."[20] In the fit between the fable Griffith proposed for the polity and its own fable, *Ulysses* hosts a meditation on individuality and community, a fresh stage in the migration of the epic tradition.

This meditation integrates materials with a more comprehensive focus than the Emersonian confluence of biography and history. For Emerson, "the emphatic facts of history" refer ultimately to individual experience.

> All history becomes subjective ... there is properly no history; only biography. Every mind must know the whole lesson for itself—must go over the whole ground. What it does not see, what it does not live, it will not know. What the former age has epitomized into a formula or rule for manipular convenience, it will lose all the good of verify-

ing for itself, by means of the wall of that rule. Somewhere, sometime, it will demand and find compensation for that loss by doing the work itself.[21]

As the epic fable elaborates its approach to communal definition, the fable draws away from possible individual awareness. The design raises the possibility that we require a specifically crafted historical sense for it to turn legible.

Chapters 4 and 5 examine the possibility of closure in this discursive context. At stake is the possibility of representing a stable, lasting collective subject of nationalism, a figure adumbrated by the correspondence between the sequence of chapters and the human organs assigned them in the schemata. The possibility of closure in such a frame appears as a remembering, a recovery of the discursive process, a reflection that results in the simulacrum of an integrated subject.

The call of closure is a call to impersonal objectivity. Throughout *The Odyssey*, J. M. Perl notes that "nostalgia . . . is equivalent to slaughtering Penelope's suitors." With Book 24 "such a bloodbath impends that the gods are moved to impose a definitive public settlement between the claims of a cloying, parasitic present and an avenging, heroic past."[22] The epic function in *Ulysses* appeals to a more generous, pluralistic standard of authenticity. We are invited to explore an approximation of community that curbs the claims of consanguinity. We examine the myth of distinct national origins while noting the resistance of otherness and historical accident to this kind of homogenization.

The possibility of closure is explored through a meditation on the aesthetics of the photographic image, a figure of closure conversant with the ideal of the self-reflexive constitution of the self in *Portrait*. The end of "Penelope," the series of "yeses," the event likely to have announced the conception of Milly, who was to be born eight months after the actual wedding and who, in her turn, is associated with photography and serial replication, extends the syntactical relevance of this way of conceiving the self to the limits of the work.

Chapter 4 examines Milly's characterization in such a focus. Bloom had intended it for Stephen to sleep in Milly's empty bed. Stephen puts an end to the rapprochement by singing the ballad "Hugh of Lincoln," targeting Bloom's Jewishness and charging the Jew's daughter with ritual murder. The chapter investigates the narrative coherence that this role for Milly implies. The performance focuses on the issue of national identity. "The borders of the nation are constantly faced," Homi K. Bhabha observes, "with a double temporality: the process of identity constituted by historical sedimentation (the pedagogical) and the loss of identity in the signifying process of cultural identification (the performative)" coexists.[23] Stephen's performance draws attention to Milly's role at this frontier, to her importance to closural gesture deriving from the fable.

Chapter 5 returns to the possibility of closure, still in the lexicon of the epic fable but in gestures independent of the Griffith parallel. "In *Ulysses*," Henry Staten has written, "realist mimesis is reconceived as the isomorphism of two decompositional series, one involving language and the other the body."[24] *Ulysses*, I seek to show throughout this study, fashions this realist mimesis so that it should coexist with an epic mimesis, a sustained meditation on collective identities, a performance *à rebours* the decompositional process, as an inquiry into the constitution of shared historical identity and the possibility of collective agency.

These approaches, distinct from Griffith's argument but alike in their testimony to "a hidden teleology," in John S. Rickard's phrase, suggest "a destined development that operates outside of the characters."[25] Chapter 5 argues that independent life of the material to which attention has been drawn in this way adds up to a claim to a separate epic mimesis, a textual stance with independent authority.

The "Book 24 aspect of the modern *nostos*," writes Perl, "surfaces mainly in those theorists who identify the twentieth-century return with precedent epochs of Renaissance or renascence."[26] As *Ulysses* revisits the foundational design of the new Ireland, the transformation of the lexical borrowings from the Griffith parallel, we do witness the simulacrum of a rebirth, a massive affirmation of emergent identity, with the whole of the text as stage.

Epic mimesis builds to this climax. It accommodates a fluctuating composite identity through a range of particulars, each with a claim to the totality deployed as the fable. The particulars include the visitations of Ulysses Browne, the one Irish Ulysses who is so named in *Portrait* and *Ulysses*; the anticipation of Bloom's odyssey in Dublin by his forebears' travels in eastern Europe, an odyssey that ends in Dublin; coronation imagery associated with Stephen; and finally the harmony that I shall be describing as the epic rhyme, linking Buck Mulligan in the opening pages of "Telemachus" and Milly Bloom at the conclusion of "Penelope," a harmony that invokes aspects of the continuity of concern to the fable but configures these as belonging to a more comprehensive syntax, to a more elemental approach to national culture.

The focus of the epic function in *Ulysses* is this deployment of the historical drama in the interstices of individuality and seriality, personal and communal self-definition, inheritance and creativity. The motivation of the deployment is *Ulysses'* self-reflective promotion of this pattern as an alternate model of historiography.

Chapter 6 considers the limitation on this overview of epic mimesis and the limitation on transmission of historical identity as such. The representation of national awareness partakes of error and forgetfulness. The limitation on the overview tempers the finality of the design. In counterpoint to the heuristic results, to the celebration of a construal deriving from the epic function, the chapter details an adjacent design, a self-reflective commentary on the epic function, still open-ended, still concerned with the lexical items and political outcomes already analyzed, but tantamount nevertheless to a distinct approach.

The recognition of the limits to the epic mode of synthesis argues for different assumptions about the text, for the recognition of *Ulysses'* ultimately comic provenance and of images, not concepts, as the parameters for critical approaches to the text. Writing of *elocutio* in his interpretation of the compositional practice of Giambattista Vico, John Milbank insists that "the very instance of the utterance" is the climax of invention and judgement.[27] In responding to ideological challenges to the iterated identities necessary for the epic design, images find voice, complicating the renewal of tradition. Synthesis in the epic mode as practiced in *Ulysses* is not a formula but a critical probing.

The renewal of the epic tradition requires a deliberately self-conscious refusal of easy sentiment. Instead of allowing narcissistic self-indulgence to provide the rule for historical continuity, *Ulysses* postpones closure. The syntax of the epic fable uses the incoherence to complicate expectations. Instead of conforming to a sentimentalized ideal of tradition, we adjust to a logic that includes nescience and amnesia, to a difficult model of deliberate historical agency that accommodates semiconsciousness and self-betrayal.

Chapter 6 traces three such modifications of the epic argument. The first occurs in the characterization of Milly, the second in Bloom's inadvertent self-historicization when he confuses operas by Meyerbeer and Mercadante. The final deferral of closure according to the epic design occurs in the overlapping features of Lipoti Virag and the Dublin eccentric "Endymion" Farrell. Throughout the reader is asked, it seems, to admit ignorance, error, and blind will as formative powers of epic scope.

The characterization of Milly casts doubt on her paternity. The drama of Bloom's confusion of operas suggests that misperception and nescience might issue from the most elaborate historical argument. Lipoti Virag, genealogically an ancient premise of the argument, and Farrell, an eccentric instantly recognizable in contemporary Dublin, share an extravagantly vocal voluntary paralysis.

Ulysses annexes these reservations to its radical orientation to the present. The contemporaneity which, as I have argued, is the raison d'être of the epic design is also "an essential feature," Zack Bowen notes, "of comedy."[28] Bowen directs attention to a passage in James Kern Feibleman's *In Praise of Comedy* (1939) that illustrates this focus:

> Sherwood Anderson is speaking for all comedians when he exclaims, "I want to take a bite of the now." Comedy epitomizes the height of the times, the Zeitgeist. Hanging upon the vivid immediacy of actuality, it touches the unique particularity embodied in the passing forms of the moment. A criticism of the contradictions involved in actuality, it must inevitably be concerned with the most ephemeral of actualities.[29]

The epic design, like the telos of comedy, aims at "a bite of the now." The confluence unsettles all generalizations about the result.

With *Ulysses'* articulation of the epic tradition, we move from a cognitive mode that involves "an outside relation between knower and object" to a practical understanding of how the "truth" of the present moment, to paraphrase Vico, has been made ("factum").[30] The articulation of the design recovers intimate aspects of our relationship to the text and distributes these as immanent anticipations of the direction of the argument. On the margin of the applicability of the epic design, we discover the force of historical constraint.

The position is a challenging one. The doubt cast on the genre's ability to order historical experience smacks of the formative energy of Stephen's determination in *Portrait* to forge the conscience of a new Irish race. Seamus Deane, reflecting on the problem of defining national identity, contrasts "the spiritual heroics of a Yeats or Pearse," their faith in "the incarnation of the nation in the individual," and the "fetish of exile, alienation, and dislocation," a skeptical emphasis on the noncoincidence of individual need and national expression of Beckett and of Joyce.[31] At least Joyce's appreciation of the need to constitute a communal "we" is much more complex than any dichotomy of belonging and nonbelonging allows.

"The task of the historian," writes Maurice Mandelbaum, "is to analyze a complex pattern of change into the factors which serve to make it precisely what it was."[32] *Ulysses'* engagement with "the epic" in the predualistic manner of Vico, its treatment of the genre as both function and emergent design, in fact, a topos, a commonplace, a position recurrently indicated as relevant to the representation of communal experiences, incorporates the ideal of adequate historical representation as an epic undertaking.

2

The Ascent of Stephen Dedalus from Messianic Ambition to Epic Discourse

"All of Joyce's works might be understood," writes Umberto Eco, "as a continuous discussion of their own artistic procedures."[1] When Stephen Dedalus reappears in *Ulysses*, without the historic role he had aimed to fashion for himself in line with his epic ambition, the new site bristles with aesthetic issues. What has become of the heuristic value of narrative progression through modes of free indirect discourse to first-person diary testimony? Stephen's highly personal appropriation of linguistic expression in *Portrait* was billed as preliminary to a new moment of communal expression and self-definition. How do we situate the character now that he has reappeared as a response to a new environment?

At the minimum, his reappearance in defeat has to confirm that the progression of narrative devices in *Portrait* was inadequate to the challenge that the *Kunstlerroman* envisioned. The defeat further implies that the accentuation, as such, of Stephen's individuality was altogether mistaken. Such a postscript to Stephen's effort would nearly mirror T. S. Eliot's view of genuine artistic expression as a movement of "continual self-sacrifice, a continual extinction of personality" culminating in "the historical sense," which Eliot deemed indispensable.[2] The appreciation of Stephen's failure would coexist with an appreciation for "not only of the pastness of the past, but of its presence . . . [compelling] a man to write not merely with his own generation in his bones, but with a feeling that the whole literature of Europe has a simultaneous existence and composes a simultaneous order."[3] As the counterpoint to Stephen's failure, this complex awareness of the past and present has to accommodate the contemporary demand for national coherence, the telos that had defined *Portrait* and which the imminent Irish political independence rendered a live issue. For Stephen, "[h]istory is a nightmare from which I am trying to awaken" (2.377). His ignominious return to Ireland proves that he is mired in "the pastness of the past."

Tom Nairn attributes the pressures of national self-definition to "specific deep-communal structures perturbed or challenged by modernization in successive *ethnies*."[4] Through its treatment of Stephen, *Ulysses* revisits these disturbed foundations. The design supplements the heuristic force of reflection, the experiments with free indirect discourse and first-person diary narrative in *Portrait*. The itinerary allocates allusions to frame the epic horizon for the polity from the character's frustrated efforts to represent his situation. In *Portrait*, Stephen had aimed to seize his surroundings and, through the force of his personality, so transform these that, in the future, his compatriots would have to abide his creation as a new constraint: he meant, to repeat the oft-quoted phrase, "to forge the conscience of [his] race in the smithy of [his] soul" (*P*, 253). In reconceiving Stephen's messianic project, the new environment replaces ironic implication with a new lexicon. The new context reformulates the need of a fresh starting point for national self-definition with which Stephen has become identified.

The new environment recycles the materials at different levels of relevance for Stephen's ambition. The new orientation, Stephen's novel stance, is a fresh connection with the epic tradition. To foreground this new affiliation, I will present analyses that go against the grain of the narrative progression in the Telemachiad chapters. The theme of the affiliation is alienation. I look at the seal in "Proteus" that separates the new Ulyssesean portrait of Stephen from Homer's legacy. I look at Stephen's characterization in "Nestor" in relation to the model of imitation in successive genres, the model of achievement mirrored in the career of the English poet John Milton. I briefly note the symbol of the mirror in "Telemachus," emblem of the reduced range of the character to the undertaking.

The displacement of Stephen's self-portrait in *Ulysses* derives from his concern with transcending the merely personal. Stephen in *Portrait* would readily have agreed with F. W. Schlegel that even as conscience "draws us back toward ourselves, back toward our person and individuality," it is not to our empirical self that we are drawn. The movement is toward "the *general Individual*," toward a "consciousness of consciousness" and an affirmation of the "life of life."[5] *Ulysses* depicts this proclivity to abstraction as separation and isolation from the action. The progression I will be analyzing from "Proteus" to "Nestor" to "Telemachus" configures this distance as indicative of a new relationship, with heuristic range comparable in suggestiveness to the commentary achieved through *Ulysses'* juxtaposition of chapters governed by radically different stylistic criteria.

The only stretching of metaphor in the description of Stephen's efforts in "Proteus" as attempts at a self-portrait consists in not emphasizing that Stephen merely reasons toward such a representational effect. Whereas *Portrait* featured an album of styles in developmental sequence, "Proteus" gives us Stephen dramatizing his inescapable visibility. He is committed to an epistemological investigation that returns him to a liminal stance among different alternatives—conceptual, visual, tactile, aural—to apprehending and representing his situation. Invoking Aristotle's distinction of the *diaphane*, or visible (the medium of plastic representation), and the *adiaphane* (the stuff inexpressible as light, resistant to light), he mimes his moment to moment contact with the perceptual world. Having proposed the fiction that, like the reader, he is deciphering two-dimensional signs, Stephen sets out to traverse the multidimensional medium before him bodily. In the passage, he rifles Aristotle (the bald millionaire) and Bishop Berkeley for means to situate the resistance.

> Ineluctable modality of the visible: at least that if no more, though through my eyes. Signatures of all things I am here to read, sea spawn and seawrack, the nearing tide, that rusty boot. Snotgreen, bluesilver, rust: coloured signs. Limits of the diaphane. But he adds: in bodies. Then he was aware of them bodies before of them coloured. How? By knocking his sconce against them, sure go easy. Bald he was and a millionaire, *maestro di color che sanno*. Limit of the diaphane in. Why in? Diaphane, adiaphane. If you can put your five fingers through it is a gate, if not a door. Shut your eyes and see. (3.1–9).

He might be trying to find his way into or out of a prison. In any event, he wills himself blind. Only the reader sees. The willed blindness is self-portraiture.

R. J. Schork has observed that the initial adjective in the passage, "ineluctable," sets up a false etymology. The root "luc" is only apparently connected to the Latin word for light. The word at the root is *lucto*, which means to "wrestle, to grapple with." For Stephen, the "ineluctable modality" seems to be the modality of the world as such. As readers, we misperceive Stephen's struggle if we found it on the visible. We do not "see" his struggle anymore than Stephen, his eyes closed, sees the world around him.

The adjective "ineluctable" derives, "with no visible mediation," according to Schork, "from Virgil's *Aeneid*." As Aeneas recounts the fall of Troy to Queen Dido in Carthage, he reports that "a priest of Apollo had solemnly announced that the city's end was at hand." The phrase *"venit ineluctabile tempus* (time that could not be wrestled away has come)" belongs in the announcement.[6] The allusion is a concise summing up of the detour that the representation of Stephen in *Ulysses* must include. Unlike in *Portrait*, the rhythms of his developing maturity no longer rule the prose.

What do we make of the difference? Ezra Pound had proposed the term *vortex* as a synonym for *image*, distinguishing both terms from mere ideas. "The image is not an idea. It is a radiant node, or cluster; it is what I ... must perforce call a VORTEX, from which, and through which, and into which, ideas are constantly rushing."[7] In *Ulysses*, Stephen has something of the fixity of the idea. He has, Joyce complained, a shape that cannot be changed.[8] He has come to represent a solution to a compositional dilemma. In this role, he enacts a self-referentiality so analytically acute that his thoughts, in a kind of ecphrastic doubling, bespeak the independent motivation of the text as the successor of *Portrait*.

Guided by sound and touch, Stephen in quest of order is depicted as reaching out for help to the two fundamental terms that Lessing had used in *Laocoön* to distinguish the rhythm of verbal arts from those of plastic arts: *Nacheinander* (after one another) and *Nebeneinander* (beside one another). Shod in borrowed boots, invisible to himself, he listens to the rhythm of his progress along the shell-strewn seashore. En passant, his mood appropriates something of Hamlet's brooding darkness. He dramatizes his progress, his stick a royal ash, coeternal with the unseen world, scanning the marks of his passage through the darkness with it.

> Stephen closed his eyes to hear his boots crush crackling wrack and shells. You are walking through it howsomever. I am, a stride at a time. A very short space of time through very short times of space. Five, six: the *Nacheinander*. Exactly: and that is the ineluctable modality of the audible.
> Open your eyes. No. Jesus! If I fell over a cliff that beetles o'er his base, fell through the *Nebeneinander* ineluctably! I am getting on nicely in the dark. My ash sword hangs by my side. Tap with it they do. My two feet in his boots are at the end of his legs, *nebeneinander*. Sounds solid: made by the mallet of *Los demiurgos*. Am I walking

through eternity along Sandymount strand? Crush, crack, crick,
crick. Wild sea money. Dominie Deasy kens them a'.
Won't you come to Sandymount,
Madeline the mare?
Rhythm begins, you see. I hear. Acatelectic tetrameter of iambs
marching. No, agallop: *deline the mare*. (3.10–24)

Unseeing, Stephen's awareness of rhythm (*Nacheinander*) is the measure of the *Nebeneinander*—the contiguity that his voluntary blindness has rendered problematic.

The measure? His ear encodes something—perhaps the sound of his step crushing shells, the rhythm of the phrase his steps suggest—as iambic tetrameter. In any event, the phrase brings to mind his employer, Deasy, the schoolmaster, an Englishman who by virtue of nationality can advertise a claim to the rhythms of the English language Stephen, his subordinate, perforce uses.

The theme of usurpation sets up the italicized line: *Madeline the mare*. The reference might be to the French watercolorist Madeleine Lemaire or to the Paris church of Mary Magdalene where a Pierre Joseph Henri Lemaire, according to Gifford and Seidman, "created a relief sculpture of the Last Supper" (G&S, 46). Both allusions bring futile flight to France to mind. The noun "mare" echoes with the French homonyms, *mer* (sea) and *mère* (mother), words resonant for Stephen with defeat. The important point, however, from which no plethora of allusive incertitude should distract us, is the aural portrait Stephen is attempting and the aspects of the composition that escape him

"Rhythm begins, you see. I hear." What does he hear? Who sees? Stephen's analysis—"Acatelectic tetrameter of iambs marching"—refers to the italicized line "*Won't you come to Sandymount.*"[9] It does fall one syllable short of iambic tetrameter; with only seven, not eight, syllables, it is "acatelectic."

The remainder outpaces him. "Agallop" is an anapest. Presumably, Stephen has recalled the Mother Goose rhyme often used to illustrate rhythms. In the last example, "The footman lags behind to tipple ale and wine" and is said to go "gallop, a gallop, a gallop to make up his mind" and to go "a gallop, a gallop, a gallop, to make up his time."[10] And *deline the mare?* It returns us to the shore, to the sea, *mare* in both Latin and Italian. "Line" from *deline* calls attention to the verse and shore.

Stephen prepares to open his eyes. The wit, come full circle, should not distract us from the readiness with which Lessing's categories assimilate to Stephen's playfulness. The ease represents a change in Joyce's treatment of the German thinker. In Joyce's earlier writing, the references to Lessing's categories tended to be admonitory. *Stephen Hero* deemed *Laocoön* to be irritating and filled with "fanciful generalizations."[11] *Portrait* has the doltish Donovan praise the "idealistic, German, ultraprofound" nature of *Laocoön* (P, 211). Stephen goes on to issue a sententious warning against *Laocoön*. "Lessing should not have taken a group of statues to write of. The art, being inferior, does not represent the forms [lyric, epic, dramatic] clearly from one another" (P, 214). Stephen's quasi-blind singsong clowning in "Proteus" is pedantic play with Lessing's categories. Granted that Lessing's theory of genre is unsatisfactory, does not the dissatisfaction particularly befit the despairing figure of the artist manqué particularly well?

The sardonic mood also appears to blend with Stephen's motive when he mimics the image that is Lessing's concern in the treatise—the scream that tore the figure of the Trojan priest as he was enveloped and broken in the coils of Apollo's vengeful serpents. However, just as the environment of "Proteus" has tended to outpace Stephen's responses, the signature of this final bit of clowning invokes a context for Stephen's self-portraiture that connects it to his role in *Ulysses* and to the epic design.

Stephen's mimicry in the episode is self-parodic. Through extravagant distortion, he is sardonically returning to the forecast of creative exile in the April 16 diary entry of *Portrait*. When Stephen had left Ireland for a heroic future, fearless, he anticipated the welcome of distant lands and terrible companions:

> Away! Away!
> The spell of arms and voices: the white arms of roads, their promise of close embraces and the black arms of tall ships that stand against the moon, their tale of distant nations. They are held out to say: We are alone. Come. And the voices say with them: We are your kinsmen. And the air is thick with their company as they call to me, their kinsman, making ready to go, shaking the wings of their exultant and terrible youth. (P, 252)

Back on the morning of June 16, 1904, in Ireland, he finds himself the victim of the destiny he thought to meet across the seas. He had hoped to be a heroic adventurer. Instead, the reversal—complete with a distended exaggeration of the diary's opening "Away! Away!"—renders Stephen as the home port for a grotesque, and apparently malevolent, airborne being:

"He comes, pale vampire, through storm his eyes, his bat sails, bloodying the sea, mouth to her mouth's kiss." (3.397–98) Stephen dutifully records the vision. Experimenting with sound, he writes the result at the bottom of a letter about cattle disease, which he has been asked to take care of for his employer.

> Here. Put a pin in that chap, will you? My tablets. Mouth to her kiss. No. Must be two of em. Glue em well. Mouth to her mouth's kiss.
> His lips lipped and mouthed fleshless lips of air: mouth to her womb. Oomb, allwombing tomb. His mouth molded issuing breath, unspeeched: ooeeehah: roar of cataratic planets globed, blazing, roaring wayawyawayawaway. Paper. The banknotes, blast them. Old Deasy's letter. (3.399–405)

The frustration of Stephen's grandiose airborne hopes of destiny is the obvious object here. The vampire has been variously identified with *dio boia*, the hangman god, with the Holy Spirit, with death, with the Greek Daedalus, with Simon Dedalus, with Stephen himself, with the black panther of Stephen's nightmare, and with the female "batlike souls" who haunt Stephen's libido.[12] Only the multiple possible identities of the victim limit the diversity. He or she might be Stephen's mother, or Stephen, or the Virgin Mary, or God.[13]

The point left out of these accounts is the studied exaggeration of the gesture. *Laocoön* had weighed the appropriateness of strongly expressed emotion in different arts. Stephen appears to have depicted himself so as to flout Lessing's prescription. Imagining himself to be at the crux of deliberate representation, Stephen does not pay attention to the "picture" he mimes as such. His pose is graphic and rendered through indirect discourse and onomatopoetically. The passage, which he hears and we see, expressly embraces the freedom Lessing held out to the poet.

The historical background of Lessing's treatise provides the exaggeration and Stephen's expressive self-indulgence with the likely subtext. Lessing's *Laocoön* originated as a disagreement with an interpretation offered in the German classicist Johann Winckelmann's *History of the Art of Antiquity* (1764). For Winckelmann the surviving statue of Laocoön, stoically undergoing agony in his serpent coils, attested a greatness of soul which he judged Virgil's representation of the same scene in *The Aeneid* had not achieved. For Winckelmann, Virgil's inferiority was proven by his having Laocoön emit an "agonizing cry."[14]

Lessing objected that Winckelmann had confused the medium with the achievement. The stoic depiction of the cry in the marble had nothing to with the artist's greatness of soul. Sculpture, by its nature, requires restraint. Beyond the moment represented in sculpture "there is nothing further, and to show us the uttermost is to tie the wings of fancy and oblige her, as she cannot rise above the sensuous impression, to busy herself with weaker pictures below it, the fullness of expression acting as frontier which she dare not transgress."[15] The plastic artist had to stop before the climax of the action that he wants to represent: "The mere opening of the mouth—apart from the fact that the other parts of the face are thereby violently and unpleasantly distorted—is a blot in painting and a fault in sculpture which has the most untoward effect possible."[16] Such criteria, inevitable in the arts concerned, like sculpture, with the disposition of coextensive relations (*Nebeneinander*), simply do not apply in judging poetry. The poet is free to prolong the expression of feelings. Words do not offer the kind of resistance to impression that plastic materials do. "When Virgil's Laocoön cries aloud, to whom does it occur then that a wide mouth is needful for a cry, and that this must be ugly? Enough, that *clamores horrendos ad sidera tollit* is an excellent feature for the hearing, whatever it might be for the vision."[17] Well, it certainly did occur to Joyce, and Stephen appears to be acting precisely to parody the suggestion that language has this freedom.

Consider how similar the description of the vampire kiss and the cry *clamores horrendos ad sidera tollit* (appalling cries rising to the stars) are in point of fact. Laocoön, according to John Conington's 1886 translation, goes into agony and

> ... to the unregarded skies
> sends up his agonizing cries.
> A wounded bull such moaning makes
> when from his neck the axe he shakes.[18]

According to W. F. Jackson Knight's prose translation, "His shrieks were horrible and filled the sky, like a bull's bellow when an axe has struck awry, and he flings it off his neck."[19] Stephen takes up the same posture. He dramatizes Laocoön's agony, exaggerating the force of the cry and its direction toward the heavens, now graphically rendered: "His mouth molded issuing breath, unspeeched: ooeeehah: roar of cataratic planets globed, blazing, roaring wayawyawayawayaway."[20] Stephen records his inspiration on "Old Deasy's letter" about cattle disease, making the cry congruent with something "like the bellows of a wounded bull." In the context, it is a rare touch, *non plus ultra*.

In the new epic medium, there is still more to the effect. As I noted earlier, Stephen is celebrating his freedom from, in Lessing's terms, coextensive relationships (*Nebeneinander*). The onomatopoeic repetitiveness of his self-indulgence is so protracted that the distinction between the syllables as successive and as coexistent gets lost. This is not the artist remaining hidden "within or behind or beyond or above his handiwork, invisible, refined out of existence" (*P*, 215). The representation emphasizes the visibility of speech.

Stephen has, in fact, struck the pose of Laocoön. The doomed Trojan priest had tried, unsuccessfully, to warn Troy against admitting the wooden horse. Virgil spells out the consequences of what Laocoön's success at Troy would have meant. Here is Virgil's account in Jackson Knight's prose translation:

> But there, in front of all, came Laocoön, hastening furiously down from the citadel with a large company in attendance. While still far off he cried: "O my unhappy friends, you must be mad indeed. Do you really believe that your enemies have sailed away? Do you think that a Greek could offer a gift without treachery in it? Do you know Ulysses no better than that?"[21]

His interrogation of the stratagem culminates in this way:

> "Whatever it proves to be, I still fear Greeks, even when they offer gifts." As he spoke, he powerfully heaved a great spear at the horse's side, into the firm timber-work of its rounded belly, and there it stood, quivering. At the impact, the echoing spaces of the cavernous womb growled and rang; and if the destined will of Heaven had not been set against us, and our reason had not been deranged, Laocoön had surely driven home a thrust till the iron tore open the Greek lair. Troy would then have survived till now; and O proud Citadel of Priam, you would have been standing still.[22]

If Troy had stood, Homer would not have written either *The Iliad* or *The Odyssey*. Aeneas would never have sailed to found Rome. *Ulysses* would not have been written.

Stephen has inadvertently separated his presence from the transmission of the epic tradition. The irony at Stephen's expense here constitutes the invocation of a lineage. Stephen, self-parodied, has nevertheless invoked Calliope, the epic muse—in Greek, "beautiful voice." The voice inaugurates a departure—integrating the text with a classical tradition, the *translatio studii*, the cultural analogue of the *translatio imperii*, the transmission of legitimacy from Troy through Greece and Rome, westward through titles as various as Caesar and kaiser and czar westward.[23]

Stephen at the western tip of Europe is to be translated into this tradition in a world that in J. M. Perl's deft phrase "misordered in pursuit of phantoms."[24] He is not in touch with the muse. The epic environment "re-imagines" Stephen through parameters altogether different from the progression toward full presence indicated by the movement from free indirect discourse to the direct discourse of the transcribed diary entries and by the summative title *A Portrait of the Artist as a Young Man*. Stephen's perspective is no longer the point. Indeed, "seeing" and "portraiture" are beside the point.

Rather than offer a "picture," *Ulysses* re-members the polity.[25] It re-members by reasoning about the constitution of the polity in stylistically heterogeneous chapters, for each of which Joyce advertised a different corresponding organ of the human body. Joyce reported that he was losing interest in Stephen during the composition of *Ulysses*. Stephen's shape is subsidiary to this enterprise. The totality at stake, like the body of the king in medieval political theory, supplies communal experience with a "body politic . . . a body that cannot be seen or handled, consisting of Policy and Government, and constituted for the Direction of the People and Management of the public weal, and this body is utterly void of Infancy and old Age, and other natural defects, which the Body natural is subject to."[26] In the re-membering, the three chapters of the *Telemachiad* have no bodily organs corresponding to them according to the schema of correspondences that Joyce publicized.

As the section of *Ulysses* that draws most immediately on *Portrait*, the problem in the *Telemachiad* is how to come to terms with this legacy. The salient point in the orientation is the emerging relationship of the material to the fable. The orientation requires a holistic grasp of the constraints and implications of genre.

The mark of Stephen's inaptness for the task is his failure to deal with cheating in his examination of memory work in the Dalkey schoolroom. Preoccupied with thoughts of a Blakean demiurge, Stephen is about to test his students' memorization of Milton's *Lycidas*. Talbot, the student he calls on, cheats. He is reading from the text, which he has kept open just beneath Stephen's line of vision. Stephen does not seem to care. Indeed, he has not been listening to the surreptitious reading and, capping the odd emphasis that this absentminded involvement with Milton's poem brings to the poem, confesses his inattention.

> Have I heard all? Stephen asked.
> Yes, sir. Hockey at ten, sir. (2.91–92)

Talbot might be telling the literal truth. Perhaps the issue is the portion of the poem assigned for memorization, and he has indeed rendered it. It is certain that Stephen's "all" brings to mind the complete poem.[27] And the final portion of the poem, the eight-line coda of *Lycidas*, suggest a powerful model of self-determination.

Its significance as a model derives from the rhetorical shift that occupies the eight-line coda of *Lycidas*. Milton has a new voice appear without warning. Just as in the Telemachiad we must come to terms with an authorial presence who is clearly not Stephen, in the coda we must cope with "a detached observer, whose poise and serenity," to quote Louis Martz, "give a new vitality to the shepherd singer, as we see him move into the sunset."[28] It is an adjustment analogous to Stephen's changed roles between *Portrait* and *Ulysses*. In both the *Telemachiad* and *Lycidas* we have to identify a new source of epic authority, entailing a shift away from the first-person mode.[29]

> Thus sang the uncouth Swain to th' Oaks and rills,
> While the still morn went out with Sandals gray,
> He touched the tender stops of various quills,
> With eager thought warbling his Dorick lay;
> And now the Sun had stretched out all the hills,
> And now was dropt into the Western Bay;
> At last he rose, and twitch'd his Mantle blew;
> To morrow to fresh Woods, and Pastures new.[30]

Described in the terms of Stephen's theory of genre, the coda reveals that the "personality of the artist [has passed] into the narration itself" (*P*, 215). The change signals the need to adjust our initial understanding of *Lycidas* to include a programmatic statement that views original voice as dependent on a hitherto unseen narrative presence.

Until the change prophesied in the coda, Stephen's life and Milton's show a rough similarity. For both, a period of voluntary absence from home was followed by an anticlimatic return. At home, both found themselves keeping school.[31] Both needed to come to terms with death: Milton with the death of Edward King, Stephen with the death of his mother. Finally, both must face the possibility that the poetic career on which so much had been staked might never amount to anything: Milton in the proxy of King's disappointed hopes, Stephen in the unsatisfactory round of daily life in Dublin.[32]

With the announcement in the coda, the parallel ends. In this, the eleventh stanza of *Lycidas*—and eleven, Hugh Kenner notes, is "Joyce's number of regeneration"—Milton looks to future.[33] The meter changes. The lines are in ottava rima, the stanza form appropriate to "a poet's epic intention."[34] Stephen has no comparable show of self-determination to offer. The counterpart of his performance before the class to Milton's decisive change of direction is the riddle that he unexpectedly poses to his students.

This is Stephen's own "ghoststory." And in comparison with the decisive change in *Lycidas*, Stephen's performance is indeed ghostly. In Blakean language, he has had to become reconciled to a flat, Ulro-like space.[35] In comparison with the decisive change in *Lycidas*, Stephen's performance is similarly insubstantial. Unlike the "detached observer whose poise and serenity give a new vitality to the shepherd singer," Stephen's performance is pointedly disjointed. He has had no success in shaping his experience. Compared to the decisive change that he, apparently, recalls for the reader without himself reflecting on it, his performance verges on incoherence.

He proposes to ask a riddle. His riddle is, in fact, a non sequitur. No one, as P. W. Joyce noted, could have guessed the answer.[36] In fact, only for Stephen does the performance have a point. An "itching" heralds it in his throat. The solution comes in a "shout of nervous laughter" (2.112, 114). The performance, with a rare economy of means, allows him to display some of the contradictions that impede his assuming a public poetic stance.

We are a world distant from the scope of the conscience to which he had dedicated himself in *Portrait*. Walter Pater, in *Marius the Epicurean*, had ascribed the following characteristics to conscience:

> A sense of conscious powers external to ourselves, pleased or displeased by the right or wrong of very circumstance of daily life ... [and] the old fashioned, partly Puritanic awe, the power of which Wordsworth noted and valued so highly in a northern peasantry ... symbolic usages ... a great seriousness—an impressibility to the sacredness of time, of life and its events, and the circumstances of family fellowship; of such things to men as fire, water, the earth, from

labour on which they live, really understood . . . as gifts—a sense of religious responsibility in the reception of them. A religion for the most part of fear, of multitudinous scruples, of a year-long burden of forms; [and also] . . . heavenly powers . . . a welcome channel for the almost stifling sense of health and delight . . . relieved as gratitude to the gods."[37]

Stephen, in contrast, takes refuge in the boastful cunning of a fox. The great advantage of the performance is to permit Stephen's self-exposure with no chance of the audience's penetrating his private purpose.[38]

The cock crew
The sky was blue:
The bells in heaven
Were striking eleven.
'Tis time for this poor soul
To go to heaven. (2.102–7)

The traditional answer, "The fox burying his mother under a holly tree," could not, in any case, have been guessed from the clues.[39] But Stephen even wants insurance against the possibility that his preoccupations might be deciphered. His students ask to hear the clues twice.

—What is it, sir? We give up.
Stephen, his throat itching, answered:
—The fox burying his grandmother under a hollybush.
He stood up and gave a shout of nervous laughter to which their cries echoed dismay. (2.113–17)

As performance this is not communication but display.

Stephen has no substantial message. He is entangled in genealogies. His vision is intransitive.

In "Telemachus," the heuristic value of reflectivity as such is a subject for mockery. The emblem of art, the analogue for *Portrait*, is Buck Mulligan's shaving mirror. Mulligan taunts Stephen's preoccupation with reflection and representation.

—The rage of Caliban at not seeing his face in a mirror, he said. If only Wilde were alive to see you. (1.143–44)

Mulligan's allusion is to Oscar Wilde's *Picture of Dorian Gray*. His paraphrase, Gifford and Seidman point out, is from the preface: "The nineteenth century dislike of Realism is the rage of Caliban seeing his own face in a glass. The nineteenth century dislike of Romanticism is the rage of Caliban not seeing his own face in a glass" (G&S, 16).

Stephen, unable to offer an alternate decorum, can only react. Much like it makes use of Buck Mulligan's gesticulating at the Mass and lightheartedness, *Ulysses* incorporates and fits Stephen's appearance to its own measure.

—Drawing back and pointing, Stephen said with bitterness:
—It is a symbol of Irish art. The cracked lookingglass of a servant.
(1.145–46)

In the most literal sense, the fiction achieved through Stephen at this point cannot be anything else.

3

Joyce and the Fate of Arthur Griffith's *Resurrection of Hungary* in *Ulysses*

Nationalism subordinates the significance of experience to an ideal order abstracted from the experience of the community. The process is innately historical. The Literary Revival claimed to have recovered the ideal order from the experience of pagan Ireland. The Gaelic League aimed to achieve authenticity through the materiality embodied in language. Stephen Dedalus aspired to inculcate the self-understanding of the Irish people with a new moral referent. Whether it involves the recovery of an original geography, a racial, linguistic, or religious integrity, nationalism confronts the problem of historical knowledge.

What is to be done with the legacy of the past? How does one translate nationality into nationalism? How does one configure an imaginative space, order it temporally, populate it with heroic individuals and their deeds so that it partakes of this past and inspires compatriots to behave as though the vision were a direct expression of their shared nationality?

The importance of Arthur Griffith's Sinn Fein for Joyce was that it pointed Ireland toward Europe. "For the Irish, the dates of Luther's Reformation and the French Revolution mean nothing," Joyce had complained in "Ireland, Island of Saints and Sages." "The wave of democracy that shook England at the time of Simon de Montfort, founder of the House of Commons, and later, at the time of Cromwell's protectorate was spent when it reached the shores of Ireland."[1] Irish nationalism had to look outward. The challenge was to craft an understanding that took note of the diverse sources of common identity and allowed for a historical vision that pointed beyond self-glorification, resentment, and repetition.

> Our civilization is a vast fabric in which the most diverse elements are mingled, in which nordic aggressiveness and Roman law, the new bourgeois conventions and the remnant of a Syriac religion are rec-

onciled. In such a fabric it is useless to look for a thread that may have remained pure and virgin without having undergone the influence of a neighboring thread. What race, or what language (if we except the few whom a playful will seems to have preserved in ice, like the people of Iceland) can boast of being pure today?[2]

To Joyce, it was not at all evident that this reconfiguration of Ireland's legacy could be achieved. He hedges his appeal to Irishness by observing parenthetically that nationality might prove to be "a convenient fiction like so many others to which the scalpels of present day scientists have given the coup de grace."[3] He commends Irish eloquence but notes that "a revolution is not made of human breath and compromises."[4] In a word, the shaping of Irish nationality had to take account of European civilization and envision the continuity of Irish history in new ways.

Through Bloom's link with Griffith, the fable of *Ulysses* returns to Stephen Dedalus's claim to mold Irish experience. The turn to Griffith is highly critical. Sinn Fein is not represented as fit for the historic task for which Stephen was not. *Ulysses'* critical adaptation of Griffith's argument elaborates the lexicon of the constitutional proposal beyond what had been offered in *The Resurrection of Hungary*. This chapter will look at the historical provenance of the lexicon of Griffith's argument and its deployment among the exaggerations of "Cyclops" and according to the stylistic decorum of "Circe," the chapter that disrupts contextualization altogether by suspending communicative addressivity. The deployment of the lexicon of Griffith's argument in such stylistically skewed forms emphasizes its self-referential nontransitivity. The traits associated with the characters do not result in interpersonal contact. Instead, they cluster. Without a consensually transparent line dividing foreground from background, the result is frequently grotesque.

For Stephen, the issue, as the opening adjective "stately" suggests, is still the ownership of the formative action. The prominently placed adjective carries portentous intimations. As an allusion to Stephen's dispossession, it recalls Horatio's report of the ghost in *Hamlet* who had appeared before the watch and moves "slow and stately by them" (1.1.201–2). Mulligan unknown to himself calls Stephen to his responsibilities. In the broader, less character-bound context, it alludes to Tennyson's invocation of Virgil:

> I salute thee, Montavano
> I loved thee since my day began
> Wielder of the stateliest measure ever moulded by the lips of man.[5]

This second context implies that the distribution of formative aspects of the Irish political landscape in the syntax of the fable is anticipated from the outset.

Ulysses elaborates its distinctive epic perspective on modern Irish nationality through Bloom's efforts to make sense of his genealogy. Bloom faces several different obstacles. First, he just does not know enough. He has only approximate information about his family's roots in central Europe. Rumor links his European origins and Griffith's program, but he does not know this. He has no earthly reason for imagining that his personal history might have public relevance.

Contemporary scholarship offers no help. The interest in historical continuity, especially in nationalist circles, tends to self-inflation and hysteria. Standish O'Grady had endorsed a historical imagination that allowed a nation to recover its own mythology, which for Ireland meant "a value far beyond the tale of actual events and duly recorded deeds."[6] Lady Gregory was committed to the kind of historiography that turned readily into myth, and myth that as readily "turned into history."[7] To integral nationalists, like the Citizen in "Cyclops," the chapter subordinate to stylistic decorum of this approach to Irish national identity, Bloom's very presence in the country is a symptom of national decline.

The fable reconfigures these limitations by confronting them and pointing beyond the difficulties. From this perspective, the issue is not whether Bloom is believable as pater patriae or whether the Griffith analogy between Anglo-Irish and Austro-Hungarian constitutional developments adequately expressed the complexities of Ireland's historical situation. What matters is the ongoing effort to represent the contradictions and reservations entailed in the parallel in recognizable narrative progression. The fable subordinates the Griffith analogy to the narrative progression implicit in the succession of generations in Bloom's family. The problems of continuity and family inheritance incorporate the problematic of conceiving of a new Ireland on Sinn Fein's prescription.

Bloom would like to continue the hereditary family practice of naming sons Rudolph and Leopold in alternate generations. Memories of his son, Rudy, and his father, Rudolph, figure in his thoughts throughout the day. The family's past connection with the Hapsburg dynasty might seem to have nothing to do with his environment, but Bloom is trying to forge a raison d'être through the narrative order that the names suggest.

To Joyce, composing *Ulysses* first in Hapsburg Trieste, then in a Swiss exile from a continent-wide war, these connections between the family and supranational Hapsburg entity were, as I argued in the Introduction, more problematic and suggestive. The straightforward "analogy between family feeling and national feeling overlooks the fact," Jonathan Ree has noted, "that you cannot have a sense of belonging to the same nation as your neighbors unless you are aware of it as one nation among others and part of an imagined totality of nations forming, eventually a kind of world system." Joyce would have had daily reminders that "nations only exist in the plural" and that "the principle of nationality" required the phenomenon of internationality.[8] Bloom's connection with the Hapsburg dynasty through his family history embodies this practical complication of the claim to national authenticity. It foreshadows his vulnerability and the hostility of the nationalists who will find him alien. Once the fable annexes the associations that Stephen Dedalus has focused on, the odyssey of the connectivity fluctuating between them becomes a measure of national self-awareness.

The rhetorical deliberation that I am ascribing to the fable dovetails with what we know of Joyce's hesitations concerning imminent Irish independence. In 1906 he had written to his brother, Stanislaus: "If the Irish [Sinn Fein] programme did not insist on the Irish language I suppose I could call myself a nationalist. As it is, I am content to recognize myself as an exile."[9] His familiarity with the Dual Monarchy was far more comprehensive than Griffith's. By 1915, the second year of the composition of *Ulysses*, when Italy's declaration of war on Austria-Hungary forced him from Trieste into his second exile, he had spent eleven years, a third of his life, living under Hapsburg rule.[10] He was never to idealize the vanished imperium. From Paris, he was to look back on his experience of Hapsburg government as having been one of the lesser evils among the forms of rule he had known. "They called it a ramshackle empire.... I wish to God there were more such empires," he told his friends, the Colums.[11] He liked "the mellowness of life there ... [and] the fact that the state [had] tried to impose so little upon its own or upon other people. It was not war-like, it was not efficient, and its bureaucracy was not strict, it was a country for a peaceful man."[12] Unlike Griffith, Joyce would have known the workaday nuts-and-bolts of the Sinn Fein model for Anglo-Irish cooperation.

The details of the arrangement that he could not have idealized are flagrant. It was a state that could imprison an Italian worker, Anton Zamparetti, in Trieste in 1906 "for *lèse-majesté* because he persisted in calling the emperor 'king,'" the title that was the legally obligatory form of address for the same monarch in Hungary.[13] The 1867 compromise had established three governing bodies, an arrangement that had to be renegotiated every ten years. Public institutions were designated royal (*königlich*) kingdom of Hungary, imperial-royal (*kaiserlich-koniglich* or k. k.) in the Austrian crown lands, imperial-and-royal (*kaiserlich und königlich* or k. u. k.) if they belonged to the constitutionally joint ministries—foreign affairs, defense, and the offices associated with their financing.¹⁴ This complicated compromise was Robert Musil's *Kakkania*. On paper, it called itself the Austro-Hungarian monarchy. In daily speech, it was still called "Austria, . . . a name that it had as a state, solemnly renounced by oath, while preserving it in all matters of sentiment."¹⁵ Acquaintance with such a complex historical formation could not bow to allegorical simplification.

Ulysses emphasizes the vulnerability of the arrangement. As the First World War continued with massive Austro-Hungarian defeats, the survival of the exemplum, never mind the argument Griffith derived from it, was open to question. And Bloom? Like the hereditary House of Austria, he is besieged by nationalists who challenge his legitimacy. Like the dynasty, he is being forced, willy-nilly, to represent a vaguely cosmopolitan ideal.

The catechetical narrative voice of "Ithaca" provides a cameo view of the roles ideally available to this troubled model of legitimacy. Bloom owns an "indistinct daguerreotype of Rudolf Virag," his own father, and his father's "father Leopold Virag executed in the year 1852 in the portrait atelier of their respective 1st and 2nd cousin, Stefan Virag of Szesfehervar, Hungary" (17.1875–77). Hidden in a drawer, the dramatis personae of the fable have all been rendered members of the same family.

This is more than the fable itself could do. Isolated between two Rudolfs —his father, who committed suicide, and his malformed son, Rudy, a misbirth—Bloom, the last male of the lineage, is threatened with the extinction of his name. His isolation in 1904 Dublin between the two deaths resonates with a notorious Hapsburg parallel: the death of the imperial heir, Crown Prince Rudolf, under mysterious circumstances on January 30, 1889, a harbinger of the doom that seemed to cling to the Hapsburg emperor who had lost his brother, Maximilian, to a Mexican firing squad and would loose his empress, Elizabeth, to an assassin's bullet.

Rudy Bloom had died from his birth defects, and Rudolph Virag-Bloom poisoned himself. The death of Crown Prince Rudolf was never explained but continued to fascinate Europe. The sheer pointlessness of the death and the helplessness of the king-emperor and his family held the public's attention. The thirty-year-old crown prince died at a private hunting lodge at Mayerling. The bodies of the crown prince and his eighteen-year-old mistress, Maria Vetsera, were discovered, shot to death, side by side in bed. Nothing more was known. A suicide pact was rumored.

The scandal was long and trying for the Hapsburg court. Why should a young man, the only son and heir of the Emperor Franz Joseph and the Empress Elizabeth, in apparent good health, have suddenly killed himself? The act defied the empire's apparent baroque stability. The Court issued contradictory accounts of the death. At first apoplexy was blamed. There were rumors of an accident, a fatal, self-inflicted gunshot wound. Although suicide was officially confirmed as the cause of death, rumors continued to circulate. The government's verdict did not end either the general fascination with the case or the Hapsburg discomfort with the revelations.

Despite the persistent interest, the Austrian court refused to offer further clarification. Officials refused all comment. Every effort was made to sever the observance of Vetsera's death from the prince's. Her body was secretly moved from Mayerling. Unofficial speculation mentioned a malformation of Rudolf's skull and an inherited "Wittelsbach" madness. Conflicts with his father were recalled.[16]

The mystery persisted even as Rudolf's role as crown prince went to Franz Ferdinand, Franz Joseph's nephew, who would, in turn, fall to the assassin's bullet in Sarajevo. The emperor was rumored never to have reconciled to the loss. When the Countess Marie Larisch-Wallersee, who had been the go-between in Rudolf's love affair, tried to publish her memoirs in 1897, Franz Joseph bought and burned the manuscript.[17]

Bloom recalls his father's death in a hotel room "with hunting pictures" (6.360). Little Rudy was born malformed. Bloom's isolation is threatened by shapelessness and death. He gives Molly *Ruby: The Pride of the Ring*; he puts a ruby ring on the phantom finger of his one-time flame Josie (Powell) Breen (15.468–69). As he prepares to give the volume to Molly, he notes:

> *Ruby: Pride of the Ring* ... Fierce Italian with carriagewhip. Must be Ruby pride of the ring on the floor naked. Sheet kindly lent. *The monster Maffei desisted and flung his victim from him with an oath.* Cruelty behind it. Doped animals ... (4.346–49)

As he holds Josie's hand, his gesture inverts the role of his eponym in the fable "Androcles and the Lion." He does not claim the injured lion's injury and will not act the lion. The lines in Italian belong in *Don Giovanni*, part of the program Boylan was to deliver to Molly that afternoon. The opening phrase from *Hamlet* bespeaks his irresolution.

> The witching hour of night. I took the splinter out of this hand, carefully, slowly. (tenderly, as he slips on her finger a ruby ring) *Là ci darem la mano*. (15.467–69)

Bloom would seal the moment.

Whereas Rudolf/Rudy signals death, suffering, and metamorphoses, Lipoti Virag, Bloom's grandfather, appears to be a forceful identity, overdetermined and unfocused. Bloom seeks refuge in the role in the "Cyclops" episode when he finds himself attacked by nationalists. When the fiery (and beery) patrons at Barney Kiernan's want to deny him his right to call himself an Irishman, Bloom would, by preference, remain strictly rational. He contends that he is Irish because he is himself. The place he lives, this moment in time, should be sufficient warrant.

> A nation? says Bloom. A nation is the same people living in the same place.
> —By God, then, says Ned, laughing, if that's so I am a nation for I'm living in the same place for the past five years.
> So of course everyone had the laugh at Bloom and says he, trying to muck out of it:
> —Or also living in different places.
> —That covers my case, says Joe.
> —What is your nation if I may ask? says the citizen.
> —Ireland, says Bloom. I was born here. Ireland.
> The citizen said nothing only cleared the spit out of his gullet and, gob he spat a Red bank oyster out of him right in the corner. (12.1421–34)

Bloom protests the hostility by insisting on the reality of the suffering for which the prejudice against him is responsible.

> —And I belong to a race too, says Bloom, that is hated and persecuted. Also now. This very moment. This very instant. (12.1467–68)

As far as he is concerned, history, at best, has been a nightmarish distraction from what really constitutes life. Sensible people would not intentionally force history into such a mold:

> [It is] no use . . . Force, hatred, history, all that. That's not life for men and women, insult and hatred. And everybody knows that it's the very opposite of that is really life. (12.1481–83)

The problem is that Barney Kiernan's patrons do not care about the existential coloring of the moment. They want him to be responsible for a logos operant in the moment. He is the "perverted jew . . . Ahasuerus . . . [cursed] by God" (12.1635, 1667). He is "Virag from Hungary!" (12.1666–67). The anonymous narrator declares him responsible for the "Hungarian system" identified with Sinn Fein and with

> all kinds of jerrymandering, packed juries and swindling the taxes of the government and appointing consuls all over the world to walk about selling Irish industries. (12.1575–77)

The logos of persecution prompts Bloom to claim kinship with Christ, and the drunken Citizen, enraged by Bloom's presumption, threatens to crucify him to revenge the blasphemy and flings a "biscuit box" (a mock ciborium, a symbolic casket) at him.

This culmination of his symbolic elevation-execution launches Bloom on a kind of historical odyssey. He initiates a symbolic regression along the trajectory of Rudolph Virag-Bloom's emigration. Conforming to the decorum of the chapter, Bloom's evolution is atavistic. He, too, ends up by seeking justification in (what is for him) the archaic past. With crowds of well-wishers cheering, the fleeing Bloom turns into his own grandfather: "Nagyaságos [sic] uram Lipóti Virag" (12.1816). (The translation of the middle-class honorific term is "esquire.")[18] In exchange for safety, he seems to abandon all that Rudolf Virag had accomplished through his emigration, including Ireland.

Lipoti Virag's destination, appropriately celebrated by orchestras and bonfires, is "the distant clime of Százharminczbrojùgulyás-Dugulás (Meadow of the Murmuring Waters)" (12.1818–19). The choice of address is scatological. The Hungarian part of the address—allowing for the misspelling of "borju," not "broju," that is "veal" or "calf"—translates as "one hundred and thirty veal gulyas blockage or constipation." The street address links Hungary's national dish and constipation.[19] The flowery English pseudotranslation in the brackets is sheer misdirection. Taken together with the first two parts of the address, however, it implies that the ultimate destination of Leopold-become-his-own-grandfather odyssey is the water closet: the "Meadow of the Murmuring Waters." There, presumably, the blockage of generation, the extinction of Rudolph, father and son, the end of the "dynasty," will find proper issue. In terms of the family continuity, Bloom's escape from the Cyclops still leads to an end. This time the end comes in an anatomically ludicrous and alimentarily precise sense.

It should be evident that the parody has a broad scope: nationalist posturing is one object. Bloom's return to the role of Lipoti Virag comments on Standish O'Grady's ideal historiography as inherently heroic. The phrasing of the toilet-bowl description aims at the pretentious stylistic decorum of the Literary Revival pseudoepic, which the chapter mocked earlier:

> In Innisfail the fair there lies a land, the land of holy Michan. There rises a watchtower beheld of men afar. There sleep the mighty dead as in life they slept, warriors and princes of high renown. A pleasant land it is in sooth of murmuring waters, fishful streams where sport the gunard, the plaice, the halibut, the gibbed haddock, the grilse, the dab, the brill, the flounder, the pollock, the mixed coarse fish generally and other denizens of the aqueous kingdom too numerous to be enumerated. (12.68–75)

We are being invited to contemplate communal values of the generality with which Stephen Dedalus was concerned.

With his forced withdrawal to the role of Lipoti Virag, Bloom appears about to surrender his personal identity to an epic progenitor as wrapped in myth and unreason as any idol whom the Cyclops might revere. However, the telos of the epic fable is intelligent rather than atavistic. The uncertain step backward into the toilet turns out to be only a prolegomenon to a fresh act of filiation.

When the biscuit box strikes the ground, it signals Bloom's incarnation as "ben Bloom Elijah"—still a son the Hebrew "ben" insists—but a son with the role of mediating between the archaic fathers and their epigones.

> lo, there came about them all a great brightness and they beheld the chariot wherein He stood ascend to heaven. And they beheld Him in the chariot, clothed upon in the glory of the brightness, having raiment as of the sun, fair as the moon and terrible that for awe they durst not look upon Him. And there came a voice out of heaven, calling *Elijah! Elijah!* And He answered with a main cry: *Abba! Adonai!* And they beheld Him even Him, ben Bloom Elijah, amid clouds of angels ascend to the glory of the brightness at an angle of fortyfive degrees over Donohoe's in Little Green street like a shot off a shovel. (12.1910–19)[20]

As "ben Bloom Elijah" Bloom has a mission. The prophet Elijah, we recall, had meant to "turn the heart of the fathers to the children and the heart of the children to the fathers..." [Mal. 4:6]. Bloom has achieved this acme of self-filiation in a transcendent, albeit parodic, exile.

The Citizen's biscuit box striking the roadway starts an earthquake. It is followed by "eleven shocks, all of the fifth grade of Mercalli's scale... [and] a violent atmospheric perturbation of cyclonic character" (12.1859–60). The eleven seismic shocks of the catastrophe echo the eleven days of Rudy's short life, the need for beginning after beginning, the serial repetition of singularity.

The deployment of Griffith's argument in "Circe" defies the application of this seriality. What can possibly correspond to the referent of the argument in a discursive space that does not lend itself to public address and public assertion as the adjective had been understood in previous episodes?

The problem is analogous to the challenge that arises from periodization in history. Once the domain under study is known to have been actuated by principles and a spirit qualitatively different from the principles and spirit that rule the time of the historian's writing, how is the historian to establish that his or her analytical procedure does not contaminate the object of study, the past, through the introduction of alien criteria, but fashions an expression according to its native telos?

"Circe" responds to this challenge by warping the medium. It is not that the elements germane to the fable do not appear or combine. If anything, they do so too readily and cohere with too much force. The way in which they behave challenges the ideal of representational stability as such. They appear overdetermined in a way that defies coherent analysis.

Kant argued that without categories, perceptions, whether of the world without or of the world within, of sense, imagination, or self, would belong to no world at all. The perceptions "would be without an object." The result would be a "blind play of representations—less even than a dream." The possibility of experience depends on an a priori "permanent synthetic unity of perception." Without this transcendental foundation, he surmised, "a whole crowd of phenomena might rush into our soul, without ever forming real experience."[21]

"Circe" postulates that something like this crowd, an emergent totality, in form at times quasi-human, at times bestial, at times a random variation of objects animate and inanimate, concrete and abstract, has usurped the transcendental foundation. We cannot schematize events according to a univocal matrix of space-time.

Addressivity has run amok. Because all sorts of phenomena, "objects, animals, abstract ideas ... are all given lines to speak," Steven Connor writes, "... events, ideas, and objects decline to settle for the ignominious condition of a mere referent, energetically refusing to be spoken *of*." We cannot discuss the goings-on properly because "there are no objects of discourse in this chapter, but only subjects of discourse, restlessly surging up into speech."[22] The chapter dramatizes the relativism consequent on the recognition of qualitatively different modes of perception and ways of proceeding to a conclusion in different historical eras.

What has become of the parallel between Griffith's constitutional proposal and the characters? Of the fable? Gertrude Himmelfarb reproaches social historians for devaluing "the political realm." In subordinating political history to the effects of social forces, social history "makes meaningless those aspects of the past which serious and influential contemporaries thought most meaningful. It makes meaningless not only the struggle over political authority but the very idea of legitimate political authority."[23] The reader expecting to refer to the fable as guide must make do with a composite entity, something like mob or rumor or an enchanted landscape with animals and objects that can speak.

As a result the political allegory, by way of the fable, gets occluded. Allegory depends on the successful transfer of information from one context to another. The ongoing disruption of context in "Circe" preempts such a transfer. Self-reflexivity is impossible in a medium where the reflective surface, the light, the message, all are likely to become animate.

In terms of the parallel between Griffith's historical argument and the narrative progression, the reader lacks an appropriate measure. "Addressivity is ... so constitutionally jammed, impeded and scrambled in 'Circe,'" Steven Connor writes, "as to disallow any of its solidary effects to hold long. Acclamation, proclamation, exclamation, annunciation, accusation, interrogation, declaration and denunciation cross and propagate uncontrollably through the chapter." The medium is active, alive in some way. "Circe" "resists the various public address systems for forming cultural identities.... [Its] sheer excess of interference between the voices and their lines of utterance ... prevents the crystallization of either addressor or addressee as 'I' or 'you.'"[24]

The domain has to be taken on its own terms. The philosopher of history Michael Oakeshott serves as a good guide to the circumspection that such a recognition of the independence of the object of the discourse entails. The historical past is so complicated, so entirely composed of contingencies, that it has "no unity or feeling or clear outline," Oakeshott writes, "no over-all pattern or purpose." Its intelligibility derives from the "circumstantial relations established by the historian."[25]

Each piece of historical writing is an independent exercise, "a picture drawn to its own scale, eliciting a coherence in a group of contingencies of similar magnitude." What matters to the historian are effects, not causes. The historian's concern is not with "a single ideal coherence of events which may be said to be true to the exclusion of all others; there are only a multitude of 'coherences' of different orders and on different scales."[26]

Oakeshott is a particularly appropriate guide to the phantasmagoria of "Circe" because his distrust of generalities is no methodological platitude. To produce an account of the effect of the past, Oakeshott requires a special sense, "an attitude unique to history as such." It is a sense thoroughly embroiled with, in fact indistinguishable from, the present. "The activity of the historian," he writes, "is pre-eminently that of understanding present events—the things that are before him—as evidence for past happenings."[27] Since it is from this foundation that the historian "imparts to the past, and so to the world, a peculiarly tentative and intermediate kind of intelligibility," the insistence on relativity becomes an affirmation of singularity.[28]

The encounter with the past has this special character, irreducible to law. Oakeshott gives the following example:

> The historian although he sometimes writes of the outbreak of war a "conflagration," nevertheless leaves us in no doubt that he knows of no set of conditions which may properly be called the necessary and sufficient conditions of war. He knows only a set of happenings which when fully set out make the outbreak of *this* war seem neither an "accident," nor a "miracle," nor a necessary event, but merely an intelligible occurrence.[29]

The specific requirement of the historian is to be able to envision "an intelligible convergence of human choices and actions."[30] Aside from this requirement, the historian postulates nothing as necessary.

The equivalent in "Circe" to this openness and the configuration of the energies, which we have associated with the fable as intelligible, is the figure of Lipoti Virag. The concentration of energy through the figure is such that the pressure for self-expression precludes the self-awareness of Oakeshott's "genuine historian."

"Circe" caps the progression of historical styles from Anglo-Saxon to

Harlem English in "Oxen of the Sun" and stylistically is, according to the reader's taste, their proper climax or immediate echo. Lipoti Virag is a convulsive reaction, the final expression, or the prolongation of the exhausting historical progression of the styles. "Circe" depicts Lipoti Virag as a convulsive, mechanical, ill-focused dispenser of pornographic lore, the author of a multivolume *Fundamentals of Sexology*, which makes public "the Sex Secrets of Monks and Maidens" (15.2423, 2547). Spasms make him twitch grotesquely and spurt out polysyllabic examinations of the anatomies of the Nighttown whores and unpredictable animal sounds. It is in this figure that the fleeing Bloom is supposed to find the "father of all his race," the archaic progenitor to rival the Citizen's Gaelic sires, the father of a father such as he himself is precluded from becoming, his "granpappachi."[31]

The role of Lipoti Virag is an uncomfortable demand on Bloom. As the last Leopold to have fathered a Rudolph, Lipoti confronts him as an embodied concentration of libidinal energies more potent than he himself can comprehend. Lipoti Virag is the counterpart of the malformed Rudy. He is excess about to turn incomprehensible. He is the threat of experience about to turn illegible. While an earlier draft of "Circe" had designated Lipoti "Bloom's double," he also embodies a kind of surplus in the fable, an anonymity, a tendency to stand in for the writing as such, the fable in surplus basking in self-reference:[32]

> *Lipoti Virag, basilicogrammate, chutes rapidly down through the chimney flue and struts two steps to the left on gawky pink stilts. He is sausaged into several overcoats and wears a brown mackintosh under which he holds a roll of parchment. In his left eye flashes the monocle of Cashel Boyle O'Connor Fitzmaurice Tisdall Farrell. On his head is perched an Egyptian pshent. Two quills project over his ears.* (15.2304–10)

The term "basilicogrammate," or lord of language, recalls Stephen's antinomian claim in the hospital to be "Bous Stephanoumenos, bullockbefriending bard, lord and giver of life" (14.1115). The caricatured Egyptian Thoth on "gawky pink stilts" is a distorted version of Stephen's vision of the bird-girl in the "likeness of a strange and beautiful seabird [with] . . . long slender bare legs delicate as a crane's," the vision that seemed a harbinger of Stephen's vocation in *Portrait* (P, 171). The "brown mackintosh" refers to the enigmatic stranger at Paddy Dignam's funeral whose coat became "M'Intosh" in the press report while the print diminished Bloom himself to L. Boom, a noise (16.1260).³³ The "monocle" of the automaton-like Cashel Boyle O'Connor Fitzmaurice Tisdall Farrell, who "parafes his polysyllables" in the "constant readers' room" of the National Library (9.1115), that is, writes his multisyllabic name paragraph-size, alludes to the ultimate visibility of the process. The strain here is tremendous. The embodiment of locomotor ataxia—and the locomotor apparatus is the organ of "Circe"—Lipoti embodies a form of writing, or self-inscription, the logos all but falling short of coherent expression, an expression that gestures at extinction and explosion, a parodic approximation of fulfillment.

"Circe" registers the rhetorical and historical associations of the figure on at least three separate occasions. Each approximates the perspective of the totality with a different bias. Like Lipoti Virag, the scenes are convulsive approximations of the narrative progression. Each blends allusions to Griffith's historical arguments for a new Irish constitution with details from Bloom's domestic drama. Each strikes a balance with the aspect of the totality that falls short of narrative approximation, the call to authenticity that Joyce in his early piece, "Drama and Life," had described as existing

> before it takes form, independently ... conditioned but not controlled by its scene. It might be said fantastically that as soon as men and women began life in the world there was about them, a spirit, of which they were dimly conscious, which would have had to sojourn in their midst in deeper intimacy and for whose truth they became seekers in after times, longing to lay hands on it.³⁴

This spirit is the inspiration of the fable.

In apparent response to a prostitute's suggestion that he "make a sump speech out of it" (15.1352), the active speech mode transforms Bloom. He becomes "Leopold the First," the "undoubted emperor-president and king-chairman, the most serene and potent and very puissant ruler of [the] realm" (15.1471–72). Borrowing from Griffith's description of the coronation of Franz Joseph, he approximates the active mode, the sudden break with context of the rhetorical apostrophe, crowned with "St. Stephen's iron crown" (15.1439), anointed with "a cruse of hairoil ... [and assuming] a mantle of cloth of gold."³⁵ He "puts ... a ruby ring" on his own finger and then he "ascends and stands on the stone of destiny" (15.1490–91) or Stone of Scone, the site traditionally identified with the Tanist Stone or the Lia-Fail, "the monolith erected by the ancient Gaelic kings at their coronations."³⁶

In a fantastically parodic fashion, Bloom has found a way to Tara. As

Leopold the First, wearing both crown and ruby ring, Bloom stands sovereign and complete. The embodiment of sovereign Ireland, he chooses a new consort. He bestows his "royal hand upon the princess Selene, the splendor of the night" (15.1506–7), the goddess of the moon.

Of special relevance to this transcendent union is the tradition of the English coronation ceremonial, which deemed the finger on which the ring was to be placed "the 'marrying finger' [and] . . . the coronation ring . . . 'the wedding ring of England.'"[37] By putting the ring on his own finger, Bloom, like Napoleon, who had placed the crown on his own head, is making a rare claim to autonomy—to the right to remake the conditions that have made him, a right that, like Napoleon's, would be sui generis. While Molly entertains Boylan, Bloom marries himself. The scene is massively overdetermined. The ceremony recalls Buck Mulligan's projected production of *Everyman His own Wife* (9.1171). Bloom, in the guise of Ireland triumphant, is also a celebrant of Onan.

The approximation of the totality recurs in this lexicon in the accusatory mode. The agent of the transformation is Bello Cohen, the Circean male avatar of brothel owner Bella Cohen, a possible allusion to the short-lived Communist reign of Bela Kun and the punishing postwar confusion in Hungary following the fall of the Hapsburgs. Just as the turn to Communism rendered the contradictions of the modus vivendi of the ancien régime visible, Bello's torture of Bloom's indicates the bias of self-division.

The dominatrix forces Bloom to undergo a series of bestial metamorphoses that recall the "doped animals" in Molly's circus novel, *Ruby: Pride of the Ring*. Bello orders him to "shed [his] male garments" and decrees that he is to be called Ruby Cohen (15.2967–68). Then Bello, in emulation of Bloom's courting of Josie, "places a ruby ring on [Ruby Cohen's] finger." He insists on gratitude: "And there now! With this ring I thee own. Say, *thank you, mistress*" (15.3067–69). Bloom, with gratitude sadistically enforced, complies. He has been inscribed as his own wife and his own child. He has made good the requirement of his connection with Lipoti and Rudolf/Rudy through his own body.[38]

The culminating scene of "Circe" engages these associations but with a difference. Stephen has been knocked down after a drunken assault by British soldier, Private Carr, who had judged him guilty of lèse-majesté toward the British sovereign. Stephen is lying unconscious on the ground. Bloom is engaged in a recognizable action in an interpersonal context. He is trying to wake Stephen up. He first calls him by his family name and then, on the one occasion in the text when this happens, by his Christian name.³⁹ Stephen is too drunk to respond. For a moment, he confuses Bloom's interruption of his sleep with Haines's nightmare of the night before in the Martello Tower. Then, still more intimately, he imagines Bloom to be the visitant creature of the vampire poem he had composed at noon. Finally, mumbling lines from "Who Goes with Fergus?" he turns off the whole troubling prospect. In his drunken sleep, he seeks the more profound rest from worldly care that the glades of Yeats's Fergus had promised, the consolation he had offered his mother. Meanwhile, Bloom stands above him, looking concerned and looking for something practical to do:

BLOOM
Eh! Ho! (*There is no answer. He bends again.*) Mr. Dedalus! (*there is no answer*) The name if you call. Somnambulist. (*he bends again and, hesitating, brings his mouth near the face of the prostrate form*) Stephen! (*There is no answer. He calls again.*) Stephen!

STEPHEN
(*frowns*) Who? Black panther. Vampire. (*he sighs and stretches himself, then murmurs thickly with prolonged vowels*)
  Who ... drive ... Fergus now
  And pierce ... wood's woven shade?
(*He turns on his left side, sighing, doubling himself together.*)

BLOOM
Poetry. Well educated. Pity. (*he bends again and undoes the buttons of Stephen's waistcoat*) To breathe. (*he brushes the woodshavings with light hand and fingers*) One pound seven. Not hurt anyhow. (*he listens*) What?

STEPHEN
(*murmurs*)
  ... shadows ... the woods
  ... white breast ... dim sea
(*He stretches out his arms, sighs again and curls his body ...*)

At best, Bloom's appreciation of Stephen's artistic ambitions would be minimal, but his actual response compounds a series of errors. He mishears Stephen's mumblings. He cannot imagine their solipsistic inspiration. He does recognize May Goulding Dedalus's features in Stephen's face, but then he mistakes the name Fergus from the lyric "Who Goes With Fergus?" for the name of a girl. He imagines that he has made out Stephen's beloved's name in the mumbled poetry. Respecting the unasked-for confidence, he is prepared to treat the accidental revelation as a secret.

He invokes his Freemason oath for emphasis. He has made Stephen himself the poem's context.

> (... *Bloom, holding the hat and ashplant, stands erect. A dog barks in the distance. Bloom tightens and loosens his grip on the ashplant. He looks down on Stephen's face and form.*)
> BLOOM
> (*communes with the night*) Face reminds me of his poor mother. In the shady wood. The deep white breast. Ferguson, I think I caught. A girl. Some girl. Best thing could happen to him (*he murmurs*) . . . swear that I will always hail, ever conceal, never reveal, any part or parts, art or arts . . ." (15.4924–53)

The oath is redundant. Bloom cannot deliberately "reveal" the poem in his hearing.

The stance is highly suggestive. As in the figure of Dante when he meets Virgil in the Dark Wood in the opening of the *Inferno*, the composition of the work finds voice here.[40] The recognition points to the possibility of the tradition enfolding the moment. The gesture adumbrates a claim of "higher universality" which Hans-Georg Gadamer had described as "the basic tendency of the historical spirit; to recognize itself in other beings."[41] However, the mode of synthesis associated with Lipoti Virag rules here.

Bloom, inadvertently, reflects his concern for Stephen back on himself. The encounter ends up intransitive. When he mistakes "Fergus" for "Ferguson," the suffix "-son" deflects his concern for Stephen to his preoccupation with his own incompleteness. For Bloom, the meaning of the transition, ultimately of the encounter with Stephen, is Rudy, his lost son.

> (*Silent, thoughtful, alert he stands on guard, his finger at his lips in the attitude of secret master. Against the dark wall a figure [appears] slowly, fairy boy of eleven, a changeling, kidnapped, dressed in an Eton suit with glass shoes and a little bronze helmet, holding a book in his hand. He reads from right to left inaudibly, smiling, kissing the page.*)
> BLOOM
> (*wonderstruck, calls inaudibly*) Rudy!
>
> RUDY
> (gazes, unseeing into Bloom's eyes and goes on reading, smiling. He has a delicate mauve face. On his suit he has diamond and ruby but-

tons. In his free left hand he holds a slim ivory cane with a violet bow-knot. A white lambkin peeps out of his waistcoat pocket.) (15.4956–67)

There is no possibility of a coherent overview of events here. Because the moment bears the impress of the mode of synthesis associated with Lipoti Virag, it will conflate any number of contradictory emphases. We can treat the moment as a reward Bloom has merited, as does Elliot B. Gose; or, with Karen Lawrence, as testimony to irretrievable and premature aspiration to closure, which the text mocks; or, with Marilyn French, for whom the details of Rudy's costume are inescapably parodic, as a silly fantasy.[42] "One of the ways Joyce supersedes Flaubert," writes David Weir, "is in his ability to maintain the seemingly contradictory narrative modes of sympathy and irony simultaneously."[43] The end of "Circe" does not so much invite closure as point to the need for other discursive alternatives— a welcome that the last three chapters of this book gleefully trump and exercise as a warrant to reconceive the totality of the fable.

4

Closure and Millicent Bloom

Hayden White notes that "in addition to the level of conceptualization on which the historian emplots his narrative account of what happened, there is another level on which he may seek to explicate 'the point of it all' or 'what it all adds up to in the end.'"[1] Narrative progression contributes to the chiaroscuro of this understanding through the marks left by the action of *Ulysses* as the fable follows in the wake of the sun. The design deploys the conjunction of Stephen Dedalus and Milly Bloom, the alternative to Bloom's tentative equation of Stephen and Rudy, as approximations of the communal "we," the attribution of collective agency that renders membership in a community thinkable.

The parallel is a prolegomenon to an examination of birth as a metaphor for the making of a new Irish political landscape. Initially, Stephen and Milly are linked through associations with novelty and pictorial representation. Stephen, of course, carries these allusions as a result of *Portrait*. Milly, referred to metonymically as "photo" on two occasions (1.685, 14.1535), has a "hereditary taste" for pictorial representation (8.176) and is linked to an heirloom daguerreotype, inherited from the Bloom ancestor Stefan Virag.

The text readily accommodates inquiry into the relationship between Stephen and Milly as symbols of complementary modes of representation. Stephen writes with darkness. He is fascinated by his own shadow impinging on the world, leaving an impression on the imaginable cosmos as backdrop, an impress, an analogue of letters, in ink, in print, darkening the page.

In a many-sided ludic performance in "Proteus," Stephen actively contemplates imprinting darkness. He probes the properties of shadows, the darkness beyond the solar light, the darkness identified with subjectivity. He dramatizes the dark materiality of letters on the printed page and reaches out to annex viewers and readers to the performance that is a parody of Bishop Berkeley's epistemologically derived, theologically sanctioned idealism. Interrupting himself with dramatic promptings, he envisions the empirical world in distinct stages of genesis, as seen and known. The performance starts with darkness. It is self-consciously adjusted for imaginary bifocal viewing and is only a breath distant from casting the world around him as a writing with light, or photography.

> His shadow lay over the rocks as he bent, ending. Why not endlessly till the farthest star? Darkly they are there behind this light, darkness shining in the brightness, delta of Cassiopeia, worlds. Me sits there with his augur's rod of ash, in borrowed sandals, by day beside a livid sea, unbeheld, in violet night walking beneath a reign of uncouth stars. I throw this ended shadow from me, manshape, ineluctable, call it back. Endless, would it be mine, form of my form? Who watches me here? Who ever anywhere will read these written words? Signs on a white field. Somewhere to someone on your flutiest voice. The good bishop of Cloyne took the veil of the temple out of his shovel hat; veil of space with coloured emblems hatched on its field. Hold hard. Coloured on a flat: yes, that's right. Flat I see, then think distance, near, far, flat I see, east, back. Ah, see now! Falls back suddenly, frozen in stereoscope. Click does the trick. You find my words dark. Darkness is in our souls, do you not think? (3.408–21)

Stephen identifies himself with the imprint of letters. "The signs on a white field" rule Berkeley's derivation of the phenomenal world from sense impressions and Stephen's mimicry of the epistemic constitution of the multicolored, three-dimensional world.

Milly is associated with light giving shape to darkness. In the "Oxen of the Sun" chapter, she takes the shape of a zodiac sign and metamorphoses into a kind of skywriting through light. Her youth and fertility shape Alpha—the first letter of the alphabet. Much like the daguerreotype heirloom, the metamorphoses accommodates and accords significance to the dramatis personae of the fable. Greeted as a "wonder of metempsychosis," the letter A metamorphoses into the image of swirling, snakelike filaments, an umbilical confusion, an organic approximation of a birth, a new beginning, and the prognostication of an eventual legibility.

> And lo, wonder of metempsychosis, it is she, the everlasting bride, harbinger of the daystar, the bride, ever virgin. It is she, Martha, thou lost one, Millicent, the young the dear, the radiant. How serene does

she now arise, a queen among the Pleiades, in the penultimate antelucan hour, shod in sandals of bright gold, coifed with a veil of what do you call it gossamer. It floats, it flows about her starborn flesh and loose it streams, emerald, sapphire, mauve and heliotrope, sustained on currents of cold interstellar wind, winding, coiling, simply swirling, writhing in the skies a mysterious writing till, after a myriad metamorphoses of symbol, it blazes, Alpha, a ruby and triangled sign upon the forehead of Taurus. (14.1099–109)[2]

The image has a broad resonance. Stephen's and Bloom's attempts to detach themselves from the environment and to achieve a more rounded, more autonomous conception of their roles have an echo here. The connection with Stephen takes shape in the prominent allusion in Milly's metamorphosis as "Alpha, a ruby and triangled sign upon the forehead of Taurus" to the schoolboy cry *bous stephaneforos*, or crowned bull (Taurus crowned), the early mockery that had dogged Stephen's dreams of greatness in *Portrait* (P, 168). The vision in the sky also recalls the firedrake during Anne Hathaway and Shakespeare's nights of lovemaking, the symbol of suffering and compensatory prominent in Stephen's theory of Shakespeare's life and work. Milly's apotheosis has, it seems, inscribed the contact and destiny of which Stephen dreams "among the stars" (9.932).

The connection with Bloom appears in the metamorphosis's climactic reference to his birth sign, Taurus. The "ruby and triangled sign" of Bloom's house makes Milly the giant red star Aldebaran on the star map. In terms of Bloom's personal symbolism, it identifies her as Rudy's sibling and as a female: the new beginning of the ongoing metamorphosis of his lineage.

There is a dynamic relationship between this image of fertility and the components of the images expressing Stephen's struggle to find a fresh beginning. The many-stranded spreading presence in the night sky evokes the imagery of Stephen's bitter conflation of paradisiacal hope, midwifery, birth, and death at the sight of the *Frauenzimmer* in "Proteus." There, too, the issue had been the possibility of a new beginning. Stephen recalled his own birth. Then, in a comic twist, he imagined a trail of umbilical cords reaching all the way back to Creation. The reiteration of A—once in Greek, once in Hebrew—translates into numerical notation as eleven.

> One of her sisterhood lugged me squealing into life. Creation from nothing. What has she in the bag? A misbirth with a trailing navelcord, hushed in ruddy wool. The cords of all link back,

strandentwining cable of all flesh. That is why mystic monks. Will you be as gods? Gaze in your *omphalos*. Hello! Kinch here. Put me on to Edenville. Aleph, alpha: nought, nought, one. (3.35–40)

The entire supposed telephone number to "Edenville" translates numerically as 11,001; a lesser version of Millicent, which translates numerically as 1,000,100. Both numerical transpositions offer extension of the eleven days, fantastically extended at the end of "Circe" to eleven years, as I noted, of Rudy's life.[3]

Stephen envisions his struggle as subterranean. He dreams of earning a full understanding of light. In *Portrait*, in expressly anti-Platonic language, he resists the separation of form from matter. He determines "to try slowly and humbly and constantly to express, to press out again, from the gross earth or what it brings forth, from sound shape and colour which are the prison gates of our soul, an image of the beauty we have come to understand" (*P*, 207).[4] The imagery recurs in the "Wandering Rocks" chapter, with Stephen struggling in a birth fantasy that invokes the bifurcation of experience as form and matter. The detail compares with the range of reference in the representations and unifying role we associate with Milly; however, we are underground.

Stephen's fantasy takes wing in front of the shop of Thomas Russell, "lapidary and gemcutter, 57 Fleet Street" (G&S, 275). The name Russell has, in all probability, moved Stephen to remember George Russell (AE), the mystic Neo-Platonist with whom he has just spoken in the National Library. In that chapter, Eglinton had mocked Stephen's literary ambitions as the "Sorrows of Satan" (9.19).[5] In this passage, Miltonic references do recover something of Stephen's once proud *non serviam*. The overwhelming impression left by the passage, particularly the phrase "fallen archangels," is brooding defeat. The allusion to Bloom's family hopes appears in the female dancer's navel (*omphalos*): a "ruby egg." Imagining the "ruby egg" on "her gross belly" to be enticing "a sailorman," Stephen has spontaneously come up with a parodic version of Bloom, Joyce's modern Ulysses, enticed by his longing for Rudy.

> Stephen Dedalus watched through the webbed window the lapidary's fingers prove a timedulled chain. Dust webbed the window and the showtrays. Dust darkened the toiling fingers with their vulture nails. Dust slept on dull coils of bronze and silver, lozenges of cinnabar, on rubies, leprous and winedark stones.
>
> Born in all the dark wormy earth, cold specks of fire, evil, lights

shining in the darkness. Where fallen archangels flung the stars of their brows. Muddy swinesnouts, hands, root and root, gripe and wrest them.

She dances in a foul gloom where gum burns with garlic. A sailorman, rustbearded, sips from a beaker rum and eyes her. A long and seafed silent rut. She dances, capers, wagging her sowish haunches and her hips, on her gross belly flapping a ruby egg.

Old Russell with a smeared shammy rag burnished again his gem, turned it and held it at the point of his Moses's beard. Grandfather ape gloating on a stolen hoard.

And you who wrest old images from the burial earth? (10.800–815)

This is the closest Stephen comes to conceiving the plot in which he is involved.

The daguerreotype associated with Milly offers a more exact approximation of his situation. The imagery concurs with the image of burial. The address of the "portrait atelier of Stefan Virag," perhaps of the original home of Stefan Virag, is "Szesfehervar, Hungary."

The town Székesfehérvár—there is no "Szesfehervar"—had in Joyce's day, as it does today, only one major claim to notice.[6] Until the Turkish conquest in the sixteenth century, Székesfehérvár—in Latin, Alba Regia or Alba Civitas—repeated in Hungarian coronation ceremony the ritual role of Tara for the Irish kings and the ritual role of Rheims for French monarchs. In all, "thirty-five [Hungarian] kings [had] been crowned under ... the Cathedral dome." Of these, sixteen remain "interned in its vault."

The most significant of these, both for Hungary and for Stephen's self-definition, is the "sarcophagus of King Stephen I." The Stephen at Székesfehérvár had been Hungary's first Christian king, the eponym of the crown of St. Stephen, which Arthur Griffith made the symbol for Ireland's constitutional salvation.[7] On a scale of which Stephen Dedalus could only dream, King Stephen I had shaped his country's faith about as much as any one individual could claim. Stefan Virag's daguerreotype holds this aspect of Stephen—the dream that has been actualized in a shape that he cannot access.

The inaccessibility and separation appear to be formally motivated. Joyce's Paris notebook of 1903 observes that while photography does dispose "sensible matter ... for an aesthetic end," this disposition is not "a human disposition of sensible matter."[8] In other words, the photographer may "write with light," but the bluntness of the instrument, a hostage to the obtuseness of matter, rules the result. Stephen is not to have a complement in Milly.

Still nothing prepares us for Stephen's anti-Semitic outburst—rendered almost pathos-neutral by the panoptic gaze of "Ithaca." Its target is Milly Bloom. As Michael Seidel writes, epic seeks the standard for formative events it records.[9] As far as culture goes, Bloom is no more Hebrew than Stephen is Gaelic. Milly's Jewishness is, nevertheless, the fulcrum of Stephen's attack. Stephen Dedalus insists on spelling this out precisely. He puts an end to the rapprochement between his Gaelic and Bloom's Jewish legacy by singing a ballad that depicts "the Jew's daughter" as a ritual murderess.

The ballad roundly rejects any role for Stephen in any version of the Virag-Bloom family saga and puts an end to a search for common meaning in their joint examination of the Gaelic and Hebrew alphabets. In his exposition of the autobiographical unity of Shakespeare's oeuvre, Stephen had approvingly quoted Maeterlinck on the final solipsistic closure that draws all imaginative activities:

> "If Socrates leave his house today he will find the sage seated on his doorstep. If Judas go forth tonight it is to Judas his steps will tend. We walk through ourselves, meeting robbers, ghosts, giants, old men, young men, wives, widows, brothers-in-love, but also meeting ourselves." (9.1042–46)

Hereafter, he and Bloom will travel together no further in search of a common script. Stephen's personal negotiations with the "playwright who wrote the folio of this world and wrote it badly" (9.1047) require a change of direction.

Bloom has sung a part of the *Hatikvah*, the anthem of the Zionist movement, to Stephen, and in return asked him to sing of "a strange legend on an allied theme" (17.795–96). Stephen evidently hears a threat of some sort in Bloom's song:

> Kolod bejwaw pnimah
>   Nefesch, jehudi, homijah. (17.763–64)

> (As long as deep within the heart
>   The soul of Judea is turbulent and strong)
> (G&S, 578)

He senses the essential presence of Christ in Bloom (17.783–85), but, as we might expect from his anticlericalism, the vision only compounds his unease. He meets Bloom's request for "a strange legend" not with a celebration of ancient Ireland but with a declaration of independence. His language breaks with the understanding between them.

The text of the ballad, together with Bloom's reaction and Stephen's commentary, appears below. The accompanying text identifies Bloom in terms of his lineage: he is the "son of Rudolph" and the "father of Millicent" (17.809, 829). The topic of the ballad is the ritual murder of a Christian child by Jews. Stephen sings:

Little Harry Hughes and his schoolfellows all/Went out for to play ball./And the very first ball little Harry Hughes played/He drove it over the jew's garden wall./And the very second ball little Harry Hughes played/He broke the jew's windows all.//

. . . .

How did the son of Rudolph receive this first part?
With unmixed feeling. Smiling, a jew, he heard with pleasure and saw the unbroken kitchen window.
Recite the second part (minor) of the legend.
Then out there came the jew's daughter/And she all dressed in green./"Come back, come back, you pretty little boy,/And play your ball again."//"I can't come back and I won't come back/Without my schoolfellows all./For if my master he did hear/He'd make it a sorry ball."//She took him by the lilywhite hand/and led him along the hall/Until she led him to a room/Where none could hear him call. //She took a penknife out of her pocket/And cut off his little head. /And now he'll play his ball no more/For he lies among the dead.
. . . .
How did the father of Millicent receive this second part?
With mixed feelings. Unsmiling, he heard and saw with wonder a jew's daughter, all dressed in green.
Condense Stephen's commentary.
One of all, the least of all, is the victim predestined. Once by inadvertence, twice by design he challenges his destiny. It comes when he is abandoned and challenges him reluctant and, as an apparition of hope and youth, holds him unresisting. It leads him to a strange habitation, to a secret infidel apartment, and there, implacable, immolates him, consenting.
Why was the host (victim predestined) sad?
He wished that a tale of a deed should be told not by him should by

him not be told.
Why was the host (reluctant, unresisting) still?
In accordance with the law of the conservation of energy?
Why was the host (secret infidel) silent?
He weighed the possible evidences for and against ritual murder; the incitations of the hierarchy, the superstition of the populace, the propagation of rumour in continued fraction of veridicity, the envy of opulence, the influence of retaliation, the sporadic reappearance of atavistic delinquency, the mitigating circumstances of fanaticism, hypnotic suggestion and somnambulism." (17.802–49)

The episode can, and has been made, consistent with a variety of interpretations, the majority of them versions of the *Kunstlerroman* approach to *Ulysses*, which highlight Stephen's growing self-mastery. C. H. Peake argues that, for Stephen himself, the material does not have "racial and religious features" but "symbolizes acceptance of his vocation as artist."[10] The anti-Semitism can be discounted altogether. For William Empson, Stephen and Bloom have entered into a "joking relationship (as defined by anthropologists)" so intimate that Stephen can no longer offend Bloom in the public meaning of an insult.[11] Minimizing the unpleasantness still more, Zack Bowen sees the comparison of Celtic and Hebrew alphabets and the drinking of cocoa as the prelude to the two men's symbolically becoming a single artist-Jew. In this reading, the term *victim* applies to them both. "The Jew's daughter who will perform the potential destruction on Harry-Stephen-Bloom," Bowen writes, "is both daughter and mother and Molly and Milly. . . . It may be that Stephen's warning is as much for Bloom as for himself and a realization of the consubstantial status."[12] One more shift in emphasis and the contretemps vanishes completely. The point of the exchange for Suzette Henke is that, like "Harry Hughes, [Stephen] experiences ritual annihilation of the ego and escapes from the intellectual bondage of his own head."[13]

What is seriously amiss in these interpretations is their interchangeability. They are all plausible. Each presupposes a stage of narrative development and then imagines the dialogue to derive from the projection. What about the role of the stylistic medium in such a deduction? Should it not be accorded independent weight? Should the postponement of meaning resulting from such a step stop at some point?

Marilyn Reizbaum offers such a semantically open-ended reading of the Harry Hughes performance, bolstered by a contrast with "Eumaeus." Whereas in that earlier chapter, "seeming acts of conversion were undermined or rewritten by acts of wandering," in "Ithaca" occurrences that appear to be "interchanges of mutuality become acts of mimicry."[14] The point of the song, in Reizbaum's reading, is its specularity. "The boldness of Stephen's act is graphically displayed through the musical notation of the song, included in the text as if parodically to provide for the reader's arsenal. Simply put, the accusation of ritual murder, as we know, is an old tune, easily recoverable." From Stephen's performance having been displayed as text within the text, we are to interpret Stephen's behavior as "countering Bloom the Jew with a specularity of threat or danger."[15] The style, in other words, displays action without motive. The phenomenon, the contact between the two individuals, is not affected.

The manner in which Bloom's response to Stephen's performance is recorded sustains this emphasis. He is "sad." The reason for his sadness is conveyed in an awkward refrain, which twice invokes the same ungainly passive grammatical structure to establish agency. Bloom wishes that "a tale of a deed should be told not by him" and wishes it "should by him not be told." The point is the refrain "not by him" and its transposition as "by him not."[16] This is not the action in which he believed himself to have been engaged. He notes and regrets the difference.[17] The contact remains without issue.

Narrative progression forces the reader to note the irrevocable divorce of the two men. Stephen's action belies the serio-comic equivalence between Stephen and Rudy at the end of "Circe." On the kindest interpretation, Stephen has been "accidentally, [and] not designedly, offensive."[18] In any event, there is nothing for Bloom to do with the charge. He falls silent.[19] The figural equivalence of Rudy and Stephen dissolves. He and Stephen are not traveling parallel courses, not heading toward one end.

Bloom on his own, quite apart from Stephen, is heading ostensibly toward Molly and, through her, inevitably, even further back in time, toward his daughter. Molly's closing "yes" in "Penelope" takes her back to September 10, 1888, one month before the wedding. Milly's birth followed on June 15, 1889, exactly nine months (forty weeks) after this first embrace but eight months after the Blooms' wedding night (17.2276–78). The climax of her dramatic return to her first lovemaking with Bloom: "then I asked him with my eyes to ask again yes and then he asked me would I say yes my mountain flower and first I put my arms around him yes and drew him down to me so he could feel my breasts all perfume yes and his heart was going like mad and yes I said yes I will Yes" (18.1605–9)—was presumably the conception of the child.

Horace had praised Homer for the dramatic sense of not having begun *The Odyssey* at the natural beginning of the tale and for instead having begun the story of the Trojan War starting with "the twin eggs of Leda"—*ab ovo*, from the egg.[20] *Ulysses* goes the Latin critic one better by proceeding *ad ovo*—to the egg.[21] The theme inevitably calls to mind the narrator's meandering effort to get past the parental act of coition and a proper beginning to the narrative in Laurence Sterne's *The Life and Opinions of Tristram Shandy, Gentleman*. *Ulysses* also makes the conception the inescapable destination of efforts to arrive at a synoptic view of the fable.

With the conception of Milly, we literally are in media res, inoculated against the boredom and predictability that Horace foretold would result from chronicle-like fidelity to temporal succession. In Milly, Joyce offers us not only a capstone for the past but the promise of the future. She is not only the material echo of the climactic moment on Ben Howth binding Bloom and Molly, but her physical being also coincides with the continuity latent in the present moment.

June 16, 1904, is the first anniversary of her first nine-month menstruation cycle, plus one extra day (17.2289–90). In other words, Bloomsday is the first day on which Milly could have borne a full-term child.[22] The first full term of fertile potential coincides with *Ulysses'* commemoration of the life of Dublin's streets. This congruence with Milly may be the nearest a book can come to claiming that it is alive. Stephen had imagined an Eve who "had no navel," an absolute beginning whose belly was "without blemish, [while] bulging big, a buckler of taut vellum" (3.42–43).[23] In Milly, *Ulysses* leaves us with a vision of Eve, on whose belly the events and styles of Bloomsday have been figuratively inscribed.

As the telos of the fable, Milly is a starting point. Associated with serial creativity, her figure incorporates a challenge to fixed teleology per se. Benedict Anderson has noted the discrepancy between "narratives of person and nation":

> In the secular story of the "person" there is a beginning and an end. She emerges from parental genes and social circumstances onto a brief historical stage, there to play a role until her death. After that nothing but the penumbra of lingering fame or influence.... Nations however have no identifiable birth, and their death, if ever they happen are never natural. Because there is no Originator, the nation's

biography cannot be written evangelically, "down time," through a long procreative chain of begettings.[24]

The serial novelty associated with Milly points beyond the culmination of the epic fable. The etymology of her name, "mill-" (thousands), recalls benedictions of natural increase, such as Moses' blessing on Israel in Deuteronomy: "The LORD GOD of your fathers make you a thousand times so many more as ye *are*, and bless you, as he hath promised you!" (1:11). As a woman, she is "the link between nations and generations . . . the sacred lifegiver" (15.4648–49).[25] She represents the essential middle term *begat*, which all the patriarchal genealogies take for granted. Through Daguerre, she is metonymically linked to "physical process which gives Nature the ability to reproduce herself."[26] These associations combine to make her a symbol of impersonal increase and immortality. "Aristotle explicitly assures us," Hannah Arendt writes, "that man, insofar as he is a natural being and belongs to the specie mankind possesses immortality; through the recurrent cycle of life. . . . Being for living creatures is life and being-for-ever . . . corresponds to procreation." Through procreation humans are like "things that are and do not change."[27]

As the culmination of the Austro-Hungarian, Anglo-Irish parallel, Milly is the common denominator of "the democratic dispersal of monarchical hubris." She is the symbolic equivalent of the perspective from which, in Jonathan Ree's phrase, "each national subject can proclaim, 'la nation, c'est moi.'"[28] As story, at the end of "Ithaca," the name *Millicent*'s numerical translation links her, by way of the Dublin pantomime *Sinbad the Sailor* (G&S, 571, 606), to *A Thousand and One Nights* and to the rhyme ushering Bloom through "Ithaca."

> Sinbad the Sailor and Tinbad the Tailor and Jinbad the Jailor and Whinbad the Whaler and Ninbad the Nailer and Finbad the Failer and Binbad the Bailer and Pinbad the Pailer and Minbad the Mailer and Hinbad the Hailer and Rinbad the Railer and Dinbad the Quailer and Linbad the Yailer and Xinbad the Phthailer. (17.2322–26)

The narrative progression, the succession of closural gestures, signals the effortless translation of Bloom into a multiplying Odyssean identity.

The original narrative suspense is lost in this environment. Scheherazade had constructed her nightly tales for her new husband, the murderous Sultan Schahriar, so that daybreak always leave a cliffhanger. Were the sultan's curiosity to find out what happened next not strained to the limit, he would have been reminded of his earlier resolve always to put to death his new bride of the night before. By hiding the outcome of the tale, Scheherazade was buying a new day's life, one day at a time.

It is important to point out that this return to narrative progression occurs in the Ithacan environment where thought can go everywhere and everything is known. Nietzsche identified this bias as "deep-seated illusion first manifested in Socrates: the illusion that thought guided by thread of causation, might plumb the farthest abysses of being and even *correct* it."[29] The reach of theory, like the reach of art, "is potentially all that exists." The difference is that "the artist having unveiled the truth garment by garment, remains with his gaze fixed on what is still hidden, [while] the theoretical man takes delight in the cast garments and finds his satisfaction in the unveiling process." It is the process "which proves to him his own power."[30] Science and the impersonal catechistic technique of "Ithaca" almost stifle the power of narrative.

Milly's association with *A Thousand and One Nights* returns the abstraction from lived experience in the Ithacan performance to the life her representation in *Ulysses* repeatedly recontextualizes. The text, as a totality, is so diverse that it "acts as if it were cut off," notes Karen Lawrence, "from any creating consciousness."[31] The informing vision is Blakean, with "the largest of things contained in the smallest . . . [in] minute particulars" and extremes tending to identity.[32]

Milly's role in relation to this tension is to temper the abstraction. In the broadest frame of reference, she seems to be the vehicle for the assertion that the personal is, to adapt a slogan, the historical.

The fable does not readily defer to such a summary overview. It insists on a countervailing organization of the text that accords with Aristotelian dramatic unities. The time, after all, "is one day . . . ; the place is one city . . . ; the plot is a single action—the meeting of Stephen Dedalus and Leopold Bloom."[33] Milly is an alternative to abstraction, not an abstract qualification to a formal argument. She embodies a privileged association with the origination of life, with its continuity, and with the performance of the narrative.

At issue is the romantic inheritance of history as a formative power. Rinehart Kosseleck has drawn attention "to a shift in the boundary distinguishing history and poetics" in late-eighteenth-century German-language usage to the attribution of creative potential to historical process as such, and to the recognition of history—*Geschichte*—as a source of novelty, a force independent of its actual representation in individual histories.

The word *Geschichte* shifted from an accepted plural form to a collective singular. It became a singular substantive. The change displaced "the naturalized foreign word *Historie*" with which the plural form of *Geschichte* had coexisted. Even in the plural form, *Geschichte* had "referred more to an incident" than "to an account of it."[34] Now, in the guise of collective singular, it encouraged the perception of a role for "history pure and simple." In this process of aggrandizement, it became commonplace to contrast history (*Geschichte*) with empirical histories (*Geschichte, Historie*), which finally derived from the more comprehensive instance.

History, the totality, included partial approximations and conditioned, individual accounts of historical processes.[35] The challenge of historical narrative was to take these centrifugal accounts and provide them with "the unity found in the epic derived from the existence of Beginning and End."[36]

Milly embodies something of this formative function. The relationship, as I argue in the remaining chapters, is distinct from equivalence. Joyce does not seem to have been attracted by the notion of history as an abstract, creative order of experience that was greater than the sum of its representations. Milly's role overlaps with pluralities of *Geschichte* and *Historie* without initiating a dialogue with the avuncular understanding of historical process that, "from around 1780," Kosseleck notes, made it possible to "talk of *history in general, history in and for itself, and history pure and simple.*"[37]

The representation is a challenging one for the reader. "The autotelic Modernist work of literature was said to remove the reader," Jonathan Levin states, "from a false sense of time and subjectivity" in order to force a confrontation with "the impersonal, eternal tradition that underwrites and authorizes all mere[ly] subjective and temporal experience."[38] Joyce's history lesson requires that the reader be more proactive, to make the odyssey through the text the occasion for unforeseen patterns of significance and alternative readings of history. While the epic fable enacts an approximation of a comprehensive grasp on events, the lacunae point to the need for a different order of hermeneutics.

5

Epic Mimesis and the Syntax of *Ulysses*

How do we talk about the epic fable once the integrity of history and historical context have been bracketed so as to preclude the unification of the theme? Can the level of analytical abstraction that I have identified as the epic fable endure as a stopping place: a third-person position that demystifies cultural engagement? Or is it too fragile? Are we bound to follow Joyce in the eternal recurrence of infinite digression through *Finnegans Wake* to ALP's extinction, "mememormee! Till thousendsthee" (*FW*, 628) to a condition past all bearing with generalities? Is it meaningful to ask how the epic fable belongs to the syntax of *Ulysses*?

"Telemachus" had introduced a world in which to be properly represented Buck Mulligan's *Introibo ad altare dei* would, according to Hugh Kenner, need six sets of quotation marks since "Mulligan's pretending to be a Black Mass celebrant, who is going through the motions of an Irish priest, who is reciting from the *Ordo*, which quotes from St. Jerome's Latin version of Hebrew words ascribed to a psalmist in exile."[1] Milly Bloom at the end of *Ulysses* seems to recede from the reach of discourse in analogous, incremental steps. What sort of context do these different modes of deferral bestow on the odyssey of Stephen and Bloom? ALP rushing, carried into the arms of her father the sea, is not until the instant of joining, stilled in extinction: "Lps. The keys to. Given! A way a lone a last a loved a long the" (*FW*, 628).

The value Milly approximates points to nature, to procreative increase, and to storytelling without end. As the culminating instant of "Penelope" belongs to myth, the fixity and generative force of the occasion recall Mikhail Bakhtin's univocal order of "beginnings ... fathers ... founders of families ... 'firsts' ... 'bests.'"[2] In Bakhtin's world, she stands for the instant "when epic distance [is] disintegrating," the moment that the "comic familiarity" of the novel makes individuality thinkable.[3] Her individuality is pristine and elemental. As I noted, she is hardly thinkable without contradiction. Her antithetical characterization, partaking equally of universality and seriality, continues to include her in contexts that project the various contradictions serially.

Can one maintain a naive faith in narrative progression *via* the fable when we have to make progression fit such antithetical contexts? Do the dramatis personae of the fable detach from the epic argument? What becomes of the syntax that had appeared to rule there? The proliferation of heuristic alternatives seems to require a unified historical understanding, a first-person recognition that "expressive individuality and myths of endless proliferation of differences have," in Charles Altieri's words, left "rationalism itself suspect."[4] Where does such a recognition lead?

In a very Russian response to marginalization, Dostoyevsky's Underground Man had wanted inclusion in the historical process, whereas Stephen Dedalus, notes M. Keith Booker, with "the full burden of Ireland's misshaped legacy [on him] . . . wants out."[5] *Ulysses* accommodates synechdochal visitations to the discursive region where reason should rule but complexities only multiply. The synoptic approximations of closure in the lexicon of the fable complicate the medium, mimicking the redundancy of actual historical processes.

The Griffith parallel does not rule teleology. The lexicon is amenable to syntactical arrangements and a temporal horizon in which the proclamation of the Irish Free State is an outcome of secondary interest. The approximations continue to invoke the ongoing compositional focus of the work and to rework aspects of the fable spanning the text. It is the receptivity to other possible outcomes, other arrangements, that is responsible for the simulacrum of historicity.

The first such alternative surfaces in the visitations of the Irish expatriate Ulysses Browne, the one Irish character to bear the hero's name.[6] Potentially, the figure belongs with *Ulysses'* concern with self-definition, with the function that shapes Stephen's meditations in the *Telemachiad*. Unlike Stephen's, Ulysses Browne's deployment features no critical self-awareness. The figure has the role of a blind spot, a quasi-totality indicative of the parallel between Stephen-Bloom and Griffith's historical argument. By means of Browne, the fable of *Ulysses* profiles this self-reference without any further elaboration on the theme.

In *Portrait*, Stephen had recoiled from the entity. At the time, he was still a very young boy. Ulysses Browne was a ghost to be feared: the spirit of the scion of the Browne family from whom the Jesuits had purchased the buildings of Conglowes Wood College in 1813.[7]

Ulysses Browne had been a marshal in the service of the Hapsburg queen Maria Theresa. After he died in battle during the Seven Years War, his ghost returned to haunt Conglowes. Lying in bed at night, Stephen dreaded his "figure [coming] up the staircase from the hall [in] . . . the white cloak of a marshal; his face . . . pale and strange . . . [with] his deathwound [from] the battlefield of Prague far away over the sea." Stephen's childish imagination took refuge in the homely and familiar:

> O how cold and strange it was to think of that! All the dark was cold and strange. There were pale strange faces there [in the dark], great eyes like carriagelamps. They were the ghosts of murderers, the figures of marshals who had received their deathwound on battlefields far away over the sea. What did they wish to say their faces were so strange?
> *Visit, we beseech Thee, O Lord, this habitation and drive away from it all* . . . (P, 19)

In *Ulysses*, Hapsburg-ruled Europe persists as a region beyond the shaping power of Stephen's imagination. Its most prominent embodiment in Dublin is, of course, Bloom. In Bloom, Stephen's dream of "Europe . . . beyond the Irish sea, [the] Europe of strange tongues and valleyed and woodbegirt and citadelled" (P, 167) has achieved epic scale. The irony is that Stephen's relegation to the status of a failed epic poet bars him from understanding that Bloom substitutes for the crucial experience of exile that *Portrait* had seemed to reserve for him.

Public opinion in *Ulysses* is no more successful in accounting for Ulysses Browne than for Bloom. John Wyse Nolan, the same individual who had, inadvertently, conferred public epic stature on Bloom with the claim that "Bloom gave the idea for Sinn Fein to Griffith" (12.1573–74), makes Ulysses Browne the climax of a litany of Irish military achievements overseas. The catalog of heroic self-sacrifice ought to fill the Irish patriots gathered in Barney Kiernan's tavern with an appropriately magnified sense of their national significance. The Ireland of Nolan's imagination is the homeland to heroes and unmerited suffering:

> We fought for the royal Stuarts that reneged us against the Williamites and they betrayed us. We gave our best blood to France and Spain, the wild geese. Fontenoy, eh? And Sarsfield and O'Donnell, duke of Tetuan in Spain, and Ulysses Browne of Camus that was fieldmarshal to Maria Theresa. What did we ever get for it? (12.1379–84)[8]

Unfortunately, the attempt at epic magnification falls into incoherence because Ireland's overseas heroes were also fighting each other.

Specifically, the one Irish Ulysses in *Ulysses* could not be found consistently allied with "France and Spain." During the battle of Fontenoy, where the expatriate Irish Brigade in the service of France fought so valiantly against the British that it was held "the Boyne [was] avenged," Catholic Austria, and so perforce Ulysses Browne, had been allied with the English.[9] The climax of Nolan's litany only testifies to the cross-purposes and bloodletting among Ireland's "best blood." Intending to show the patriots icons of self-sacrifice, Nolan has extolled the behavior of isolated self-regarding Cyclops.[10]

The intended lesson was self-reliance. Europe has failed Ireland. The call of the outsider cannot be trusted. In the National Library, while Ireland's literati ponder Dr. Sigerson's observation that Ireland's "national epic has yet to be written," the reader could not but note Stephen's silent presence (9.309). Nolan's final question, "What did we ever get for it?," invites the comparison. Just as the Cyclops Polyphemus, struck blind, had failed to see Odysseus, the chauvinists in Barney Kiernan's are blind to the epic connection with Europe through Bloom, which they readily mock and demean. The figure of Ulysses Browne is a synecdoche for the blindness. It represents the limit to the characters' ability to see themselves and adequately reflect.

The insistence on the opaque recalcitrance of the past recurs in the presentation of the oldest recollection in Bloom family lore, his father's recollection of "his grandfather having seen Maria Theresia [sic], empress of Austria, queen of Hungary" (17.1909–10).

The material is inert without the link between Austria-Hungary and England-Ireland. Once we note the appositeness of the recollection to the concern with continuity and legitimacy, we find that we have only broached the difficulty. The marker that reaches furthest back into Bloom's past receives very different treatment from Griffith.

For Griffith, Maria Theresa is a false, self-serving opportunist. When the Prussian Frederick the Great held Silesia and a European coalition contested her right to her remaining inheritance, she struck the pose of a princess in peril and appealed for support from Hungary. The plea succeeded. In a gesture of misguided noblesse, in 1741, chivalric Hungary accepted the embattled Hapsburg as the nation's queen, rightfully crowned with the crown of St. Stephen. But Maria Theresa's reconciliation with Hungary's ancient constitution proved perfidious:

"My brave brethren," ... the beautiful young queen [had said], "my enemies assail me. I am a woman, and a woman appeals to you, chivalrous Hungarians!" And with a mighty shout Hungary went forth to battle for the beautiful young queen, and so well did it battle that it fixed the lady as securely as lady can be fixed on her throne, and placed her pretty foot as neatly as it might be placed on its own neck. And the lady did not die of laughter.[11]

She repaid the support of the great nobles by turning them into Germanicized courtiers. She discharged her debt to the Hungarian peasant by sending Austrian colonists "trooping into the fertile plains of the Magyar's land."[12] In Griffith's account she is Hapsburg perfidy incarnate.

Ulysses supplies Bloom with no comparable analytical context. No politics are hinted at. There is not even a date. This perhaps is the point. The Virag-Bloom recollection of Maria Theresa recalls early historical annals. The vagueness of outline involves the kind of distance that establishes Stephen and Leopold's role in the fable. Even though the date is undetermined, the mention of Maria Theresa's name indicates a potentially verifiable public realm of experience. The fable alludes to a comparable domain of reference, to the objective historical record available to a public historically distanced from the foundation of Irish state.

For such a public, the names of Leopold and Stephen, like the name of Maria Theresa for Bloom and his father, would serve as markers of an objective, transpersonal world. The effect is not unlike the multiple embedding of citations in "Telemachus" to which Hugh Kenner directed attention. The cost of disregarding a set of quotation marks is a naive reading of *Ulysses* modeled on this anecdotal specimen of Bloom family lore.

The name Maria Theresa is only a marker. For Bloom and for his father, the essential narrative was the odyssey of the Virags toward Ireland. The goal preempts the relevance of any drama of Maria Theresa. For an early medieval historian, such as the anonymous annalist of St. Gall, the chronology of imminent Christian salvation similarly deprived political and natural events of autonomous significance.[13]

Bloom's essential story traces a migration route comprised of seven stopping points, all political capitals of some kind (except Szombathely, the first in the sequence), and culminating in Dublin, "the seventh city of Christendom" (*P*, 167).[14] Milan and Florence had been the chief cities of Hapsburg-ruled Italy. Florence had been the capital of a separate though Hapsburg-ruled principality, the Grand Duchy of Tuscany. Milan had been designated the capital of a separate Kingdom of Lombardy-Venetia, which the Austrian emperor refused to recognize through a separate coronation and attempted to rule as though it were an Austrian province.[15] Vienna and Budapest, emblems of the constitutional partnership Griffith admired, had not appeared in the Rosenbach holograph and came to be inserted into the paragraph in late 1921 or early in 1922 when Joyce was correcting Darantière's proofs.[16] It seems evident that at least part of the effect sought is the forging of continuity between Ireland and the continent.

> What first reminiscence had [Leopold] of Rudolph Bloom (deceased)?
> Rudolph Bloom (deceased) narrated to his son Leopold Bloom (aged 6) a retrospective arrangement of migrations and settlements in and between Dublin, London, Florence, Milan, Vienna, Budapest, Szombathely with statements of satisfaction (his grandfather having seen Maria Theresia [sic], empress of Austria, queen of Hungary), with commercial advice (having taken care of pence, the pounds having taken care of themselves). Leopold Bloom (aged 6) had accompanied these narrations by constant consultation of the geographical map of Europe (political) and by suggestions for the establishment of affiliated business premises in the various centers mentioned. (17.1905–15)

The tragedy of Bloom's life is that with himself, this line of patrilineal transmission has stopped. His young son Rudy's death means that there is "none now to be for Leopold, what Leopold was for Rudolph" (14.1076–77). The link with the past manifest in the "family custom of giving Hapsburg names to males (Leopold—Rudolph—Leopold—Rudolph)" has been broken.[17]

The reference to Maria Theresa is apparently an aside. It belongs with other parenthetical intrusions, mostly whimsical, which lend an idiosyncratic tinge to the Latinate flow of the summary. In fact, it enhances the pathos of Bloom's situation without expressly naming it.

War had begun during Maria Theresa's reign because her father, the Emperor Charles VI, had died without a male heir. The Spanish branch of the Hapsburgs had died out in 1700. One of the most frequently repeated stories told of Maria Theresa was her joy at the birth, which guaranteed that the Hapsburg succession crisis would not be repeated.[18] When she got news of the birth of her first grandson, Maria Theresa shattered baroque decorum, rushing to the "imperial playhouse [where in the middle of the performance] flushed with excitement [she] leaned forward over the front of her box and, speaking in the broadest of Viennese, imparted her news ['Der Pold'l hoat a Buabn!' (My Poldy's got a boy!)] to the amazed spectators."[19]

The allusion to Maria Theresa's joy, if it is the scene referred to, ironically underscores his haplessness. The allusion is the reverse of the standing allegorical equivalence. The theme of orderly "retrospective arrangement of migrations and settlements" is sustained by the transmission of the narrative from great-grandfather Rudolph to his grandchild, Rudolf, Bloom's father, and finally to Leopold Bloom. The dramatic point of the parallel is Bloom's isolation.

Without knowing it, Bloom is looking for a term, a translation of this prehistory of his odyssey with Stephen, that would encompass past and present. The link between the historical Maria Theresa and the epic fable's use of Griffith brings the themes of isolation, vulnerability, and violence to the fore.

We do not have the historical perspective for a comparable contextualization of the epic design of *Ulysses*. When "the genuine historian, working under complex constraints puts together a configuration of change and gives it a name (usually not his own and reluctantly appropriated), by calling it 'the Carolingian Empire,' the 'Protestant Reformation,' 'the Intellectual Revolution of the Seventeenth Century,' 'the Peninsular War' or 'European Liberalism,'" writes Michael Oakeshott, "we must understand him to be begging us not to place too much weight on these identifications, and above all not to confuse his tentative multiform identities with the stark, monolithic products of practical and mythological understanding which these expressions may also identify."[20] Instead of historical contextualization, we are offered intimations of such a perspective in the imagery and design of the epic argument. Poetics supplements *Ulysses'* reasoning from historical data with a perspective derived from its assimilation of the epic tradition.

J. M. Perl is much too tentative in proposing that "it might not be inaccurate to describe [*Ulysses*] as an odyssey of modern Western history."[21] The grand unification of experience of which Stephen had dreamed in *Portrait* and which is assayed through the fable of *Ulysses* remains intrinsic to the design. With appropriate modifications to include the displacement of final significance through the seriality, note the syntax of crowning in the sequence of *novae coronae*—that is, new stars, or, etymologically from the

Latin, *new crowns*—which had more or less coincided with the respective births of Stephen and Bloom's ideal complements, Shakespeare and Rudy. Looking up at the night sky, the two discuss, we are told,

> the posited influence of celestial on human bodies: the appearance of a star (1st magnitude) of exceeding brilliancy dominating by day and night (a new luminous sun generated by the collision and amalgamation in incandescence of two nonluminous exsuns) about the period of the birth of William Shakespeare over delta in the recumbent neversetting constellation of Cassiopeia and of a star (2nd magnitude) of similar origin but lesser brilliancy which had appeared in and disappeared from the Corona Septentrionalis about the period of the birth of Leopold Bloom and of other stars of (presumably) similar origin which had (effectively or presumably) appeared in and disappeared from the constellation of Andromeda about the period of the birth of Stephen Dedalus, and in and from the constellation of Auriga some years after the birth and death of Rudolph Bloom, junior, and in and from some other constellations some years before or after the birth or death of other persons . . . (17.1118–32)

The vision is utopian, and the equivalences are qualified as approximate. From the perspective of the fable, the important phrase is "and in and from some other constellations some years before or after the birth or death of other persons." Serial multiplication opens up the design to history.

This opening is consistent with narrative momentum in the earliest episodes in *Ulysses*. When in "Telemachus" Buck Mulligan mocks Stephen, the action appears to be retrograde. Mulligan's ironic welcome is the embrace of the future clerically minded Irish state. The Ireland in which an Irish Catholic like Mulligan enjoys "the social advantages of Protestant education and feels himself to be a natural member of a [changing] Ascendancy" would accord Stephen a priest's tonsure.[22] This is the Ireland Joyce scorned, the country in whose anticipated independence he claimed to foresee only reasons for animosity.[23]

Apparently inspired by sweetness and light, Mulligan's opening words offer the priestly tonsure to Stephen, "Come up, Kinch! Come up, you fearful Jesuit!" (1.8). In fact, the words resonate with a violent context. The invitation preserves the taunts of children who had mocked the prophet Elisha with "Go up, thou baldhead, go up, thou baldhead." Elisha had turned on mockers with a curse, and "two she bears [came] out of the wood and tare forty-two [of them]" (2 Kings, 2:24).[24] The succession that Mulligan invites is atavistic. The communion offered predates national allegiance. The subtext sounds death-wishes.

Although he detests the performance, Stephen obeys. It only becomes evident in "Proteus" what a multifaceted threat to autonomy he had perceived in the parodied role of priest. Stephen's grief, in a figurative sense, has already committed him to baldness, "a sign of mourning" in the Bible.[25] The danger is that he will make resentment his life's theme. The Latin quotation, from the *Vaticano Pontificum* (Venice, 1589) attributed to Joachim Abbas, has been altered.[26] It now reads as "Descend bald man, so that you do not become more bald than you are."[27] The "garland of grey hair" belongs to the priest he saw near the rock where Mulligan dove into the sea (1.689, 739), and the remainder of the sentence conflates Stephen with the priest.

> The oval equine faces, Temple, Buck Mulligan, Foxy Campbell, Lanternjaws. Abbas father, furious dean, what offence laid fire to their brains? Paff! *Descende calve, ut ne amplius decalveris*. A garland of grey hair on his comminated head see him me clambering down the footpace (*descende!*), clutching a monstrance, basiliskeyed. Get down baldpoll! A choir gives back menace and echo, assisting about the altar's horns, the snorted Latin of jackpriests moving burly in their albs, tonsured and oiled and gelded, fat with the fat of kidneys of wheat. (3.111–19)

The "basiliskeyed" priest, his gaze, like that of the king of serpents (*basileus*, in Greek, "king"), "reputed to be capable of looking anyone dead on whom it fixed," belongs as much to him as it does to any baleful priest.[28]

In "Telemachus," atop the mock altar of the Martello Tower, feeling cursed and powerless, Stephen "half expect[ed] to see a shaven crown, as of a priest or monk" in Mulligan's "light untonsured hair" (1.15).[29] The ersatz priest, sweeping the horizon with the shaving mirror, Stephen's "symbol of Irish art" (1.146), fills the sea and sky of the "tidings" that Stephen suffers from "GPI"—the general paralysis of the insane (1.131–32).

The totality of the text elides the negativity of the moment by linking Mulligan's intrusion to Milly's intercession on Bloom's behalf. The two events are simultaneous.

Mulligan inadvertently saves Stephen. Momentarily alone, Stephen gets wrapped in a vision of a cannibalistic mother. As he is "trembling at his soul's cry" (1.282) before "eyes, staring out of death, to shake and bend [his] soul" (1.273), he discovers Mulligan to be life, to be "warm running sunlight and in the air behind him . . . friendly words" (1.283). The moment coincides with Milly's rescue of Bloom in "Calypso." There Bloom sees Palestine, the promised land, turn into

> barren land, bare waste. Vulcanic lake, the dead sea: no fish, weedless, sunk deep in the earth. No wind . . . [to] those waves, grey metal, poisonous foggy waters. Brimstone they called it raining down: the cities of the plain: Sodom, Gomorrah, Edom. All dead names. A dead sea in a dead land, grey and old. . . . Dead: an old woman's: the grey sunken cunt of the world. (4.219–23, 228)

The memory of his daughter intervenes. He recalls her presence as

> [q]uick running sunlight [that] came running from Berkeley road, swiftly, in slim sandals, along the brightening foot path. Runs, she runs to meet me, a girl with gold hair on the wind. (4.240–42)

Pivoting on the coincidence, narrative progression, on both occasions, has turned away from death.

The simultaneity of the roles draws attention to links between these very different figures. Joined by a shaft of sunlight, we are prodded to recall that Mulligan and Milly, apparently the antithetical ends of the narrative, the apparent embodiments of the Alpha and Omega of the Dublin odyssey, the terminal points of the day and the action, the first presence that the narrative notes and the last character whose imminent conception echoes in the final affirmation of "Penelope," these two very different figures seem to belong together.

There is nothing intuitively self-evident about this equivalence. As characters whom the reader feels for, they share only a common humanity. Yet light and the imagery of crowns figure in both characterizations.

Milly the photo girl is, as we saw, associated with writing through light. Mulligan, too, would represent himself through sheer light. In the event, he does so for the briefest time span, in duration a flash. When he sweeps the sea before him with his shaving mirror, he intends to display a lighthearted freedom from the ties of convention. He means to display a Hellene inclusiveness that can transmute blasphemy, mockery, and prurience as sweetness and light—"in sunlight now radiant on the sea" (1.131). Inadvertently, he mimics the *exemplum* of Plato's contempt in *The Repub-*

lic. He represents the quickest, most indiscriminate way to the Universal: the mode of an artist who chooses the least demanding and most transitory way of imitating the "essential nature of things":

> The quickest [way], perhaps would be to take a mirror and turn it round in all directions. In a very short time you could produce sun and stars and earth and yourself and all the other animals and lifeless objects.[30]

It is in the slightest, most impermanent of mimetic modes that Mulligan pretends to communicate "tidings," and it is in the shortest possible time frame that he would have the apotheosis, the promise of Stephen realized.

> —O won't we have a merry time,
> Drinking whisky, beer and wine!
> On coronation,
> Coronation day!
> O, won't we have a merry time
> On coronation day! (1.300–305)

Stephen's coronation day is payday at Deasy's school: Mulligan would share in Stephen's coming into his "crowns" on the strength of his friendship and his earlier loans to Stephen.[31] The coronation of Stephen, which elsewhere is the theme of complex historical negotiations, is a familiar item on the daily menu he anticipates.

The transcendence achieved through Milly encompasses the *longue duree*. It comes about through figurative triangulation between the temporal coincidence of her role vis-à-vis Bloom in "Calypso" and Mulligan's vis-à-vis Stephen in "Telemachus." "Ithaca" recalls the moment of observation shared without either man's having been aware of it (17.41–42). It was a phenomenon of the day, an instance of parallax, which matters to the text and to the unity of the day. The perspective that could take note of the effect would be on an epic scale, remote from the ordinary at every point.

The partial rhyme Milly(cent)—Mulligan seems to be a closural allusion to this impractical perspective. To achieve it requires the convergence from points of view at the beginning and at the end of the fable. The effect of the calibration is disorienting. The vista transcends ordinary time scales. The grandeur of the perspective evokes the Ithacan appeal to

> the parallax or parallactic drift of the socalled fixed stars, in reality ever moving wanderers from immeasurably remote eons to infi-

nitely remote futures in comparison with which the years three score and ten of alloted human life formed a parenthesis of infinitesimal brevity. (17.1052–56)

The perspective foreshortens the quotidian.

We are in the approximate conceptual neighbourhood of Ezra Pound's notion of the "epic as a poem including history," but this moment of figural closure in *Ulysses* is a specific effort at metaphorical adequacy.[32] To soar to a hypothetical distance on June 16, 1904, to something like "the parallax of subsolar ecliptic of Aldebaran" (15.1656) in "Circe"—that is to say, to the point of the angle formed of "a line from the center of earth to Aldebaran and line from the center of the sun to Aldebaran" (G&S, 478)— is to invite a fall with the all-encompassing consequences of HCE's fall in *Finnegans Wake*, the shattering of language, form, and all established cosmologies. The perspective raised by the rhyme questions the feasibility of essaying interpretation with the aid of such abstraction, the role of such grand flights from the everyday *tout court*.

As we "mull it again," the final rhyme of *Ulysses* evokes a coherence on the verge of this dissolution. The consequence of this insecurity, however, is not fragmentation but an appeal to the mathematical sublime, to a perspective that incorporates multiple agencies.

The tension for coherence is powerful. "The repetitive, the irrational, the quasi-instinctual may be the substratum of history—but it cannot be the subject matter of history itself," writes H. Stuart Hughes. "This can only be what is capable of coherent explanation in logically delimited time sequences."[33] A preference for the epic since the eighteenth century has signaled a pronounced bias for order. Epic, Hayden White reminds us, has "presupposed the cosmology represented in the philosophy of Leibnitz, with its doctrine of continuity as its informing ontological principle, its belief in analogical reasoning as an epistemological principle, and its notion that all changes are nothing but transformation from one state or condition to another of a 'nature' whose essence changes not at all."[34] The rhyme, encompassing the day and the book, revisits and in petto caps this possible holistic perspective.

Robert Spoo notes that "the fluid succession of presents" in *Portrait* results in a structure that "quietly resists the taut progression of pasts characteristic of developmental histories and autobiographies."[35] Coherence presupposes that interpersonal relationships are the "ontological basis of history," and "the individual 'I' exists only against the background of the community."[36] In *Ulysses*, we are invited to contemplate the displacement of narrative-historiographic equivalents to a different setting, but the epic sweep remains profoundly democratic.

Ezra Pound imagined history to be "a school book for princes."[37] Yeats and the Celtic Revival turned to mythology "for the stories of continuity that history refused them ... on the assumption that ... timeless ancestry might heal the scars of temporal division."[38] Joyce reasons about the historical situation of the polity through the final rhyme, the most comprehensive pedestal available in *Ulysses*.

The site is "a new place, a no-place," to borrow from Richard Kearney's description of the anti-ideological character of Joyce's legacy, a "*u-topos* of alternative and hitherto impossibilities ... open to a multiplicity of futures."[39] It is a take on history and nationality from the bottom up. It accepts the site as beset with conflict, multiplicity, contradiction, and error. It is sufficiently democratic to entertain possible solutions and mistakes as simply more facts, additional complications of the site.

Ulysses insists on this distance from simplification in the articulation of its position on Irish nationalism. The vantage point, made possible in part by Joyce's exile, in part by an atavistic loyalty to the fallen Parnell, facilitated the insight that antithetical aspects of Irish reality—Milly and Mulligan—sustain a common rhyme.[40] The repetition prefigures an understanding of the nation as an amalgam of formative instances, repeated negotiations among expressions of individuality and national collectivity. The epic muse marshals an array of potential identities and possible perspectives.

The inclusiveness of the gesture demands attention. Surveying antithetical approaches to the depiction of nationality, Anthony Smith contrasts the "perennialist paradigm [which] looks for continuity and rootedness" with "postmodern modes of analysis [which] seek out and discover contestation, flux and fragmentation."[41] The epic site of *Ulysses* accommodates this discursive reach: we only credit the rhetorical force of the occasion once we recognize its dynamism and commitment to the communal reality of the nation.

The aim of populism, Nebosja Popov has noted, is the "fulfilling [of the] destiny of the nation as a whole, as a collectivity. The concept of the individual is foreign to it. For populism, history is a totality, the future is a totality."[42] *Ulysses* couples this collectivist teleology to the recognition that the observer and the phenomenon, the event and the outcome, the reader and the character, are all, on Horace's prescription, in media res.

"The epic is a totalizing form," writes Philip Hardie, "the agents in epic are... expansive, striving for a lonely pre-eminence and ultimate omnipotence."[43] *Ulysses* repeatedly returns to representations of the totality in media res. The rhyme based on the two ends of the work serves as a metaphor for this domestication of the epic tradition.

The full application of the insight would correspond to the nation's finding voice through this tradition. From the more limited, more abstract standpoint of scholarship, the task involves learning to read the new "single sense of nationhood or creed ... [as an] embedded record of literary genealogy ... a movement of culture from nation to nation, language to language, religion to religion."[44] Politically, the full application envisions a dispersal of authority among members of the community, a dispersal so comprehensive and extreme that it would finally be congruent with Ernest Renan's view of the "nation's existence [as] ... a daily plebiscite" in the same sense that "an individual's existence is a perpetual affirmation of life."[45] *Ulysses* as an epic performance aims at distinguishing and isolating the site of this dialogue unaffected by the critical biases foregrounded in the rhetorically stylized later chapters.

The epic genre lends itself to this kind of isolation. As a genre, it is a measure removed from the ideological distortion that rules individual expression and the ongoing self-definition of individuals and society in the social environment. "A literary genre, by its very nature," Mikhail Bakhtin writes, "reflects the most stable, eternal tendencies in literature's development. Always preserved in genre are undying elements of the archaic.... A genre is always the same and not the same, always old and new simultaneously."[46] Genre, in a manner, is partly autonomous. It embodies an apparently inescapable manner of apprehending and representing the world. "Every genre represents a special way of constructing and finalizing a whole, finalizing it essentially and thematically, not just conditionally or compositionally."[47] The epic genre avoids the intimacy, the sentiment, and the familiarity that result in what Hannah Arendt called "*worldlessness*, [the] solipsistic, inbred condition that leads nowhere, is nowhere," while, according to Bakhtin, it postulates a "single-voiced" condition, refusing social complexity and heteroglossia.[48] The epic performance in *Ulysses* fashions a distinctive site for reflection with a degree of traditional autonomy in the critical environment from all these biases.

6

Other Alternatives

Nationhood and Forgetfulness

When *Ulysses* configures the link to the epic tradition, it allows for constraining negotiations between historiography and the genre. Along with the celebratory synthesis in the figure of Millicent and in the epic rhyme, the register of the epic fable accomodates a nonprogressive, countervailing movement. This new argument, a kind of anticlimax, challenges the continuity necessary to the design, stresses the roles of error and forgetfulness in the making of national identity, and portrays the transmission of tradition as passive, as achieved between semiconsciousness and paralysis, as a state where the will is both engaged and alienated.

Consider, for example, the treatment of the choric affirmation culminating in Milly's conception—the capstone of Bloom's homecoming, the seal of his triumph and his one hope of practical, if not personal, immortality. To account for Milly's apotheosis in the fable, we found it necessary to re-imagine the situation of discourse; however, she is also there to sustain speculation and lewd innuendo. The qualification undercuts her transcendent role and, with it, the dramatic culmination of the fable.

Is she his daughter at all? Her blondness and green dress amaze Bloom. The green dress fuses her active sexuality—the sixteenth-century equivalent of the expression "roll in the hay" was "to give a girl a green gown"—symbolically with Ireland's reproductive future.[1] It marks her as separate. At the minimum, it embodies the strangeness, the alienation with which each generation has had to come to terms in the maturing physical anatomies of its children. It is the mark of her separate role and right to a separate future, to a destiny separate from Bloom's.

And what are we to make of her blond hair? The alienation on this point is even more fundamental. In the most comprehensive perspective, it may be reassuringly inclusive and a sign of the medieval Norse addition to the

Irish population.[2] As we encounter it, however, the detail questions legitimacy in the Virag-Bloom family. A "blond, born of two dark, [Milly] had blond ancestry, remote," through violation by an identified "Herr Hauptmann Hainau, Austrian Army" and through an intervention "proximate" by a "hallucination" of Molly's first love, "lieutenant Mulvey, British navy" (17.868–70).[3] Furthermore, Bloom himself discovers the figure of Milly, "fairhaired [and] greenvested," in the female shape he mistakes for his wife in "Circe" (15.3162–71).

The missing syntax is painfully insecure. Bloom craves Milly, confuses her with the threat to his possession of Molly, and shares an ancestral violation with her, present in his body as in hers. Most troubling from the perspective of the epic syntax I have been tracing is the presence of another sailor, "lieutenant Mulvey," a figure who would not figure among Penelope's suitors in the *Odyssey* correspondence, at the conjugal climax celebrated at the end of "Ithaca." To be in media res is to acknowledge the evidence of the pattern and the lack of final assurance.

Ulysses is indeed, as Perl has observed, "a theodicy ... a defense of the universal order."[4] However the order it invokes is so attentive to particulars, so radically democratic, that it balks at confinement. As historiography, it has reversed Leopold Ranke's disentanglement of the historical and the literary. It then proceeds to ignore the benefits of a clearly marked compositional design and revels in what Dominick LaCapra called "the great temptation of historiography," the practice of "overcontextualization." The text is saturated with "the particularities of its own time and place." The plenty does not only "impede responsive understanding" but taunts the likelihood of acceptable simplification.[5] *Ulysses* is fully occupied with the novelty of its own positioning and with the resonances of the stance.

What becomes of the epic function in such a milieu? To appreciate the challenge of this environment to simplification of the epic function, it is useful to recall the many-sided melding of the values of the play and the values of the audience at the culmination of the action in Roman comedy. There, closure hinged on the recognition of an essential connection between the ideal order dramatized and the extratheatrical word. The word *plaudite*, present only in comedy, Northrop Frye notes, prompts the audience to active participation. Comedy recognizes that comic resolution enshrines values deriving "so to speak, from the audience's side of the stage." *Plaudite* invited the audience to recognize the homology. Sometimes this meant an invitation to an imaginary banquet. "Old Comedy occasionally threw bits of food to the audience." The comic inclusion of the audience in the resolution of opposed interests approximates the final triumph of the ideal society, with which the audience has empathized through the performance as "the proper and desirable state of affairs."[6]

Epic closure in *Ulysses* undergoes a comparable complication in its navigation of impulses of eccentric provenance. The complication is distinct from, in fact, nearly the obverse of Bakhtin's notion of polyphony. In *Problems of Dostoevsky's Poetics*, polyphony hinges on the display of conscious self-involvement. "Dostoevsky's major heroes," Bakhtin writes, "are by the very nature of his creative design, *not only objects of authorial discourse but also the subjects of their own directly signifying discourse.*"[7] By contrast, the integrity of the epic design hinges on its distance from the self-awareness of the characters. Where the design threatens to impinge on the characters' awareness, as in the attribution of Arthur Griffith's ideas to Bloom in "Cyclops," the implied domestication of epic distance is parodied. The synthesis of the epic and of daily realities in *Ulysses* remains alien to awareness.

Dubliners had provided us with an image of the involuntary self-paralysis of the *sensus communis* in the poetry of Gabriel's soul, having "swooned slowly" while the snow settled "upon all the living and the dead." The epic function in *Ulysses* situates Bloom's fuzzy-headed confusion of two composers, Meyerbeer and Mercadante, as a lapse in self-awareness, a lapse needed for the constitution of modern national identity but in this instance indicating a historical horizon very different from the epic march toward national self-affirmation through political independence.

When we examine the confusion of Meyerbeer and Mercadante more closely, it dispels the common dream transposed as *Ulysses'* allegorical assimilation of the foundation of the modern Irish state. The rhythm that tends toward the affirmation of a common Irish destiny appears to be at the cusp of transposition to a different syntax.

This dramatization of confusion occurs as Bloom stands before a shop window and reads the last words attributed to the nationalist martyr Robert Emmet: "*When my country takes her place among the nations of the earth, then and not till then let my epitaph be written. I have done.*" The famous words put Bloom in mind of Mercadante's oratorio on the theme of Christ's last agony, *The Seven Last Words*. Noting "Emmet's last words," Bloom associates them with the title of Mercadante's oratorio and surprisingly attributes the music to the composer Meyerbeer: "Bloom viewed a gallant pictured hero in Lionel Mark's window. Robert Emmet's last words. Of Meyerbeer that is" (11.1274–75). The attribution makes sense in context. The mention of Meyerbeer, whose *Les Huguenots* has been in his mind all day, connects Emmet's self-sacrifice with the theme of communal massacre.

The oddity is that Bloom had gotten the Meyerbeer reference right a few hours earlier. Staring at a display in the windows of Brown Thomas, he had explicitly linked Meyerbeer with the theme of massacre. In the passage, the phrase *La causa e sante* belongs in a sextet of the conspirators readying themselves for the slaughter.

> He passed, dallying, the windows of Brown Thomas, silk mercers. Cascades of ribbons. Flimsy China silks. A tilted urn poured from its mouth a flood of bloodhued poplin: lustrous blood. The huguenots brought that here. *Lacaus esant tara tara.* Great chorus that. *Tara tara.* Must be washed in rainwater. Meyerbeer. *Tara: bom bom bom.* (8.620–24)

Bloom's confusion of the two composers is explicitly marked as such late in "Eumaeus." As he heads homeward with Stephen, he instances the two works, with composers reversed, for Stephen's admiration as exemplary achievements, along with a spurious work by Mozart (G&S, 96):

> [The] music of Mercadante's *Huguenots*, Meyerbeer's *Seven Last Words on the Cross* and Mozart's *Twelfth Mass* he simply revelled in, the *Gloria* in that being to his mind, the acme of first class music as such, literally knocking everything else into a cocked hat. (16.1737–40)

The whole sequence is on a false note.

The mechanics of Bloom's confusion are not difficult to trace. The juxtaposition may have originated in a coincidence. The performances of *Les Huguenots*, famous in Joyce's day for its seven extremely demanding roles for singers, were popularly referred to as "Nights of the Seven Stars."[8] Mercadante's *The Seven Last Words* depicts Christ's passion. "First: 'Father forgive them.' (Luke 23:34); Second: 'Verily I say unto thee, To day shalt thou be with me in paradise.' (Luke 23:43); Third: 'Woman, Behold thy son.' (John 19:26); Fourth: 'My God, My God, Why hast thou forsaken me?' (Matthew 27:46); Fifth: 'I thirst.' (John 19:28); Sixth: 'It is finished.' (John 19:30); Seventh: 'Father, into thy hands I commend my spirit.' (Luke 23:46)" (G&S, 95). Bloom's isolation—his exile from Eccles Street and his role of persecuted alien—encourages the shift from the theme of civil strife to the role of victim and the theme of sacrifice.

The surprising aspect of Bloom's error is that it should occur through material with which he is so intimately associated. Molly thinks of her husband as whistling tunes from the opera, "whistling every time were on the run again his huguenots or the frog march pretending to help the with our 4 stick of furniture" (18.1217). When she is reminded of Bloom's pedagogic heavy-handedness, it is again in connection with Meyerbeer:

> O wasn't I the born fool to believe all his blather about the home rule and the land league sending me that long strool of a song out of the Huguenots to sing in French to be more classy O beau pays de la touraine that I never even sang once explaining and rigmaroling about religion and persecution he wont let you enjoy anything naturally. (18.1187–91)

As in the scene at Lionel Marks's window, where Bloom's confusion originates, her recollection associates Bloom's interest with the opera and Irish nationalism.

The action of *Les Huguenots* culminates in the 1572 St. Bartholomew's Day massacre of French Protestants, a bloodbath prepared by stealth. The opera highlights the martyrdom of the two lovers, Valentine, a young Catholic woman who converts to Protestantism to share the death of her lover, Raoul de Nangis. They marry in the midst of the fighting.

Bloom's song for Molly, "O beau pays de la Touraine," begins as a pastoral ideal—"*Smiling gardens, green fountain / gentle stream that scarcely murmurs, / how I love to dream on your banks*"—and culminates in the reiteration of the wish to be allowed to continue to dream, consigning the world to the wars of the religious reformers:

> *Ah! to dream!*
> *Let Luther or Calvin drown the earth in blood*
> *with their religious squabbles—*
> *ministers of heaven whose stern morality*
> *affrights us in the name of heaven!* (Act 2)

The reader may wonder whether Molly's resentment at Bloom's preaching, the reproach for not letting her "enjoy anything naturally," might not be perfectly appropriate to the case.

Bloom's recollection from the opera is drawn from the voices of the Catholic conspirators, including Saint-Bris, the father of the maid Valentine. Saint-Bris has no idea what his daughter has done. He does not suspect that she is a possible victim of the plot to massacre the French Protestants. He has no compunctions about the murder of the heretics en masse.

> *Yes, we!*
> *For this sacred cause,*
> *I will obey my God*
> *and my King without fear!*
> *Count on my courage:*
> *in your hands I place,*
> *My vows and my faith.*

The final curtain closes on Catholic soldiers, having left only the dying behind them, advancing. The scene emphasizes ferocity.

> *With fire and sword*
> *let us exterminate the impious breed!*
> *Let us strike down and pursue the heretic!*
> *God wills it, God wants their blood!*
> *Yes, God wants their blood!*[9]

This is the opera Bloom appears inadvertently to have invoked as he prudently punctuates his reading of Emmet's address in Lionel Marks's shop window with a protracted fart, which he camouflages by timing it to the passing of a streetcar:

> Sea bloom, greasebloom viewed last words. Softly. *When my country takes her place among.*
>   Prrprr
> Must be the bur.
>   Fff! Oo. Rrpr.
>   *Nations of the earth.* No-one behind. She's passed. *Then not till then.* Tram kran kran kran. Good oppor. Coming. Krandlkrankran. I am sure it the burgund. Yes. One, two. *Let my epitaph be.* Kraaaaaa. *Written. I have*
> Ppprrpffrrppffff.
>   *Done.* (11.1284–94)

Read with Meyerbeer's *Les Huguenots* in mind, Bloom's gesture belongs to the rhetoric that G. J. Watson describes as a "massive attempt to deconstruct the mythology of Romantic Ireland . . . [and] blood sacrifice . . . the cult of the peasant and the corresponding hatred of the commercial and urban."[10] When read as reference to Mercadante's *Seven Last Words*, Bloom's scatological rendition of Emmet is blasphemous. "When Jesus therefore received the vinegar, he said, It is finished: and bowed his head and gave up the ghost" (John: 19:30). In Bloom's interpretation, the nationalist martyr becomes an expression of the divine afflatus.

Bloom's confusion of the composers, however, is not final. When harassed by anti-Semitic patriots in "Cyclops," who mock him as a Jew and deny his right to call himself an Irishman, the context makes it clear that, surprisingly, Bloom has once again corrected himself and gotten the link between Mercadante and *Seven Last Words* right. The passage immediately precedes Bloom's flight and Lipoti Virag's apotheosis. Including Mercadante in the series foreshadows the culmination of Bloom's argument.

> And says he:
> —Mendelssohn was a jew and Karl Marx was a jew and Mercadante and Spinoza. And the Saviour was a jew and his father was a jew. Your God.
> —He had no father, says Martin. That'll do now. Drive ahead.
> —Whose God? says the Citizen
> —Well, his uncle was a jew, says he. Your God was a jew. Christ was a jew like me. (12.1804–9)

The mention of Mercadante's oratorio foreshadows the mention of Christ. The climax of Mercadante's *Seven Last Words* is based on Jesus crying out "in a loud voice . . . Father into thy hands I commend my spirit." In his version of the Aryan heresy, Bloom marshals the contributions of his Jewish champions toward the rhetorical claim on the highest manifestation of Jewish genius he could imagine.

The problem with Bloom's progression is that his ordering principle is, at best, uncertain. Bloom appears unaware that he has no business citing these exemplars as Jews. Mendelssohn was born into a converted family; Marx's parents also converted; Spinoza was excommunicated as an apostate to Judaism; Mercadante, the most flagrant exception to the principle, was not a Jew but an Italian Catholic.[11] Of course, Bloom himself, born to a non-Jewish mother, does not belong to this series either. As a list of non-Jewish Jews, the series is more logical, with the exception, once again, of Mercadante.[12]

What could be going through Bloom's mind? Giacomo Meyerbeer was a Jew. Born Jakob Liebman Bier, he had taken the name Meyerbeer to honor a bequest from a relative called Meyer.[13] Richard Wagner, in *Judaism in Music*, an 1850 pamphlet of which Joyce had a copy, denounced Mendelssohn and Meyerbeer and Judaism as "the deforming conscience of . . . modern civilization."[14] It is hard to credit the possibility that the appearance of Mercadante in the series is not intended to bring Meyerbeer to mind. The likelihood is that Bloom thought of the celebrated Jewish composer of *Les Huguenots*. Beset by Irish chauvinists and caught up by his own rhetoric, he returned to the mistaken attribution of *Les Huguenots*, which he has been formulating, and got the attribution of *The Seven Last Words* right.

The context argues that *Les Huguenots* has been suppressed. The inclusion of Mercadante in the list registers the absence as a lapse in logic. The lapse has wide implications. Ernest Renan had cited the St. Bartholomew's Day massacre as an exemplary case of how important forgetfulness is for national identity.[15] The sine qua non of nationality, Renan wrote, "is that all individuals have many things in common, and also that they have forgotten many things." Forgetting is not to be confused with not having access to the information. It is deliberate. "No French citizen knows whether he is a Burgundian, an Alan, a Taifale, or a Visigoth, yet every French citizen has to have forgotten the massacre of St. Bartholomew, or the massacres that took place in the Midi in the thirteenth century.[16]

By way of Mercadante-Meyerbeer confusion and substitution, the epic account of Irish nationality in *Ulysses* applies the litmus of the St. Bartholomew's Day massacre to the presentation. In apparently returning to the correct attribution of *The Seven Last Words* and suppressing mention of Meyerbeer and *Les Huguenots*, Bloom has performed Renan's argument. Forgetfulness, like the snow in *The Dead*, is "general all over Ireland" and, like "the snow falling faintly through the universe and falling faintly, like the descent of their last end, upon all the living and all the dead" (*D*, 220), displaces the Jewish composer of *Les Huguenots* from the consciousness of the Jew who bears the epic signature of *Ulysses*.

Joyce never seems to have had any problem with *Historia Magistrae Vitae*, the ideal of history as the teacher of life, the didactic traditional mind-set in the writing of history that Ranke wanted to banish from modern historiography. For Ranke, the modern historian starts without pedagogical intent and "merely wishes to show how it really was" (*er will bloss zeigen, wie es eigentlich gewesen).*[17] Joyce, as his campaign to see *Dubliners* in print uncensored and thus contribute to the moral reformation of Ireland and as Stephen Dedalus's claim to a messianic vocation both indicate, wanted his writing to occupy just the discursive role for which the father of modern history faulted earlier writers. Nevertheless, the shared life of "people living in the same place" who also "live in different places," in Bloom's inept definition of common elements of a nation when the Irish patriots threaten him in "Cyclops," remains "officially inarticulate."[18]

Renan had counseled that this inarticulate common life be left undisturbed. With "all his fervently expressed belief in science," Renan did not want a role, notes Martin Thom, in "the unmasking of power by reason." The nation was to remain the province of "rite, symbol, mystery and brute force."[19] *Ulysses* evinces boundless fascination with this compromise. The whole of the epic design can be read as a protracted riposte to the dictum by Ernst Moritz Arndt, the German patriot who opposed Napoleon, contending that "all great things which a man does, forms, thinks and invents as a hero, an artist, a law giver or inventor—all that comes to him only from the nation."[20]

Some interesting conclusions follow. I have in mind, of course, the sensitivity of Joyce's prose to the tempo of civil disturbances in Ireland: the Easter Rising, the imprisonment of the Sinn Fein leadership in May 1917, the postwar troubles pitting Sinn Fein and the Irish Republican Army against the Royal Irish Constabulary and the Black and Tans, the record of violence that historian J.A.S. Grenville has described as "civil war, without battle lines, carried on by ambush, assassination and murder on both sides."[21] However, far more germane to my argument is the attention to the limits of national self-definition.

Bloom has remembered to forget. Even persecuted by chauvinists, the figure sustains a synthetic, nonsectarian approach to nationality. How does this gesture fit with the epic fable? Bloom as Christ crucified achieves too much. Certainly from the perspective of the epic design, he has transposed the threat of civil strife as necessary and as the occasion, the allusions to Christ argue, for his personal actualization.

From the perspective of the epic design, this is an ideological dodge. Lipoti Virag, the embodiment of locomotor ataxia, orders his descendent to force himself to recall Meyerbeer's opera:

VIRAG
(*Severely, his nose hardhumped, his side eye winking*) Stop twirling your thumbs and have a good old thunk. See you have forgotten.

Exercise your mnemotechnic. *La Causa e santa.* Tara. Tara. (*aside*) He will surely remember. (15.2382–86)

The Italian phrase evokes the slaughter of the Huguenots. "Tara" indicates the music and also the Hill of Tara, topography "associated with the ancient high kings of a united, golden age of Ireland" and the site of Daniel O'Connell's mass meeting in 1843 for the repeal of the union (G&S, 150).

The stakes in the division between Bloom and his ancestor on this issue, as in Irish society, are large. Disagreement over the St. Bartholomew Day's massacre is one of those threshold events that render the empathy requisite for communication difficult. Shared agency requires shared purpose. Nationalism might claim to constitute a natural, biologically and historically authentic bond; however, as Stephen Dedalus saw very clearly, the practical exercise of this bond was a moral undertaking.

David Lloyd translates the call to national authenticity as "the projective desire of nationalism," which requires the programmatic "homogenization of the people."[22] *Ulysses* returns to this call, approximating the common understanding of past and present, with the phrase "*Coactus volui.*"

The phrase is shared by Lipoti Virag and Cashel Boyle O'Connor Fitzmaurice Tisdall Farrell, a living community of grandiloquent Irish names. Gifford and Seidman translate the phrase as "I willed it under constraint" (G&S 282). *Coactus volui* originated in Justinian's IV, 2. 21. 5., as a formula for the acceptance of a legacy. The formula indicated that the legatee "would not have been willing [to accept the legacy] had it been freely offered" but deemed that "having been forced," the legatee was fearful and willing.[23] In the terms of the epic design, the sharing of the phrase distributes Farrell and Lipoti Virag as terminal points, abutting respectively on the present and the potency of sexual generation the making of the present moment from the distant past.

In "Wandering Rocks," we see Cashel Boyle O'Connor Fitzmaurice Tisdall Farrell muttering his "fierce word *Coactus volui* . . . with ratsteeth bared" (10.1111–13). In an iconic summary of *Ulysses'* transposition of Griffith's argument, he aims his rage "through a fierce eyeglass across the carriages [of the viceregal procession] at the head of Mr. M. E. Solomon in the window of the Austro-Hungarian viceconsulate" (10.1261–63). In "Circe," Lipoti Virag, in a grotesque avian metamorphosis, punctuates his version of sexual encounters with the identical phrase *Coactus volui*, to announce penetration.

Woman, undoing her sweet pudor her belt of rushrope, offers her allmoist yoni to man's lingam. Short time after man presents woman with pieces of jungle meat. Woman shows joy and covers herself with feather skins. Man loves her yoni fiercely with big lingam, the stiff one. (*he cries*) *Coactus volui.* Then giddy woman will run about. Strong man grapses woman's wrist. Woman squeals, bits, spucks. Man now fierce angry, strikes woman's fat yadgana. (*he chases his tail*) Piffpaff! Popo! (*He stops, sneezes*) Pchp! (*he worries his butt*) Prrrrrht! (15.2549–56)

In both contexts, the phrase *Coactus volui* signals the apparent practical mastery of conditions required for common life. Cashel Boyle O'Connor Fitzmaurice Tisdall Farrell's aggressive eye joins, even as it threatens, the representatives of the British and Hapsburg crowns. Lipoti Virag joins man and woman, even as he mocks and parodies the coupling.

Hans-Georg Gadamer, in an often quoted passage, observed that "understanding is not to be thought of so much as an action of one's subjectivity, but as the placing of oneself within a tradition, in which past and present are constantly fused."[24] In the epic fable, *Ulysses* negotiates such a "fusion" or, in the lexicon of *Portrait*, such a "forging," a complicated point of access that derives both from the past and from the impingement of the present. In the linkage of Lipoti Virag and Cashel Boyle O'Connor Fitzmaurice Tisdall Farrell, *Ulysses* returns to the fable with the comprehensive awareness of context postulated in Vico's *memoria*.

While apparently asserting themselves, Cashel Boyle O'Connor Fitzmaurice Tisdall Farrell and Lipoti Virag are protesting the conditions to which they have perforce had to submit. For Vico, understanding was comprised of a "philological sensibility" permitting access to "the points around which past cultures can be understood," a recollection introducing a fresh ordering of the material, "a different encompassing order of meaning."[25]

In the conjunction of Farrell and Lipoti Virag, two figures, the effort to situate continuity abuts on the breakup of tradition. Cashel Boyle O'Connor Fitzmaurice Tisdall Farrell protests the contemporary conjunction that I have argued identifies the modern Irish epic. Lipoti Virag, in bestial metamorphosis, is at grips with human reproduction. When asked in his old age whether he was "still able to have a woman," Sophocles replied: "Hush man; most gladly indeed am I rid of it all, as though I had escaped from a mad and savage master."[26] Lipoti Virag, who proleptically embodies the Bloom family continuity, is described parenthetically as *"agueshaken, profuse yellow spawn foaming over his bony epileptic lips"* with *"a flickering phosphorescent scorpion tongue"* and *"gibbering baboon's cries [as] he jerks his hips in the cynical spasm"* (15.2598, 2600–3).

We are dealing with something other than "the textual unconscious" here, the force that John S. Rickard identifies as a "metapersonal source of mind," "an involuntary spontaneous evocation of memory" that hints at "the destiny that drives toward resolution."[27] The figures span the elements of the epic fable. They are quasiconscious embodiments of its domain.

Reflecting on the riots at the performance of John Millington Synge's play *Playboy of the Western World*, Seamus Deane comments that "a community that has learned to make the distinction between history and legend . . . has disabled itself as a traditional community." When such a community is forced into denying the applicability of these distinct modes of understanding, "it turns into a mob."[28] The epic fable's constitutive negotiations with the immediate present and its defining past have frozen such a formative instant, rigid, and yet quasiconscious.

The figures register force majeure. Nancy F. Partner has referred to historiography as "the narration of the half-known," noting that "the Hebraic God of history rules the ethos of history in our culture—an ethos which subjects history to the withering attentions of logical inquiry while demanding continual renewal in acts of creative imagination."[29] In Farrell and Lipoti Virag, the will remains. The confrontation with constraint borders on nightmare; nevertheless, it has awoken and belongs also to the day.

The level of abstraction is reminiscent of the *Annales*'s detachment of historiography from the representation of individual agency and from the guiding role of a central institution such as the state. The founders of the *Annales*, Lucien Febvre and Marc Bloch, had turned from linear historical narrative toward "the aspects of feeling and experience embedded in collective mentalities."[30] At a remove from the conventional characterizations of historical agency comparable to Bertolt Brecht's treatment of "acting, music and design . . . as a bundle of separate elements . . . [operating] autonomously but . . . [also as] commentary and contradiction," the complication welcomes the prepersonal, social intentionalities informing the language, in Bakhtin's sense, with "each word [tasting] of the context and contexts in which it has lived its socially charged life."[31]

Cashel Boyle O'Connor Fitzmaurice Tisdall Farrell, Ellmann records, "carried two swords, a fishing rod, and an umbrella, . . . wore a red rose in his buttonhole and had upon his head a small bowler hat with large holes for ventilation; from a brewer's family in Dundalk he was said to have fallen into a vat and never recovered."[32] In Dublin, he was nicknamed "Endymion"—"whom the moon loved"—after the mortal beloved of Selene, whom she kept forever youthful in perpetual sleep in a mountain cave and whom she constrained to allow her to bear fifty daughters. In "Circe," Bloom, we recall, also marries Selene as he inflates in consequence as the fantastic successor of Parnell (15.1509–10).

Lipoti Virag also expands outward from a hallucination that, according to John Gordon, articulates "the andiron nearest the hatrack" in Bella Cohen's brothel. His entire performance may only amount to the observation that "life, especially female life is a crow beautified with fake feathers."[33] Zoe, the Nighttown whore whose name translates from the Greek as "life," reports that the sexual penetration which he celebrates with the cry of "*Coactus volui*" is a "dry rush" (15.2562); that is to say, the penetration is without orgasm, and probably lubrication (G&S, 497). The final wisdom he conveys in *Ulysses* is the cry, entirely cerebral, attributed only to *Virag's Head*: "Quack!" (15.2638).

Portrait had defined "epical form" as the instant that "the artist prolongs and broods upon himself as the centre of an epical event and this form progresses till the center of emotional gravity is equidistant from the artist himself and from others" (P, 215). *Ulysses* modifies this definition by opening the form to both past and future. The result is, I have sought to show, highly labile. Epic form in *Ulysses* is dialogue carried on in many tongues, engaged with multiple constituencies present and future. Thomas M. Greene has caught, I believe, the accent of this conversation in his characterization of classical imitation:

> Imitation acts out a passage of history that is a retrospective vision or construct, with all the vulnerability of a construct. It has no ground other than the modern universe of meanings it is helping to actualize and the past universe it points to allusively and simplifies. It seeks no suprahistorical order; it accepts the temporal, the contingent and the specific as given. But it makes possible an emergent sense of identity, personal and cultural, by demonstrating the viability of diachronic itineraries.[34]

This is the passage Joyce faced in the composition of *Ulysses*.

Ulysses as an epic sustains a complex supplement to comic affirmation. It celebrates "moments when individuals and communities locate themselves in relation to parents and children, ancestors and posterity, beginnings and endings."[35] As a mode of address, it sustains a determination to accord the distant future a full spectrum of possible response. It transforms this distance from this permanent audience, the distance that constitutes its most considerable investment in the regulative role of epic, into a call for communicative transparency between distant generations.

Ulysses dramatizes this fragile overview of Dublin without drawing on the retroactive transformation of everyday "motley," which Yeats found spellbinding. Instead of "retroactive foreshadowing," with narrator and audience invited to wonder at the mystery of the past and "to judge the participants" as though in some essential way, *"they too should have known what was to come,"* Ulysses tests synthetic approaches.[36]

Joyce himself reportedly described the daily encounter with his text in this vein to the Polish novelist Jan Paradowski as an imagined conversation:

> Ah, how wonderful that was to get up early in the morning, around five o'clock, and enter the misty regions of my emerging epic, as Dante entered his *selva oscura selva selvaggia.* Words cracked in my head and a multitude of images crowded around, like those shades at the entrance to the Underworld when Ulysses stood there awaiting the spirit of Tiresias. I wrote the greater part of the book during the war. There was fighting on all fronts, empires fell, kings fell into exile, the old order was collapsing with a crash; and I had as I sat down to work, the conviction that in the midst of all these ruins I was building something for the most distant future."[37]

While the claim of the epic focus to relative autonomy does not stabilize the text, it is a powerful call. It summons the contemporary audience in the name of epic futurity. It crowds habit and expectation while acknowledging the force of established readings. Thomas C. Hofheinz deems the "affirmation of *Finnegans Wake*" and of Molly's ultimate "yes" in *Ulysses* to be evanescent, "on the edge of negation and oblivion, cast in the tenuous clarity between life and death, sleep and waking, then and now."[38] *Ulysses'* achievement in the epic tradition is to bring to this sensitivity, to this appreciation of impermanence and of the demands of historical scholarship, a working commitment to the undiminished consequence of events.

Notes

Introduction. The Epic Fable: A Negotiation with History and Nationhood

1. White, *Metahistory*, 54.
2. Lewis, *Time*, 101.
3. Iggers, *Historiography*, 31–64.
4. White, *Content*, 65.
5. Ibid., 66.
6. Ariès, *De L'Histoire*, 64–68.
7. Longenbach, *Poetics*, 18.
8. Virgil, *The Aeneid*, books 1, 6, and 8.
9. The verb in Hopkins is from the final quatrain of *Pied Beauty*. The poet is considering God's Creation. "He fathers-forth," he writes, whose own "beauty is past change." The poem bids the reader, "Praise him."
10. On Tennyson's elegiac temper, see Tucker, *Tennyson*, passim.
11. Kenner, *Colder Eye*, 196.
12. Arendt, *Condition*, 8.
13. Longenbach, *Poetics*, 10.
14. Pound, *Essays*, 401.
15. Nairn, *Faces*, 17.
16. Letter to Stanislaus Joyce, November 6, 1906, in Ellmann, *Joyce*, 237.
17. Nolan, *Nationalism*, 21.
18. Dismissal of Griffith's importance to Joyce on these grounds is a critical commonplace. Nolan cites the following extract from Griffith's preface to John Mitchel's *Jail Journal* as an example of Griffith's antilibertarian nationalism: "The right of the Irish to political independence never was, is not and never can be dependent on the right of the admission of equal rights in all other peoples. It is based on no theory of, and is in nowise dependent on theories of government and doctrines of philanthropy or universalism" (Nolan, *Nationalism*, 22).

Nolan concludes that because positions such as this "are deeply at odds with Joyce's sense of himself as the victim and subject of a general British imperialism, and his hostility to racism," he would have more readily identified, in spite of his dislike of violence, with the extreme nationalists' commitment to "secular principles of universal rights" (Ibid.).

The problem with this reasoning is the assumption that Joyce was looking for a position to endorse. If his much vaunted self-exile means any one thing, the sense of it has to involve a rejection of the alternatives his connection with Ireland otherwise allowed. He could certainly be credited with a utopian political stance, which nothing in contemporary Ireland remotely resembled. In fact, his departure from Ireland would have made it practical to entertain such a utopian allegiance.

19. Nolan, *Nationalism*, 59.
20. Hofheinz, *Invention*, 70.
21. Weir, *Mediation*, 8.
22. Hegel, *Philosophy*, 60–61.
23. Adorno, *Notes*, 35.
24. Hegel, *Aesthetics*, 1044–45, in Moretti, *Epic*, 11.
25. Moretti, *Epic*, 5.
26. MacCabe, *Revolution*, 150.
27. Beissinger, Tylus, and Wofford, *Epic Traditions*, 5.
28. Propp, *Morphology*; Barthes, "Introduction to the Structural Analysis of Narratives," *Image*, 79–125; Chatman, *Story*.
29. Spoo, *Language*, 161.
30. Jameson, "History," 128. Social experience, ideally integrated in a manner that can only be suggested under capitalism, does not serve Jameson's reading of *Ulysses* as a specifically epic performance very well. To make sense of the work as "the epic of the metropolis under imperialism, in which the development of the bourgeoisie and the proletariat alike is stunted to the benefit of a national pettybourgeoisie," he has to discount the significance of Joyce's "hostility to Irish nationalism" (Ibid., 134).
31. Weir, *Mediation*, 184.
32. Brooks, *Plot*, 5.
33. Auerbach, *Mimesis*, 20.
34. Minogue, *Nationalism*, 57.
35. Barthes, *Degree Zero*, 30.
36. Hutchinson, *Cultural Nationalism*, 14.
37. Friedman, *Horizontal Society*, 93.
38. Jenkins, *On What Is History?*, 15–43.
39. Spoo, *Language*, 146.
40. Auerbach, *Mimesis*, 20.
41. Anderson, *Communities*, 19.
42. Lukacs, *Theory*, 66.
43. Hegel, *Aesthetics*, 1044–45, in Moretti, *Epic*, 11.
44. Moretti, *Epic*, 11.
45. Barthes, *Degree Zero*, 30–31.
46. Hegel, *Philosophy of History*, 61.

47. Griffiths and Rabinowitz, *Novel Epics*, 5.
48. Joyce, "Catalina," *Critical Writings*, 100.
49. Joyce, "Drama and Life," *Critical Writings*, 42.
50. Ibid., 43.
51. Joyce, "Ireland, Island of Saints and Sages," *Critical Writings*, 166.
52. James, *Nation Formation*, 45.
53. Anderson, *Communities*, 5.
54. Handwerke, *Irony*, 40.
55. Lewis, *Preface*, 27–33.
56. Smith, *Nationalism*, 140.
57. Booker, *Joyce*, 20.
58. Nuttall, *Openings*, 14–15.
59. Yeats, *Autobiographies*, 263, in Nolan, *Nationalism*, 27.
60. Rilke dramatizes the impossibility of coexisting with this formative reality. He represents it as simultaneously the extinction of individuality and the heart of the creative experience. Beauty is the inconceivable order of being apart from the poet. He presents beauty as "the beginning of a terror" prolonged until it is practically unendurable. He invites the reader to contemplate the "calm" of the postponed climax, the disdain of the "order of Angels" (The First Elegy, lines 1–7. Rilke, *Duino Elegies*, 35).
61. Canovan, *Nationhood*, 3.
62. Dilthey, *Selected Writings*, 3.
63. Manganiello, *Politics*, 138; Ellmann, *Consciousness*, 89.
64. Nolan, *Nationalism*, 50–52.
65. Duffy, *Subaltern*, 10–11.
66. Deane, "Joyce and Nationalism," *Revivals*, 107.
67. Spoo, *Language*, 159.
68. Ibid., 8.
69. Ibid., 6.
70. Ibid., 7.
71. Joyce, "Portrait of the Artist," 258.
72. The material concerning the Hapsburgs has appeared in Ungar, "Among the Hapsburgs."
73. Colum, *Griffith*, 77.
74. *An Claidhean Soluis* November 26, 1904, in Edwards, *Pearse*, 72.
75. First published in the *Pilot* (Boston) August 6, 1887. It appears in Yeats, *Variorum Edition*, 709–16.
76. Hammond, *Gladstone*, 387.
77. *Hansard*, 3rd series, Vol. 304, cols. 1037–47.
78. Griffith, *Hungary*, 2.
79. Ibid., 68.
80. Ibid., 95–96.
81. Ibid., 88–89.

82. Colum, *Griffith*, 63.
83. Manganiello, *Politics*, 136.
84. Fairhall, *Question of History*, 177.
85. The crown of St. Stephen, the symbol of the kingdom, was sent to King (Saint) Stephen by Pope Sylvester II at the beginning of the eleventh century. It was considered to have been a gift of the Virgin Mary, who is also invoked as a patron saint of the nation (Butler, *Lives*, 317).
86. John McCourt, in his valuable study of Joyce's stay in Trieste, confuses the patron saints. He attributes St. Leopold to Hungary and St. Stephen to Austria. The error excludes the allegorical potential of the fable from his careful review of possible links among the Dual Monarchy, Ireland, and *Ulysses* (McCourt, *Years*, 96).
87. Cairns, *Augustan Epic*, 61.
88. Ibid., 60.
89. Ibid., 62.
90. Fairhall, *Question of History*, 177.
91. Minogue, *Nationalism*, 32.
92. Anderson, *Communities*, 10.
93. Minogue, *Nationalism*, 22, 31.
94. Joyce, *Letters* 2, 505.

Chapter 1. The Argument of the Fable: An Overview

1. Thompson, *Working Class*, 12.
2. Ariès, *De L'Histoire*, 65. The translation is my own.
3. Ibid., 65.
4. Vico, *New Science*, Book 1, section 2, paragraph 120, 60.
5. Ibid., Book 2, section 1, paragraph 404, 129–30.
6. Ibid.
7. Schneidau, *Giants*, 13.
8. Handwerke, *Irony*, 40–41.
9. Deane, "Joyce and Stephen," *Revivals*, 80.
10. The problem with this progression is that it leads "inward" only. The imitation of epic form results in the investigation of subjectivity. The direction of this movement is independent of the starting point in classical literature and comments on it only obliquely at the starting point. To argue about a specific epic legacy in this context seems arbitrary. Watson admires the presentation of epic conflict as subjective features of the narrative, the slaughter of the tutors as "Bloom's psychological victory of equanimity" (Watson, "Joyce," 198).

Terry Eagleton draws the opposite conclusion from an appreciation of the apparent superfluity of the nature of the specific parallel. "The outrageousness of *Ulysses* is that the myth by which the experience of Dublin is welded into a synthetic unity has no inward and necessary conjunction with that experience at all. One could imagine Joyce having put quite a different myth to the same purpose with the same ingenuity" (Eagleton, *Exiles*, 171).

11. The context, the insistence on identity, argues that Gifford is mistaken in reading this as primarily a parody of Louis XIV's "L'état, c'est moi" (G&S, 53).

12. Bernstein, *Philosophy*, 201.

13. Diderot, *Nephew*, 125.

14. Meinecke, *Cosmopolitanism*, 15.

15. Ellmann, *Joyce*, 296–97.

16. Seidel, *Geography*, 84.

17. Anderson, *Communities*, 40.

18. Ree, "Cosmopolitanism," 84.

19. Marx, "On the Jewish Question," in Borneman, *Belonging*, 41.

20. Keats, letter to George and Georgina Keats, February 18, 1819, *Selected Letters*, 67.

21. Emerson, "History," 127.

22. Perl, *Tradition*, 256.

23. Bhabha, "DissemiNation," 298–99.

24. Staten, "Decomposing," 380.

25. Rickard, *Memory*, 131.

26. Perl, *Tradition*, 256.

27. Milbank, *Vico*, 296–97.

28. Bowen, *Comic Novel*, 42.

29. Feibleman, *In Praise of Comedy*, 182, in Bowen, *Comic Novel*, 42.

30. Verene, *Imagination*, 43–44.

31. Deane, "Heroic Styles," 71.

32. Mandelbaum, "Narrative," 147.

Chapter 2. The Ascent of Stephen Dedalus from Messianic Ambition to Epic Discourse

1. Eco, *Chaosmos*, 1.

2. Eliot, "Tradition and the Individual Talent," *Selected Prose*, 21–30, 26.

3. Ibid., 23.

4. Nairn, *Faces of Nationalism*, 17.

5. F. W. Schlegel, *Kritisch Ausgabe* 12, 397–99. The passages appear in translation in Handwerke, *Irony*, 41.

6. Schork, *Latin*, 125.

7. Pound, "Vorticism," 92.

8. Budgeon, *Joyce*, 105.

9. The 1922 and the 1961 editions of *Ulysses* have this line as "A catalectic..." not "Acatelectic." Gaskell and Hart prefer the latter (Gaskell and Hart, *Review*, 6, 104).

10. Here goes my lord
   A trot, a trot, a trot!
     Here goes my lady
        A canter, a canter, a canter, a canter!
           Here goes my young master

> Jockey-hitch, jockey-hitch, jockey-hitch, jockey-hitch!
> Here goes my young miss
> An amble, an amble, an amble, an amble!
> The footman lags behind to tipple ale and wine
> and goes gallop, a gallop, a gallop to make up his mind.

11. Joyce, *Stephen Hero*, 33.

12. Gilbert, *Ulysses*, 106; Unkeless, "Bats," 128–32; Cheng, "Dedalus," 167–70; Seidel, "Vampire," 422; Schutte, *Shakespeare*, 109.

13. Cheng notes that the phrase *Omnis caro ad te veniet* [All flesh shall come to you] was originally used by David addressing Yahweh (Psalms 65:2)." Cheng, "Dedalus," 166. It is also a part of the entrance chant of the funeral mass (G&S, 6).

14. Winckelmann, quoted in Lessing, *Laocoön*, 6.

15. Lessing, *Laocoön*, 14.

16. Ibid., 13.

17. Ibid., 17.

18. Virgil, *The Aeneid*, book 2, lines 222–24. Trans. Conington, 44.

19. Virgil, *The Aeneid*, book 2, lines 222–24. Trans. Jackson Knight, 57–58.

20. The need to take this irreverence into account weakens otherwise thorough source studies of the poem such as Robert Adams Day's study of Stephen's debt to Hyde and Hyde's Gaelic source, to Bram Stoker's *Dracula* (1897), to Pater's description of the *Mona Lisa*, and to W. T. Horton's *Book of Images* (1898). For Day, these sources render the significance of Stephen's experience clear. He concludes that it may be the beginning of Stephen's career as a genuine poet (Day, "Vampire Poem," 183–97).

21. Virgil, *The Aeneid*, book 2, lines 56–62. Trans. Jackson Knight, 52.

22. Ibid., book 2, lines 69–80.

> Conington's translation of the same lines is as follows:
>
> "Wretched countrymen," he cries,
> "What monstrous madness blinds your eyes?
> Think you your enemies removed?
> Come presents without wrong
> From Danaans? Have you thus
> Approved Ulysses, known so long?
> What'er it be, a Greek I fear
> Though presents in his hand he bear,
> He spoke, and his arm's full force
> Straight at the belly of the horse
> His mighty spear he cast:
> Quivering it stood: the sharp rebound
> Shook the monster: and a sound
> Through all its caverns passed.
> And then, had fate our weal designed

Nor given us a perverted mind,
Then had he moved us to deface the Greeks accursed hiding place,
And Troy had been abiding still,
And Priams's tower yet crowned the hill."
Virgil, *The Aeneid*, book 2, lines 69–80. Trans. Conington, 37.

23. See Curtius, *European Literature*, 29–30. On the impact of this tradition on the early modernists, see Schneidau, *Giants*.

24. Perl, *Tradition*, 188.

25. *Ulysses* does not offer "a picture" but re-members. It isolates body parts and reconstitutes the human body/body politic. The distinction applies Bergson's observation—"to picture is not to remember"—in a concrete manner (Henry Bergson, *Matter and Memory*, 144, quoted in Jay, *Downcast Eyes*, 193).

26. Edmund Plowden, *Commentaries or Reports* (London 1816), 233a, quoted in Kantoriwicz, *Two Bodies*, 7.

27. In his closely reasoned study, Patrick Colm Hogan concludes that the time allowed seems "too short for Talbot to have continued to the end of the poem—a further 21 lines" and that it is precisely the coda that has been excluded from the assignment (Hogan, *Influence*, 122–24). My argument only requires the emphasis on the missing segment of text as absent.

28. Martz, *Exile*, 74.

29. In *Portrait*, Stephen uses the movement from first- to third-person voice in "Dick Turpin" as the example of a narrative ceasing to be "purely personal," epic rather than lyric (*P*, 215). Joseph Wittreich and Lee A. Jacobus have both noted the resemblance between the final coda of *Lycidas* and "Dick Turpin" (Wittreich, "Pastoral," 59–80; Jacobus, "'Lycidas,'" 193).

30. Milton, *Poetical Works*, vol. 1, 426.

31. Milton, in Samuel Johnson's caustic view, managed to assuage "his patriotism . . . in a private boarding school." In Stephen's own regard, the occupation is degrading. To his cronies, he pretends that he earned his money from his writing (11.265, 14.285–87).

32. Milton's continental tour and schoolteaching (1638–39) postdate the composition of *Lycidas* (Woodhouse, *Muse*, 55).

33. "Eleven paragraphs" in the "Oxen of the Sun episode," for example, "bring Bloom inside, holding his hat; eleven more, at the end of the episode conduct the noisy crew out of the hospital and into and out of the pub" (Kenner, *Ulysses*, 109).

Alastair Fowler explains Milton's use of eleven stanzas as conventional in funeral odes. He notes that Henry King's "The Exequy" also has eleven stanzas. There was a "classical association of 11," he writes, "with mourning and specifically with its termination. Tombs were honored in February, according to Ovid . . . but this stopped on the day of the Feralia, when 11 days of the month remained" (Fowler, *Silent Poetry*, 171).

34. The use of the eight-line stanza was established as a norm by Ariosto and Tasso and commended by Samuel Daniel in his *A Defense of Poetry*. It remained the

English heroical norm until Milton wrote *Paradise Lost* (Donker and Muldrow, *Dictionary*, 112).

Penelope's eight-sentence soliloquy represents an audacious variation on this measure. Stephen's definition of the octave— "the greatest possible ellipse. Consistent with. The ultimate return"—treats the measure musically (15.2111–12).

35. Dublin rumor recognizes Stephen's private formative intensity. John Eglinton mockingly refers to Stephen's project of dictating *The Sorrows of Satan* to "six brave medicals" (9.18–28). Blake had depicted Milton's self-limitation in *Paradise Lost* as a "Sixfold Emanation scatter'd thro' the deep" (Blake, *Milton*, plate 3, l.19).

36. Joyce, *English*, 187.

37. Pater, *Marius*, 4.

38. Stephen's private strategy, in fact, might encompass materials belonging to two different riddles. The first is so shot through with disturbing associations that he permits only the opening lines (the only ones to appear in the text) to surface in his thoughts:

> *Riddle me, riddle me, randy ro.*
> *My father gave me seeds to sow.*

The two words likely to have inhibited him, Patrick A. McCarthy has argued persuasively, are *randy* and *seed*, with their suggestions of sexuality and a natural inheritance passing from father to son. The word "randy" would have had Stephen allude publicly to his sexual frustration. The word "seed" would have brought up his complex, antagonistic relationship to the idea of fatherhood: his responsibilities to Simon Dedalus, the father he has rejected, and to the mythical Daedalus, the father he has failed.

If this were not enough, the solution to the riddle would have caused him to pull back still more sharply. The answer to nine of the ten known versions of the completed riddle is "writing." "The riddle and its solution," Weldon Thornton has suggested, "remind him of his failure to justify himself as an author."

> Riddle me, riddle me, randy-row,
> My father gave me seed to sow,
> The seed was black and the ground was white
> Riddle me that and I'll give you a pipe.
>
> Thornton, *Allusions*, 30.

Archer Taylor lists nine variations of the riddle. The answers to eight of them involve writing. The solution to the ninth is "[t]he ground was covered with snow and the boy could not plant them." Taylor, *Riddles*, 438–39. Were Stephen to complete the riddle, he would, in effect, be requiring his class to draw a conclusion from which he himself shrinks.

39. Kaczvinsky notes that the "hollybush" is a symbol of eternal life and sees this interpretation as confirmed by the version of the riddle that appears in "Circe."

> *The fox crew, the cocks flew,*
> *The bells in heaven*

Were striking eleven.
'Tis time for her poor soul
To get out of heaven. (15.3577–81)
Kaczvinsky, "Cock Crew," 268–69.

Chapter 3. Joyce and the Fate of Arthur Griffith's *Resurrection of Hungary* in *Ulysses*

1. Joyce, "Saints and Sages," *Critical Writings*, 167, 168.
2. Ibid., 165–66.
3. Ibid., 166.
4. Ibid., 174.
5. Tennyson, *Virgil, Poetical Works*, 511.
6. O'Grady, *History*, 22.
7. Gregory, *Poets*, 47.
8. Ree, "Cosmopolitanism," 83.
9. Letter to Stanislaus Joyce, November 6, 1906, Joyce, *Letters,* ed. R. Ellmann, vol. 2, 187.
10. Ellmann, *Joyce*, 389. An indication of how clear Joyce was about the symbols of the regime is that much later, when he told the story of the glaucoma attack in Zurich on August 18, 1917, that led to his first eye operation, he should have recalled its having coincided with the birthday of Emperor Franz Joseph (Ellmann, *Joyce*, 417).
11. Colum, *Life*, 383.
12. Colum, "Portrait," 347.
13. Karl Kraus, "Aus dem dunkelsten Österreich," in *Sittlichkeit und Kriminilitat* (Frankfurt, 1966), 203–7, cited in Johnston, *Austrian Mind*, 48.
14. Johnston, *Austrian Mind*, 335.
15. Musil, *Qualities*, 32–33.
16. Cassels, *Generations*, 194–208.
17. Ibid., 210. The first version published was, in fact, the English edition under the title *My Past* in London in 1913. This was Eliot's source. The emperor only accepted publication with this fait accompli.
18. Joyce's use of Magyar in *Ulysses* is quirky. Sometimes he gets all the complicated agglutinative case endings exactly as he should. Sometimes, as with "Nagyaságos," he adds unnecessary syllables. I hesitate to speculate on the effects that might be intended. For more on Joyce's idiosyncratic use of the language, see Ungar, "Joyce's Hungarian."
19. The number 130 is January 30, or 1/30, the date of Crown Prince Rudolf's suicide, the date on which the Hapsburg dynasty's Mayerling ordeal began. This is an instance where Joyce has the phrase just as he should. The Mayerling reference would make an appropriate street address in terms of my interpretation.
20. The phrase "Abba! Adonai!" links Bloom's persecution with Christ's agony in the Garden of Gethsemane (Mark 14:36) (G&S, 381).

21. Kant, *Critique*, 107.
22. Connor, "I . . . AM. A," 229.
23. Himmelfarb, *History*, 16.
24. Connor, "I . . . AM. A," 230.
25. Oakeshott, *Rationalism*, 166–67.
26. Ibid., 167.
27. Ibid., 150.
28. Ibid., 159.
29. Ibid., 157.
30. Ibid.

31. Mary T. Reynolds has shown that the rendering of Lipoti Virag draws on Dante's *Paradiso*, 15–17, and on the portrait of Cacciaguida, the grandfather of Dante's grandfather. She finds parallels between the mode of descent, the warrior costumes, the recourse to Latin, and the prophetic bearing of the two figures. She also notes that Virag includes traits of devils from the *Inferno*, especially the Malebranche band of *Inferno*, 21–23 (Reynolds, *Joyce and Dante*, 66–76).

32. In the draft designated as V.A. 19, Lipoti Virag's appearance in "Circe" is rendered as follows:

> "Litpold [sic] Virag, Bloom's double, wearing Stephen's hat, Buck Mulligan's primrose vest, and a brown mackintosh under which he holds a dulcimer [sic] a book in two tomes . . ." Joyce, *Notes*, 225.

33. In Spanish, "L. Boom" would be "el Boom."
34. Joyce, "Drama and Life," *Critical Writings*, 41.

35. As Robert Tracy has pointed out, there is no "iron crown of St. Stephen" outside of Griffith's pages, and Joyce's duplication of the error is the surest evidence that he had *The Resurrection of Hungary* in mind when constructing this scene. Dominic Manganiello is mistaken in maintaining that there was an "iron crown" to discover that Tracy had not known about. Manganiello, *Politics*, 242. The one crown of St. Stephen is, as Tracy observed, not iron but "a closed diadem of gold decorated with jewels and enameled icons" (Tracy, "Leopold Bloom," 532).

The other parallels between Griffith and Joyce for Tracy include that circumstance that both Franz Joseph and Bloom ride white horses, that both wear conspicuous green socks, that a foreign language occurs at the coronation of each (Hungarian at Franz Joseph's and Hebrew at Bloom's), that "Franz Josef is hailed by 'fifty-two working men from all the counties of Hungary' while Bloom is hailed by 'thirty-two working men' from all the counties of Ireland" (Ibid.).

36. "Tanist Stone," Brewer, *Dictionary*. The connection with the Scottish regalia is presumably the reason Gifford and Seidman identify the "ruby ring" with the coronation ring of Scotland (G&S, 389). In the English coronation ceremonial, however, the coronation ring is the sovereign's personal property, and there might be any number of ruby rings. The famous ruby ring to which they are referring found its way to the Hanoverians from the original owner Mary, Queen of Scots, and by way

of the Stuarts, regnant and exiled, James II having "concealed it on his person when he fled the country in 1688" (Twining, *Regalia*, 267–68).

37. Ibid., 266.

38. Ellmann records a suggestive autobiographical parallel to this imagery. He writes that, in Trieste, one of Joyce's "favorite... superstitions was a ring, composed of different kinds of metals, which he wore on his finger as a preventative against blindness. It resembled a wedding-ring, but he denounced wedding rings as symbols of slavery to which no free man could submit. 'Then why are you willing to wear this ring?' asked his pupils. 'Because I am already the slave of my eye trouble,' Joyce replied" (Ellmann, *Joyce*, 341).

39. Ibid., 12.

40. Dante, *Divine Comedy*, vol. 1, 67–90. Mary T. Reynolds draws attention to the recognition scene between Dante and Virgil in the Dark Wood in this encounter, the one occasion in the *Commedia* that Dante calls his mentor by name. That meeting, like the Circe episode, initiates a pilgrimage-like journey involving the two men (Reynolds, *Joyce and Dante*, 36).

41. Gadamer, *Truth*, 14.

42. Gosse, *Transformation*, 150; Lawrence, *Style*, 161; French, *Book*, 187.

43. Weir, *Mediation*, 3.

Chapter 4. Closure and Millicent Bloom

1. White, *Metahistory*, 11.

2. Milly as a constellation alludes to, at least, three female roles. As a "queen," she is a version of Mary, Queen of Heaven. She is also the successor of Martha, the disguised beloved of Lionel in the popular opera *Martha*. She is also a Seaside Girl.

The first references to the opera *Martha* occur in "Aeolus" (7.58–60). These references tend to merge with the adulterous correspondence that Bloom conducts with Martha Clifford and to become the symbol of loss for Bloom in "Sirens" when Simon Dedalus sings the aria "M'Appari," Lionel's lament in the opera for his lost happiness (11.662–750).

Milly is a Seaside Girl by virtue of the phrase "simply swirling" from the song "Seaside Girls" (G&S, 434). Her morning letter to Bloom had almost attributed the song to Blazes Boylan, and she apparently continued to believe it had been composed by someone called Boylan (4.407–9). Zack Bowen has determined that the composer actually was B. Norris. The point of Milly's mistake, Bowen suggests, is that all the females who matter to Bloom are consubstantial. Her virginal zodiac-incarnation certainly points to a conflation of identity along these lines (Bowen, *Musical Allusions*, 85–86).

3. The symbolic possibilities of the number are fixed referents for Joyce's imagination. The Blooms had known Stephen, now twenty-two, as a child. Molly remembers seeing him at age eleven, eleven years before in the year Rudy Bloom lived for eleven days. At the end of "Circe," Leopold sees his eleven-year-old son rise from

Stephen's prone form. The most comprehensive summary of the patterns based on eleven is Rickard, *Memory*, 148–53.

Ira B. Nadel writes that "in the Jewish textual tradition of assigning numbers to letters, the hermeneutical rule known as *Gematria* and a practice also followed in the Hellenistic world, ALP represents one hundred and eleven (aleph = 1, amadn = 30, pe = 80) duplicating the ten *Sephiroth* ... or emanations from the Tree of Life ... plus one to mark a new beginning" (Nadel, *Joyce*, 3).

4. Noon, *Joyce*, 27. An interesting counterpoint to Stephen's anti-Platonic stance is the nineteenth-century practice of calling photography by epithets such as the "heliographic art," "solar engraving," and "sun painting." Photography casts Milly the "photo girl" (1.685) into a role as antipathic to the darkness-loving Stephen as Socrates imagines the sun to be for troglodytes in the Allegory of the Cave (Schwartz, *Art*, 112).

5. The old jeweler's intense concentration recalls the quotation from Stephen McKenna's translation of *The Enneads of Plotinus*—(The First Ennead, Sixth Tractate, Section 9)—which AE, famed, like Joyce, for a prodigious memory, was known for reciting: "Withdraw into yourself and look. And if you do not find yourself beautiful yet, act as does the creator of a statue that is to be made beautiful: he cuts away here, he smooths there, he makes this line lighter, this other purer, until a lovely face has grown upon his work. So do you also: cut away all that is excessive, straighten all that is crooked, bring light to all that is overcast, labour to make all one glow of beauty and never cease chiseling your statue, until there shall shine out on you from it the godlike splendor of virtue, until you shall see the perfect goodness surely established in the stainless shrine" (Gibbon Monk, ed., *The Living Torch*, 40, cited in Davis, *Russell*, 22–23). Allusions to the possibility of self-sculpting and reverence resonate cruelly among the precious stones (Wandering Rocks?) and among the smells, sounds, and miasma of lust.

According to James Penny Smith, the jeweler as "grandfather ape" derives from the description of a Celtic Hell in "The Eaters of Precious Stones in Yeats's The Celtic Twilight (Smith, "Allusions," 314).

6. It is possible that the abbreviation of the name intended "Szesz," Hungarian for "alcohol," a word Joyce is likely to have encountered during eleven years residence in Trieste. In the event, the phrase attempts to render the place names as "Town Drunk White." The construction is still ungrammatical: it would have to have read "Szészesfehérvár."

7. *Encyclopedia of Art*, 765.

8. Joyce, "The Paris Notebook," *Critical Writings*, 146. An indication that Joyce's reservations about the art of photography persisted is the pride of place Gertie MacDowell reserves for "the photograph of grandpapa Giltrap's lovely dog Garryowen that almost talked it was so human" in the arrangement of her future home (13.233–34).

9. Seidel, *Geography*, 84.

10. Peake, *Joyce*, 292.
11. Empson, "The Ultimate Novel," *Using Biography*, 227.
12. Bowen, *Musical Allusions*, 63.
13. Henke, *Sindbook*, 220.
14. Reizbaum, *Judaic Other*, 126
15. Ibid., 127.
16. Ellmann drew attention to an earlier instance of Stephen in a role charged with these racial overtones. He notes that the manuscript of "Cyclops" at the State University of New York at Buffalo attributes the second half of the exchange below to Stephen.

—And after all, says John Wyse, why can't a jew love his country like the next fellow?

—Why not? says J. J. [O'Molloy], when he is quite sure which country it is? (12.1628–30). (Ellmann, *Joyce*, 197 note. The manuscript has been republished in Joyce, *Notes*, 170–71.)

The transposition in the manuscript suggests that through his association with Griffith's ideal in *The Resurrection of Hungary*, the figure of Stephen may also have inherited something of "the old pap of racial hatred" (Joyce, *Letters* 2, 167), which Joyce felt Griffith and the Sinn Fein were feeding to the new Ireland. In his letters, Joyce objected to Griffith's justification of the 1904 anti-Semitic pogrom in Limerick as merited by the greedy exploitative behavior by a non-Zionist majority among the Jews. He also notes Griffith's spirited defense of the French anti-Dreyfusards (Manganiello, *Politics*, 131–32). On Griffith's anti-Dreyfus activities see Nadel, *Joyce*, 64–66.

The choice of "J.J." as the substitute for Stephen suggests another kind of memorial. In "Giacomo Joyce," the resentful Giacomo (a Joyce persona) had used the phrase to reproach his unattainable Jewish lady (Amalia Popper) for sanctioning the violence of Italian royalists against socialist dissenters.

She thinks the Italian gentlemen were right to haul Ettore Albini, the critic of the *Secolo*, from the stalls because he did not stand up when the band played the Royal March. She heard that at supper. Ay. They love their country when they are quite sure which country it is. (Joyce, *Giacomo Joyce*, xiv–xv, 9)

17. Nadel does not see any special significance to the moment. It does not detract from his reading of the relationship as the independent strengthening of the two individuals. He resolves the dissonant moment crediting the environment of "Ithaca" with a homogenizing influence. "In Ithaca, Jew and Gentile, Hebrew and Gaelic, old and young possess mutual identities.... With the singing of 'Hugh of Lincoln' by Stephen, the idea of betrayal reappears as medieval anti-Semitism is musically recalled. They separate but not before their mosaic identities interact" (Nadel, *Joyce*, 94).

18. Seidel, *Geography*, 91. Instead of trying to explain the exchange, Seidel notes

that Stephen's presence in Bloom's home, to begin with, "is odd" and that "Joyce's *Nostos* is imperfect." Daniel Schwartz, while recognizing Stephen's boorishness, suggests that "Stephen and Bloom barely respond to one another." This excuses Stephen from a charge of malevolence but only at the cost of overstating the distance between the two men. Schwartz, clearly uncomfortable with the episode, credits Joyce with possibly "using the song to laugh at the Jewish matchmaking tradition" (Schwartz, *Reading*, 249–50).

Neil Randall Davison acquits Stephen of anti-Semitism but deems that by the close of the book he is "something of a nihilist" and lacks sympathy for obvious victims of persecution (Davison, *Silence*, 362). For Nadel, the episode is benign. He notes that "the idea of betrayal reappears as medieval anti-Semitism is musically recalled." The theme does not seem to him to affect the interaction of their shared "Mosaic identities," which he takes to be the dominant achievement of the concern of these pages (Nadel, *Joyce*, 95).

19. Concerning the identity of the "victim predestined," Paul Van Caspel notes that the immediate object of Stephen's commentary is the Christian boy in the ballad. "He challenges his destiny once inadvertently, by driving his ball over the garden wall, and twice on purpose, first by breaking the Jew's windows and then by letting himself be lured into a secluded spot by the Jew's daughter" (Van Caspel, *Bloomers*, 234).

With *Ulysses'* ready welcome to shifts of identity, the domain to which Stephen's commentary applies has grown in suggestiveness. The cost of this growing significance, however, is the ongoing drama. Critics tend to read the moment as though it were a summary of the plot. Marilyn French has turned the commentary into a parable on Bloom's day. The "challenge by inadvertence" refers to the tip on Throwaway. Challenges by design are his argument with the Citizen and his masturbation with Gerty. Destiny is Stephen. The "secret infidel apartment" is the brothel (French, *Book*, 228).

Stanley Sultan makes the commentary into a parable of Stephen's fate. Stephen challenges his destiny inadvertently when he meets Bloom on the library steps. He challenges "by design ... first when he spurned Bloom in Nighttown and struck God and then when he rejected the coffee and bun" in the shelter (Sultan, *Argument*, 389–90).

Zack Bowen emphasizes the shared identity toward which the action carries Stephen and Bloom and Stephen's future as an author. From this perspective, the "victim predestined" refers both to Stephen's fate in Ireland and to Bloom's sonless destiny. The "challenge by inadvertence" designates Stephen's compromise with sensuality in the composition of the villanelle in *Portrait* and also recalls Bloom's begetting of Rudy on Molly after watching two dogs copulate. Stephen's challenge "by design" to fate is his presence in Bloom's home. Bloom's challenge "by design" is his scheme to make Stephen his son. Stephen's ballad and commentary embody his refusal to acquiesce in the domestication of his artistic mission (Bowen, "Stephen's Villanelle," 63–67).

20. The passage about the "egg" and the compositional process is ten lines down in the paragraph:

> It is difficult to write with propriety on subjects to which all writers have a common claim; and you with more prudence will reduce the *Iliad* into acts than if you first introduce arguments unknown and never treated before. A public story will become your property, if you do not dwell on the whole circle of events. . . . How much more to the purpose he, who attempts nothing improperly? "Sing for me, my muse, the man, who after the time of the destruction of Troy, surveyed the manners and cities of many men." He meditates not to produce smoke from a flash, but out of smoke to elicit fire, that he may thence bring forth his instances of the marvelous with beauty, [such as] Antiphates, Scylla, the Cyclops, and Charybdis. Nor does he date Diomedes' return from Meleager's death, nor trace the rise of the Trojan war from Leda's eggs: he always hastens on to the event: and hurries away his reader into the midst of interesting circumstances, no otherwise than if they were already known; and what he despairs of, as to receiving a polish from his touch, he omits; and in such a manner forms his fictions, so intermingles the false with the true, that the middle is not inconsistent with the beginning, nor the end with the middle. (Horace, *Poetry*, 306–7)

Precisely because of its subordination of English syntax to Latin, C. Smart's translation of *The Art of Poetry* conveys something of the rhythm of the philological allusions I have been tracing. As in the translation, each allusion is syntactically distinct and subordinate to another syntactic initiative. Smart evidently wanted to follow the Latin as closely as he could. Joyce is forcing something like the discipline of this absent Latin on his readers.

21. The argument assumes that Milly was a nine-month baby (Eggers, "Darling," 395).

22. Jane Ford treats the coincidence between Milly's menstrual cycle and Bloomsday as covert testimony that Bloom had a sexual relationship with Milly and that she has been sent to Mullingar to escape his advances. While Bloom's feelings for Milly do have incestuous overtones, Ford's "gleaning of subterranean hints" of actual incest cannot possibly prove anything since such hints do not differentiate between wish and act. To get the "evidence," she has to force all kinds of disparate events into a script of actual commission: the fact, for example, that Milly "may have sleepwalked" becomes evidence, as does the fact that the phantom-lawyer O'Molloy in "Circe" defends Bloom from the charge of sexually abusing Mary Driscoll with the phrase that she "was treated by the defendant as if she were his very own daughter." Unless we assume from the outset that Bloom is guilty as charged, the worst we can conclude from her data is that "sex was in the air" chez Bloom (Ford, "Milly," 436–49).

23. In "Oxen of the Sun," Stephen reverts to this language: this time, he is concerned with the pregnancy of the second Eve, the Virgin Mary. Christian tradition,

Gifford and Seidman note, gradually separated Mary's experience of pregnancy from everything ordinarily associated with it (G&S, 416). Accordingly, Stephen pronounces it: "A pregnancy without joy ... a birth without pangs, body without blemish, a belly without bigness" (14.309–11).

When Stephen evokes the Virgin Mary in "Oxen of the Sun," it is to reject the ascetic Christian image. Ellmann reads this as an affirmation of a life-embracing vision of art. James H. Druff Jr. argues that the rejection of Christianity does not imply any such alternative. He holds that Stephen continues to be committed to a salvationist "myth of art," which, in the final analysis, is just as restrictive and life-excluding (Ellmann, *Consciousness*, 139; Druff, "History," 310–11).

The dark side of this dream is Stephen's vision in "Circe" of the black mass performed on "*the altarstone [of] Mrs. Mina Purefoy, goddess of unreason ... naked, fettered, a chalice resting on her swollen belly*" (15.4691–92). Purefoy's labor had been associated with the historical development of the English language in the "Oxen of the Sun." According to Druff, the mass represents a perverse debunking of Stephen's religion of art (Druff, "History," 308–12).

24. Anderson, *Communities*, 205.

25. Bloom uses this characterization when appealing to Cissy Caffrey, Private Carr's girl in "Circe," to intervene to help Stephen.

26. Broadside published by Daguerre in 1838 (coll. George Eastman House; reprinted in *Image*, March, 1959, 32–36, quoted in Newhall, *Photography*, 17).

27. Arendt, *Past and Future*, 42.

28. Ree, "National Passion," *Common Knowledge* 2, 3 (1993):51, in Ree, "Cosmopolitanism," 89.

29. Nietzsche, *Tragedy*, 93.

30. Ibid., 92.

31. Ibid.

32. Damon, "Dublin," 207.

33. Ibid.

34. Kosseleck, *Futures Past*, 27.

35. Ibid., 28.

36. Ibid., 29.

37. Ibid., 200.

38. Levin, "Composition," 139.

Chapter 5. Epic Mimesis and the Syntax of *Ulysses*

1. Kenner, *Ulysses*, 35. Robert H. Bell reads the relationship as still more complicated. The bard Stephen's "first words" to Mulligan are: "Tell me Mulligan." Bell notes, "Joyce's modern epic echoes the apostrophe of the conventional invocation, with Mulligan replacing the muse of yore." Bell, *Jocoserious*, 12.

2. Bakhtin, *Dialogic Imagination*, 13.

3. Ibid.

4. Altieri, "Historiography," 117.

5. Booker, *Joyce*, 193.

6. The only other Ulysses in the text is a visitant in the folds of "Penelope": "when general Ulysses Grant whoever he was or did supposed to be some great fellow landed off the ship ..." (18.681–62). Gifford and Seidman identify this event with the stopover President Ulysses Grant made at Gibraltar on November 17, 1878, during his world tour after his second term of office ended (G&S, 618).

7. Ellmann, *Joyce*, 29.

8. Camus, the place name associated with the Browne family, accents the Irishness of the fabulous field marshal. Treating the mention of Camus as indicating a literal birthplace (and for no other reason), Gifford and Seidman believe Ulysses Browne to be a compound identity for the Hapsburg field marshal Ulysses Maxmillian, Count von Browne (1705–1757), and the czarist field marshal George, Count de Browne (1698–1792), born, indeed, at Camus, and a favorite of both Catherine the Great and Maria Theresa (G&S, 360).

9. The description continues: "Never had the Irish brigade shown to such advantage. Its survivors were feted everywhere they went, its fame became universal. The Mountcassel regiment went into action several hundred strong, they came out a mere handful." O'Donnell, *Irish*, 184.

10. Homer rendered these antisocial creatures in these lines:

> Neither assemblies, nor counsel they have, nor laws and traditions;
> Dwelling apart on the crests of the highest mountains the Cyclops
> Hollow caverns inhabit, and each gives laws to his household,
> Children and wives; nor care they at all one for the other.
>
> Homer, *The Odyssey* 9, 112–15.

11. Griffith, *Hungary*, 7.

12. Ibid., 7–8.

13. White, *Content*, 6–16.

14. Szombathely does indeed have a claim to its role of the beginning of the chain of coronation cities. The literal meaning of Szombathely is "Saturday-place," a name evoking the Jewish Sabbath and apparently setting the stage for an allegorical reading. In fact, however, the town supplies Virag's emigration with a more ancient imperial connection than the histories of either the Hapsburgs or the Hanoverians. Szombathely is "the site of the Roman town [Sabaria Savaria], ... the capital of Pannonia where in A.D. 193 Septimus Severus was proclaimed emperor by his legions" ("Szombathely," *Encyclopedia Britannica*). Often visited by emperors, it had been "the center of the Pannonian emperor cult" ("Colonia Sabaria Savaria," *Princeton Encyclopedia of Classical Sites*). Another of the town's distinctions was that Marcus Aurelius wrote the second book of his *Meditations* there. Szombathely is the oldest capital in central Europe, the first in the line of descent from the emperors of Rome, by way of the Holy Roman emperors, and after Napoleon abolished the anachronism, to the Hapsburgs as emperors of Austria, and finally, through

Disraeli's appreciation of politics and pomp, to Victoria and her immediate heirs, the English empresses and emperors of India.

15. Florence, the capital of Tuscany, was ruled by a cadet branch of the Hapsburgs until 1860. The kingdom of Lombardy-Venetia was ruled as though it were an Austrian province until the loss of Lombardy in 1859. Martin, *Red Shirt*, 207.

16. Madtes, *Ithaca Chapter*, 139.
17. Tracy, "Leopold Bloom," 227.
18. Crankshaw, *Maria Theresa*, 140.
19. Rumbold, *Austrian Court*, 4.
20. Oakeshott, *On History*, 117.
21. Perl, *Tradition*, 191.
22. Platt, "Dogsbody," 77.
23. Ellmann, *Joyce*, 399.
24. Voelker, "Marsh's Library," 139.
25. Hastings and Selby, *Dictionary*, 235. Jeremiah 48:37, 16:6, and Ezekiel 27:31 cite instances of head shaving in mourning.
26. Adams, *Surface*, 125.
27. Gifford and Seidman translate the Latin in the *Vaticano Pontificum* as: "Ascend, bald man, so that you do not become more bald than you are, you who are not afraid to sacrifice your wife's hair [i.e., the children] so that you nourish the female bears' hair" (G&S, 50). The 1961 Random House *Ulysses* ended the Latin quotation with *ut ne nimium decalveris* rather than with *ut ne amplius decalveris* (Joyce, *Ulysses*, 40). Serial publication in the *Little Review* and the *Egoist* had the *amplius* version, which Gabler has restored. Gaskell and Hart take exception to this decision (Gaskell and Hart, *Ulysses*, 194). The controversy does not appear to affect the translation.
28. Brewer, *Dictionary*, 86.
29. Van Caspel, *Bloomers*, 26.
30. Plato, *Republic* (10, 597) 325, 326.
31. The term came into use "because the pay could be reckoned in crowns (five-shilling pieces)" (G&S, 19).
32. The passage in Pound runs as follows: "An epic is a poem including history. I don't see that anyone save a saphead can know any history until he understands economics" (Pound, *Essays*, 86).
33. Hughes, *Consciousness*, 6.
34. White, *Metahistory*, 54.
35. Ibid., 63.
36. Goldmann, *Human Sciences*, 28.
37. Pound, *Cantos* 54, 80.
38. Kearney, *Poetics*, 180.
39. Ibid., 181.
40. Brown, *Politics*, 339–40, 385–87.
41. Smith, *Nationalism*, 280.

42. Nebosja Popov, "Serbian Populism: Epilogue," in *Uncaptive Minds*, vol. 8, nos. 3–4 (fall-winter, 1995–96), pp. 114, 118, quoted in Tismaneanu, *Democracy*, 77.
43. Hardie, *Epic Successors*, 3.
44. Griffiths and Rabinowitz, *Novel Epics*, 6.
45. Renan, "What Is a Nation?," 19.
46. Bakhtin and Medvedev, *Formal Method*, 106.
47. Ibid., 130.
48. Skoller, *In-Between*, 13; Bakhtin, "Discourse in the Novel," *Dialogic Imagination*, 272.

Chapter 6. Other Alternatives: Nationhood and Forgetfulness

1. The idea was that by "romping with a girl in the fields and rolling her on the grass . . . her dress is stained green." Brewer, "Green," *Dictionary*.
2. Boldereff, *Reading*, 34–35. For Joyce's views on the lack of racial homogeneity in modern Ireland, see his "Saints and Sages," *Critical Writings*, 153–74 and especially 161–62.
3. Robert Martin Adams suggests that Bloom's apparent reference to this Hainau as "my progenitor of sainted memory [who] wore the uniform of the Austrian despot in a dank prison" (15.1662–63) is probably as unreliable as any of Mr. Deasy's historical generalizations (Adams, *Surface*, 19–26). Gifford and Seidman propose that the rapist might have been Julius Jakob, Baron Haynau, the "notorious Austrian general hated throughout western Europe (to the point of being in physical danger of mob violence when he traveled) for the cruelty and viciousness with which he put down the briefly successful revolutions in northern Italy (1848) and . . . Hungary (1849)." *Hauptmann*, the German term for *captain*, would have been "the rank Haynau held before he was made colonel in 1830" (G&S, 580).
4. Perl, *Tradition*, 218.
5. LaCapra, *History*, 132.
6. Frye, *Anatomy*, 164.
7. Bakhtin, *Dostoevsky's Poetics*, 7.
8. Blyth, "Les Huguenots," 10.
9. Meyerbeer, *Grand Opera*.
10. Watson, "Politics," 41.
11. Reizbaum, *Judaic Other*, 72; G&S, 578.
12. Davison, *Silence*, 218–19.
13. *The Concise Oxford Dictionary of Music*, 416.
14. Wagner, *Judaism in Music*, 25, quoted in Nadel, *Joyce*, 53.
15. There are two references to Renan in *Ulysses*, both in "Scylla and Charybdis." Eglington invokes Renan's readings of Shakespeare's last plays as allegorical histories of eternity (9.394), and Stephen alludes to Renan's ambition to write a sequel to *The Tempest* based on Caliban (9.755–56). Joyce knew Renan's *Souvenirs* and *Vie de Jesus*. He took advantage of a holiday in St. Malo to visit Renan's birthplace at Treguier (Ellmann, *Joyce*, 193, 567).

16. Renan, "What Is a Nation?," 11.
17. Kosseleck, *Futures Past*, 133–34.
18. Hofheinz, *Invention*, 44.
19. Thom, *Republics, Nations and Tribes*, 31.
20. Arndt in Kohn, *The Mind of Germany*, 77. Kohn provides no bibliography.
21. Grenville, *World History*, 262.
22. Lloyd, *Anomalous States*, 100.
23. Schork, *Latin*, 214–15.
24. Gadamer, *Truth*, 258.
25. Verene, *Vico's Science of Imagination*, 109, 105.
26. Plato, *Republic* 1, 329b.
27. Rickard, *Memory*, 124.
28. Deane, *Strange Country*, 141.
29. Partner, "Lost Time," 86.
30. Iggers, *Historiography*, 55.
31. Brooker, *Brecht*, 62; Bakhtin, *Dialogic Imagination*, 293.
32. Ellmann, *Joyce*, 365.
33. Gordon, *Metamorphoses*, 99.
34. Greene, *Troy*, 19–20.
35. Fichter, *Poets*, 4.
36. Bernstein, "Victims-in-Waiting," 625.
37. Parandowski, "Meeting," 158.
38. Hofheinz, *Invention*, 3.

Bibliography

Adams, Robert Martin. *Afterjoyce*. New York: Oxford University Press, 1977.
———. *Surface and Symbol: The Consistency of James Joyce's* Ulysses. New York: Oxford University Press, 1962.
Adorno, Theodore. *Notes to Literature*. Ed. Rolf Tiedemann. Trans. Sherry Weber Nicholson. New York: Columbia University Press, 1991.
Alpers, Paul. "Lycidas and Modern Criticism." *English Literary History* 49 (1982): 468–96.
Altieri, Charles. "*Finnegans Wake* as Modernist Historiography." In *Canons and Consequences: Reflections on the Ethical Force of Imaginative Ideals*. Evanston, Ill.: Northwestern University Press, 1990.
Anderson, Benedict. *Imagined Communities: Reflections on the Origin and Spread of Nationalism*. 1983. Rev. ed. London: Verso, 1991.
———. "Nationalism, Identity and the World in Motion: On the Logics of Seriality." In *Cosmopolitics: Thinking and Feeling Beyond the Nation*. Ed. Pheng Chen and Bruce Robins. Minneapolis: University of Minnesota Press, 1998.
Anghietti, Paul. "Berkeley's Influence on Joyce." *James Joyce Quarterly* 19 (spring 1982): 315–29.
Arendt, Hannah. *Between Past and Future: Eight Exercises in Political Thought*. New York: Penguin, 1977.
———. *The Human Condition*. Chicago: University of Chicago Press, 1958.
———. "On Hannah Arendt." In *Hannah Arendt: The Recovery of the Public World*. Ed. Melvyn A. Hill. New York: St. Martin's Press, 1979.
Ariès, Phillipe. *Le Temps De L'Histoire*. Preface by Roger Chartier. 1954. Paris: Editions du Seuil, 1986.
Attridge, Derek. *Joyce Effects: On Language, Theory and History*. Cambridge, England: Cambridge University Press, 2000.
———., ed. *The Cambridge Companion to James Joyce*. Cambridge, England: Cambridge University Press, 1990.
Aubert, Jacques. *The Aesthetics of James Joyce*. Rev. ed. Baltimore: John Hopkins University Press, 1992.

Auerbach, Eric. *Mimesis: The Representation of Reality in Western Literature.* Trans. Willard R. Trask. 1946. Princeton, N.J.: Princeton University Press, 1953.
Bakhtin, Mikhail M. *The Dialogic Imagination: Four Essays.* Ed. Michael Holquist. Trans. Caryl Emerson and Michael Holquist. Austin: University of Texas Press, 1981.
———. *Problems of Dostoevsky's Poetics.* Ed. and trans. Caryl Emerson. Intro. Wayne C. Booth. Minneapolis: University of Minnesota Press, 1984.
Bakhtin, Mikhail M., and N. Volosinov. *Marxism and Language.* Trans. Ladislav Matejka and I. R. Titunik. New York: Deminar Press, 1973.
Bakhtin, Mikhail M., and P. N. Medvedev. *The Formal Method in Literary Scholarship: A Critical Introduction to Sociological Poetics.* Trans. Albert J. Wehrle. Foreword by Wlad Gozich. Cambridge: Harvard University Press, 1985.
Barthes, Roland. *Image-Music-Text.* Ed. and trans. Stephen Heath. London: Fontana, 1977.
———. *Writing Degree Zero + Elements of Semiology.* Trans. Annette Lavers and Colin Smith. Preface by Susan Sontag. Boston: Beacon Press, 1967.
Beissinger, Margaret, and Suzanne Wofford, eds. *Epic Traditions in the Contemporary World: The Politics of Community.* Berkeley: University of California Press, 1999.
Bell, Robert H. *Jocoserious Joyce: The Fate of Folly in Ulysses.* Ithaca, N.Y.: Cornell University Press, 1991.
Benstock, Bernard. "Telemachus." In *James Joyce's* Ulysses: *Critical Essays.* Ed. Clive Hart and David Hayman. Berkeley: University of California Press, 1974.
———. "The Temptation of St. Stephen: A View of the Villanelle." *James Joyce Quarterly* 14 (1976): 31–38.
———, ed. *Critical Essays of James Joyce.* Boston: Hall, 1985.
———, ed. *James Joyce: The Augmented Ninth.* Proceedings of the Ninth International James Joyce Symposium, Frankfurt, Germany, 1984. Syracuse, N.Y.: Syracuse University Press, 1988.
Benstock, Shari. "The Dynamics of Narrative Performance: Stephen Dedalus as Storyteller." *English Literary History* 49 (1982): 707–38.
Bernstein, J. M. *The Philosophy of the Novel: Lukacs, Marxism and the Dialectics of Form.* Minneapolis: University of Minnesota Press, 1984.
Bernstein, Michael André. *The Tale of the Tribe: Ezra Pound and the Modern Verse Epic.* Princeton, N.J.: Princeton University Press, 1980.
———. "Victims-in-Waiting: Backshadowing and the Representation of European Jewry." *New Literary History* 29.4 (1998): 625–51.
Beissinger, Margaret, Jane Tylus, and Suzanne Wofford, eds. *Epic Traditions in the Contemporary World: The Politics of Community.* Berkeley: University of California Press, 1999.
Bhabha, Homi K. "DissemiNation: Time, Narrative, and the Margins of the Modern Nation." In *Nation and Narration.* Ed. Homi K. Bhabha. London and New York: Routledge, 1990.

Blake, William, *Milton*. Ed. Kay Parkhurst Easson and Roger R. Easson. Boulder, Colo.: Shambala; New York: Random House, 1978.

Blyth, Alan. "Les Huguenots—Back to Life." Introduction. *Les Huguenots: Opera in Five Acts*. By Giacomo Meyerbeer. Text by A. E. Scribe and Deschamps. First produced at the Opera, Paris, February 29, 1836. London: Decca Record Company, 1970.

Boldereff, F. M. *Reading* Finnegans Wake. Woodward, Pa.: Classic Non-fiction Library, 1959.

Booker, M. Keith. *Joyce, Bakhtin and the Literary Tradition: Toward a Comparative Poetics*. Ann Arbor: University of Michigan Press, 1995.

Borneman, John. *Belonging in the Two Berlins: Kin, State, Nation*. Cambridge, England: Cambridge University Press, 1992.

Bowen, Zack. *Musical Allusions in the Works of James Joyce: Early Poetry through* Ulysses. Albany: State University of New York Press, 1974.

———. "Stephen's Villanelle: Antecedents, Manifestations, and Aftermath." *Modern British Literature* 5.1–2 (1980): 63–67.

———. Ulysses *as a Comic Novel*. Syracuse, N.Y.: Syracuse University Press, 1989.

Brennan, Timothy. "The National Longing for Form." In *Nation and Narration*. Ed. Homi K. Bhabha. London and New York: Routledge, 1990.

Brewer, E. Cobham. *Brewer's Dictionary of Phrase and Fable*. Ed. Ivor H. Evans. 1881. New York: Harper and Row, 1981.

Brooker, Peter. *Berthold Brecht: Dialectics, Poetry, Politics*. London: Croon Helm, 1988.

Brooks, Peter. *Reading for the Plot: Design and Intention in Narrative*. New York: Alfred A. Knopf, 1984.

Brown, Malcolm. *The Politics of Irish Literature: From Thomas Davis to W. B. Yeats*. Seattle: University of Washington Press, 1972.

Browne, Terence. *Ireland: A Social and Cultural History 1922–79*. London: Fontana, 1981.

Budgeon, Frank. *James Joyce and the Making of* Ulysses. Bloomington: Indiana University Press, 1960.

Butler, Alba. *Butler's Lives of Patron Saints*. Ed. Michael Walsh. San Francisco: Harper and Row, 1987.

Butler, E. M. *The Tyranny of Greece over Germany*. Boston: Beacon, 1935.

Cairns, Francis. *Virgil's Augustan Epic*. Cambridge, England: Cambridge University Press, 1989.

Callinicos, Alex. *Theories and Narratives: Reflections on the Philosophy of History*. Durham, N.C.: Duke University Press, 1995.

Callow, Heather Cook. "Marion of the Bountiful Bosoms: Molly Bloom and the Nightmare of History." *Twentieth Century Literature* 36.4 (winter 1990): 464–76.

Camões, Luis Vaz de. *The Lusiads*. Trans. William C. Atkinson. Harmondsworth, England: Penguin, 1952.

Canovan, Margaret. *Nationhood and Political Theory.* Cheltenham, England: Edward Elgar, 1996.
Caraher, Brian. "A Question of Genre: Generic Experimentation, Self-Composition, and the Problem of Egoism in *Ulysses.*" *English Literary History* 54 (1987): 183–214.
Cassels, L. *Clash of Generations: A Hapsburg Family Drama in the Nineteenth Century.* London: John Murray, 1971.
Castle, Gregory. "Ousted Possibilities: Critical Histories in James Joyce's *Ulysses.*" *Twentieth Century Literature* 39.3 (fall 1993): 306–27.
Chatman, Seymour. *Story and Discourse.* Ithaca, N.Y.: Cornell University Press, 1970.
Cheng, Vincent, and Timothy Martin, eds. *Joyce in Context.* Cambridge, England: Cambridge University Press, 1992.
Cheng, Vincent. *Joyce, Race and Empire.* Cambridge, England: Cambridge University Press, 1995.
———. "Stephen Dedalus and the Black Panther Vampire." *James Joyce Quarterly* 24 (winter 1987): 161–76.
Cheyette, Brian."'Jewgreek Is Greekjew': The Disturbing Ambivalence of Joyce's Semitic Discourse in *Ulysses.*" In *Joyce Studies Annual 1992.* Ed. Thomas F. Staley. Austin: University of Texas Press, 1992.
Collingwood, R. G. *The Idea of History.* Ed. Jan Van Der Dussen. 1946. Oxford: Clarenden Press, 1993.
"Colonia Sabaria Savaria." In *The Princeton Encyclopedia of Classical Sites.* 232–33. Ed. Richard Stillwell. Princeton, N.J.: Princeton University Press, 1976.
Colum, Mary. *Life and Dream.* Garden City, N.J.: Doubleday, 1947.
Colum, Padraic. *Arthur Griffith.* Dublin: Brown and Nolan, 1959.
———. "A Portrait of James Joyce." *New Republic,* May 31, 1931.
Concise Oxford Dictionary of Music. Ed. P. A. Scholes. London: Oxford University Press, 1968.
Connor, Steven. "'I . . . AM. A': Addressing the Jewish Question in *Ulysses.*" In *The Jew in the Text: Modernity and the Construction of Identity.* Ed. Linda Nochlin and Tamar Garb. London: Thames and Hudson, 1995.
Crankshaw, Edward. *Maria Theresa.* London: Longmans, 1969.
Culleton, Claire A. *Names and Naming in Joyce.* Madison: University of Wisconsin Press, 1994.
Curtius, Ernst Robert. *European Literature and the Latin Middle Ages.* Trans. Willard Trask. New York: Harper and Row, 1963.
Daly, Leo. *James Joyce and the Mullingar Connection.* Intro. Bernard Share. Dublin: Dolmen Edition, 1975.
Damon, S. Foster. "The Odyssey in Dublin." In *James Joyce: Two Decades of Criticism.* Ed. S. Givens. New York: Vanguard Press, 1948.
Dante, Alighieri. *The Comedy of Dante Alighieri: The Florentine.* 3 vols. Trans. Dorothy L. Sayers. Harmondsworth, England: Penguin, 1949, 1955, 1962.

Davis, Robert B. *George Williams Russell ("AE")*. Boston: Twayne, 1977.
Davison, Neil Randall. *Silence, Exile and Cunning: Joyce and the Construction of Jewish Identity*. Ann Arbor, Mich.: UMI Research Press, 1993.
Day, Robert Adams. "How Stephen Wrote His Vampire Poem." *James Joyce Quarterly* 17 (winter 1980): 183–97.
———. "The Villanelle Perplex: Reading Joyce." *James Joyce Quarterly* 25 (fall 1987): 69–85.
De Almeida, Hermione. *Byron and Joyce through Homer:* Don Juan *and* Ulysses. New York: Columbia University Press, 1981.
Deane, Seamus. *Celtic Revivals: Essays in Modern Irish Literature 1880–1980*. London: Faber and Faber, 1985.
———. "Heroic Styles: The Tradition of an Idea." In *Ireland's Field Day*. Ed. Seamus Deane. Notre Dame, Ind.: University of Notre Dame Press, 1986.
———. "History as Fiction/Fiction as History." In *Joyce in Rome: The Genesis of* Ulysses. Ed. Giorgi Melchiori. Rome: Bulzoni, 1984.
———. "Joyce and Nationalism." In *James Joyce: New Perspectives*. Ed. Colin McCabe. Brighton, England: Harvester, 1982.
———. *Strange Country: Modernity and Nationhood in Irish Writing Since 1790*. Oxford: Clarendon Press, 1997.
———, ed. *The Field Day Anthology of Irish Writing*. Vol. 3. Derry, Ireland: Field Day, 1991.
Diderot, Denis. *Rameau's Nephew/D'Alembert's Dream*. Trans. and intro. Leonard Tancock. London: Penguin, 1966.
Dilthey, Wilhelm. *Selected Writings*. Trans. and intro. H. P. Rickman. Cambridge: Cambridge University Press, 1976.
Donker, Marjorie, and George M. Muldrow, eds. *Dictionary of Literary-Rhetorical Conventions of the English Renaissance*. Westport, Conn.: Greenwood Press, 1982.
Donoghue, Denis. "The European Joyce." In *We Irish: Essays on Irish Literature and Society*. New York: Alfred A. Knopf, 1986.
Druff, James H., Jr., "History vs. the Word: The Metaphor of Childbirth in Stephen's Aesthetics." *James Joyce Quarterly* 19 (spring 1982): 303–14.
Duffy, Enda. *The Subaltern* Ulysses. Minneapolis: University of Minnesota Press, 1994.
Eagleton, Terry. *Exiles and Emigres: Studies in Modern Literature*. London: Chatto and Windus, 1970.
Eckley, Grace. "Beef to the Heel: Harlotry with Josephine Butler, William T. Stead and James Joyce." *Studies in the Novel* 20.1 (spring 1988): 64–77.
Eco, Umberto. *The Aesthetics of Chaosmos: The Middle Ages of James Joyce*. Trans. Ellen Esrock. Cambridge: Harvard University Press, 1989.
Edwards, Ruth Dudley. *Patrick Pearse: Triumph in Failure*. New York: Taplinger Publishing, 1978.

Eggers, Tilly. "Darling Milly Bloom." *James Joyce Quarterly* 12 (summer 1975): 386–95.
Ehrlich, Heyward, ed. *Light Rays: James Joyce and Modernism*. New York: New Horizon, 1984.
Eliot, T. S. *Selected Prose*. Ed. John Hayward. Harmondsworth, England: Penguin, 1953.
Ellmann, Richard. *The Consciousness of Joyce*. London: Faber and Faber, 1977.
———. *James Joyce*. 1959. Oxford: Oxford University Press, 1982.
Emerson, Ralph Waldo. "History." In *The Complete Essays and Other Writings of Ralph Waldo Emerson*. Ed. Brooks Atkinson. New York: Random House, 1950.
Empson, William. *Using Biography*. Cambridge: Harvard University Press, 1984.
Encyclopedia of Art. Vol. 7. New York: McGraw Hill, 1964.
Epstein, E. L. "Nestor." In *James Joyce's* Ulysses: *Critical Essays*. Ed. Clive Hart and David Hayman. Berkeley: University of California Press, 1974.
Fairhall, James. *James Joyce and the Question of History*. Cambridge, England: Cambridge University Press, 1993.
Feibleman, James Kern. *In Praise of Comedy: A Study in Its Theory and Practice*. New York: Russell and Russell, 1939.
Fichter, Andrew. *Poets Historical: Dynastic Epic in the Renaissance*. New Haven, Conn.: Yale University Press, 1982.
Flaubert, Gustave. *Madame Bovary: A Story of Provincial Life*. Trans. Alan Russell. London: Penguin, 1950.
Ford, Jane. "Why Is Milly in Mullingar?" *James Joyce Quarterly* 14 (summer 1977): 436–49.
Foster, John Wilson. *Fictions of the Irish Literary Revival: A Changeling Art*. Syracuse, N.Y.: University of Syracuse Press, 1987.
Fowler, Alastair. *Silent Poetry: Essays in Numerological Analysis*. London: Routledge and Kegan Paul, 1970.
French, Marilyn. *The Book as Word: James Joyce's* Ulysses. Cambridge: Harvard University Press, 1976.
Friedman, Lawrence M. *The Horizontal Society*. New Haven, Conn.: Yale University Press, 1999.
Frye, Northrop. *Anatomy of Criticism: Four Essays*. Princeton, N.J.: Princeton University Press, 1957.
Gadamer, Hans-Georg. *Truth and Method*. Ed. and trans. Garreth Barden and John Cumming. Rev. ed. New York: Crossroads, 1988.
Gaskell, Philip, and Clive Hart. Ulysses: *A Review of Three Texts: Proposals for Alterations to the Texts of 1922, 1961 and 1984*. Totowa, N.J.: Barnes and Noble Books, 1989.
Gellner, Ernest. *Encounters with Nationalism*. Oxford: Blackwell, 1994.
———. *Nations and Nationalism*. Oxford: Blackwell, 1983.
Gibson, Mary Ellis. *Epic Reinvented: Ezra Pound and the Victorians*. Ithaca, N.Y.: Cornell University Press, 1995.

Gifford, Don, with Robert J. Seidman. Ulysses *Annotated: Notes for James Joyce's* Ulysses. Rev. and exp. ed. Berkeley: University of California Press, 1988.
Gilbert, Stuart. *James Joyce's* Ulysses. New York: Random House, 1955.
Gillespie, Michael Patrick. *Reading the Book of Himself: Narrative Strategies in the Works of James Joyce.* Columbus: Ohio State University Press, 1989.
Gleckner, Robert F. "Joyce's Blake: Paths of Influence." In *William Blake and the Moderns.* Ed. Robert S. Berthoff and Annette S. Levitt. Albany: State University of New York Press, 1982.
Goldmann, Lucien. *The Human Sciences and Philosophy.* London: Cape, 1969.
Gordon, John. *James Joyce's Metamorphoses.* Dublin: Gill and MacMillan, 1981.
Gosse, Eliot B. *The Transformation Process in Joyce's* Ulysses. Toronto: University of Toronto Press, 1980.
Grassi, Ernesto. "The Demythologization of the Real." In *Vico and Joyce.* Ed. Donald Philip Verene. Albany: State University of New York Press, 1987.
Grayson, Janet. "'Do You Kiss Your Mother?': Stephen Dedalus's Sovereignty of Ireland." *James Joyce Quarterly* 19 (winter 1982): 119-26.
Greene, Thomas M. *Descent from Heaven.* New Haven, Conn.: Yale University Press, 1990.
———. *The Light in Troy: Imitation and Discovery in Renaissance Poetry.* New Haven, Conn.: Yale University Press, 1982.
Gregory, Augusta. *Poets and Dreamers: Studies in Translation from the Irish.* Gerrards Cross, England: Colin Smythe, 1974.
———, ed. *Ideals in Ireland.* London: Unicorn Press, 1983.
Grenville, J.A.S. *A World History of the Twentieth Century. Volume One, 1900-45: Western Dominance.* Oxford, England: Fontana, 1980.
Griffith, Arthur. Preface. *Jail Journal.* By John Mitchel. Dublin: M. H. Gill, 1913.
———. *The Resurrection of Hungary: A Parallel for Ireland.* Dublin: James Duffy; M. H. Gill and Sons; Sealy, Bryers, and Walker, 1904.
Griffiths, Frederick T., and Stanley J. Rabinowitz. *Novel Epics: Gogol, Dostoevsky and National Narrative.* Evanston, Ill.: Northwestern University Press, 1990.
Groden, Michael. Ulysses *in Progress.* Princeton, N.J.: Princeton University Press, 1977.
Hammond, J. L. *Gladstone and the Irish Nation.* London and Edinburgh: Frank Cass, 1914.
Handwerke, Gary J. *Irony and Ethics in Narrative: From Schlegel to Lacan.* New Haven, Conn.: Yale University Press, 1985.
Hansard Parliamentary Debates, 3rd series (1830-91).
Hardie, Philip. *Epic Successors of Virgil.* Cambridge, England: Cambridge University Press, 1993.
Hastings, James, and J. A. Selby, eds. *A Dictionary of the Bible with Its Language, Literature and Contents Including the Biblical Theology.* New York: Charles Scribner's Sons, 1902.

Hayman, David. "Language of/as Gesture in Joyce." In *James Joyce: A Collection of Critical Essays*. Ed. Mary T. Reynolds. Englewood Cliffs, N.J.: Prentice Hall, 1993.

Hegel, Georg Wilhelm Friedrich. *Aesthetics*. Trans. T. M. Knox. Vol. 2. Oxford: Oxford University Press.

———. *The Philosophy Of History*. Trans. J. Sibree. Intro. C. J. Friedrich. New York: Dover, 1956.

Heininger, Joseph C. "Stephen Dedalus in Paris: Tracing the Fall of Icarus in *Ulysses*." *James Joyce Quarterly* 23 (summer 1986): 435–46.

Henke, Suzanne. *Joyce's Moraculous Sindbook: A Study of Ulysses*. Columbus: Ohio State University Press, 1978.

Henke, Suzette A. *James Joyce and the Politics of Desire*. London: Routledge, 1990.

Herring, Phillip. *Joyce's Uncertainty Principle*. Princeton, N.J.: Princeton University Press, 1987.

Hill, Melvyn A., ed. *Hannah Arendt: The Recovery of the Public World*. New York: St. Martin's, 1979.

Himmelfarb, Gertrude. *The New History and the Old*. Cambridge: Harvard University Press, 1987.

Hobsbawm, Eric. *Nations and Nationalism since 1870: Programme, Myth, Reality*. Cambridge, England: Cambridge University Press, 1990.

Hobsbawm, Eric, and Terence Ranger. *The Invention of Tradition*. Cambridge, England: Cambridge University Press, 1983.

Hofheinz, Thomas C. *Joyce and the Invention of Irish History:* Finnegans Wake *in Context*. Cambridge, England: Cambridge University Press, 1995.

Hogan, Patrick Colm. "Drowning in *Ulysiadas*: A 'Subtext' for Stephen's Mourning." In *New Alliances in Joyce Studies*. Newark: University of Delaware Press, 1988.

———. *Joyce, Milton, and the Theory of Influence*. Gainesville: University Press of Florida, 1995.

Homer. *The Odyssey*. Trans. H. B. Cotterill. London: George Harrap, 1911.

Horace. *On the Art of Poetry*. In *The Works of Horace*. Trans. C. Smart. London: George Bell, 1891.

Howes, Marjorie. *Yeats' Nations: Gender, Class and Irishness*. Cambridge, England: Cambridge University Press, 1996.

Hughes, H. Stuart. *Consciousness and Society: The Reorientation of European Social Thought 1890–1930*. New York: Vintage, 1977.

Hutchinson, John. *The Dynamics of Cultural Nationalism: The Gaelic Revival and the Creation of the Irish Nation State*. London: Allen and Unwin, 1987.

Hutton, Patrick. *History As an Art of Memory*. Hanover, N.H.: University Press of New England, 1993.

Iggers, Georg G. *Historiography in the Twentieth Century: From Scientific Objectivity to the Postmodern Challenge*. Hanover, N.H.: Wesleyan University Press, 1997.

Jacobus, Lee A. "'Lycidas' in the 'Nestor' Episode." *James Joyce Quarterly* 19 (winter 1982): 189–94.
James, Paul. *Nation Formation: Towards a Theory of Abstract Community*. London: Sage, 1996.
Jameson, Frederic. *The Political Unconscious: Narrative As a Socially Symbolic Act.* Ithaca, N.Y.: Cornell University Press, 1981.
———. "*Ulysses* in History." In *James Joyce and Modern Literature*. Ed. W. J. McCormack and Alistair Stead. London: Routledge and Kegan Paul, 1982.
Jay, Martin. *Downcast Eyes: The Denigration of Vision in Twentieth Century French Thought*. Berkeley: University of California Press, 1993.
Jenkins, Keith. *On What Is History?: From Carr and Elton and Rorty and White*. London: Routledge, 1995.
Johnston, William F. *The Austrian Mind: An Intellectual and Social History 1848–1938*. Berkeley: University of California Press, 1972.
Joyce, James. *The Critical Writings of James Joyce*. Ed. Ellsworth Mason and Richard Ellmann. New York: Viking, 1959.
———. *Dubliners*. London: Jonathan Cape, 1967.
———. *Finnegans Wake*. London: Faber, 1982.
———. *Giacomo Joyce*. Ed. Richard Ellmann. New York: Viking, 1968.
———. *Joyce's Notes and Early Drafts for Ulysses: Selections from the Buffalo Collection*. Ed. Phillip F. Herring. Charlottesville: University Press of Virginia, 1977.
———. *Joyce's* Ulysses *Notesheets in the British Museum*. Ed. Phillip F. Herring. Charlottesville: University Press of Virginia, 1972.
———. *Letters of James Joyce*. Ed. Stuart Gilbert. London: Faber and Faber, 1957.
———. *Letters of James Joyce*. Vols. 2 and 3. Ed. Richard Ellmann. London: Faber and Faber, 1966.
———. "A Portrait of the Artist." In *A Portrait of the Artist as a Young Man: Text, Criticism and Notes*. Ed. Chester G. Anderson. New York: Viking, 1968.
———. *A Portrait of the Artist as a Young Man*. London: Penguin, 1976.
———. *Stephen Hero*. Ed. Theodore Spencer, Rev. John J. Slocum and Herbert Cahoon. New York: New Directions, 1959.
———. *Ulysses*. Ed. Hans Walter Gabler et al. New York: Random House, 1986.
Joyce, P. W. *English As We Speak It in Ireland*. London: Longmans Green, 1910.
Joyce, Stanislaus. *My Brother's Keeper: James Joyce's Early Years*. Ed. Richard Ellmann. New York: Viking, 1958.
Kaczvinsky, Donald P. "'The Cock Crew': An Answer to the Riddle." *James Joyce Quarterly* 25 (winter 1988): 265–68.
Kant, Immanuel. *Critique of Pure Reason*. Trans. F. Max Muller. Garden City, N.J.: Doubleday, 1966.
Kantoriwicz, Ernst H. *King's Two Bodies: A Study in Medieval Political Theology*. Princeton, N.J.: Princeton University Press, 1957.

Kearney, Richard. *Poetics of Modernity: Toward a Hermeneutic Imagination.* Atlantic Highlands, N.J.: Humanities Press, 1995.
Keats, John. *Selected Letters of John Keats (1814–1821).* Ed Hyder Edward Rollig. Vol. 2. London: Cambridge, 1958.
Kedourie, Elie. *Nationalism.* London: Hutchison, 1961.
Kelly, Joseph. *Our Joyce: From Outcast to Icon.* Austin: University of Texas Press, 1998.
Kenner, Hugh. *A Colder Eye.* New York: Alfred A. Knopf, 1983.
———. *Dublin's Joyce.* London: Chatto and Windus, 1953.
———. *Joyce's Voices.* London: Allen and Unwin, 1978.
———. *Ulysses.* London: Allen and Unwin, 1980.
Killham, John. "Ineluctable Modality in Joyce's *Ulysses.*" *University of Toronto Quarterly* 34.3 (April 1965): 269–88.
Kimball, Jean. "From Eve to Helen: Stages of the Anima-figure in Joyce's *Ulysses.*" *Mosaic* 20.2 (spring 1987): 30–40.
Kohn, Hans. *The Mind of Germany: The Education of a Nation.* New York: Harper and Row, 1965.
Kosseleck, Reinhart. *Futures Past: On the Semantics of Historical Time.* Trans. Keith Tribe. Cambridge: MIT Press, 1985.
LaCapra, Dominick. *History and Criticism.* Ithaca, N.Y.: Cornell University Press, 1985.
Law, Jules David. "Joyce's Delicate Siamese Equation: The Dialectic of Home in *Ulysses.*" *PMLA* 102 (January 1987): 197–205.
Lawrence, Karen. *The Odyssey of Style in* Ulysses. Princeton, N.J.: Princeton University Press, 1981.
Lernout, Geert. *The French Joyce.* Ann Arbor: University of Michigan Press, 1990.
Lessing, Gotthold Ephraim. *Laocoön, or The Limits of Painting and Poetry, Laocoön; Nathan the Wise; Minna von Barnhelm.* Ed. William E. Steel. Trans. William E. Steel and Anthony Dent. London: Dent, Everyman's Library. 1970.
Levin, Jonathan. "Entering the Modern Composition: Gertrude Stein and the Patterns of Modernism." In *Rereading the New: A Backward Glance at Modernism.* Ed. Kevin J. H. Dettmar. Ann Arbor: University of Michigan Press, 1992.
Lewis, C. S. *Preface to* Paradise Lost. New York: Oxford University Press, 1961.
Lewis, Pericles. "The Conscience of the Race: The Nation as Church of the Modern Age." In *Joyce through the Ages: A Nonlinear View.* Ed. Michael Patrick Gillespie. Gainesville: University Press of Florida, 1999.
Lewis, Wyndham. *Time and Western Man.* London: Chatto and Windus, 1927.
Litz, A. Walton. "The Genre of *Ulysses.*" In *The Theory of the Novel.* Ed. J. Halperin. New York: Oxford University Press, 1974.
Lloyd, David. *Anomalous States: Irish Writing and the Post-Colonial Moment.* Durham, N.C.: Duke University Press, 1993.
Long, Michael. "Eliot, Pound, Joyce: Unreal City?" In *Unreal City: Urban Experi-*

ence in Modern European Literature and Art. Ed. Edward Timms and David Kelley. Manchester, England: Manchester University Press, 1988.
Longenbach, James. *Modernist Poetics of History: Pound, Eliot and the Sense of the Past*. Princeton, N.J.: Princeton University Press, 1987.
Lowe-Evans, Mary. *Crimes Against Fecundity: Joyce and Population Control*. Syracuse, N.Y.: Syracuse University Press, 1989.
Lukacs, Georg. *The Theory of the Novel: A Historico-Philosophical Essay on the Forms of Great Epic Literature*. Trans. Anna Bostock. 1920. Cambridge: MIT Press, 1971.
Lyons, F.S.L. *Ireland since the Famine*. London: Weidenfeld and Nicolson, 1971.
Lyons, J. B. *James Joyce and Medicine*. Dublin: Dolmen Press, 1973.
MacCabe, Colin. *James Joyce: New Perspectives*. Bloomington: University of Indiana Press; Sussex: Harvester Press, 1982.
———. *James Joyce and the Revolution of the Word*. London: Macmillan, 1978.
Madtes, Richard. *The "Ithaca" Chapter of Joyce's* Ulysses. Ann Arbor, Mich.: UMI Research Press, 1983.
Mahaffey, Vicky. *Reauthorizing Joyce*. Cambridge, England: Cambridge University Press, 1988.
Mandelbaum, Maurice. "A Note on History as Narrative." *History and Theory* 6 (1967): 413–9.
Manganiello, Dominic. *Joyce's Politics*. London: Routledge and Kegan Paul, 1980.
Martin, George. *The Red Shirt and the Cross of Savoy: The Story of Italy's Risorgimento 1748–1871*. New York: Dodd, Mead, 1969.
Martz, Louis. *Poet of Exile: A Study of Milton's Poetry*. New Haven, Conn.: Yale University Press, 1980.
Marx, Karl. "On the Jewish Question." In *The Marx-Engels Reader*. Ed. Robert C. Tucker. New York: W. W. Norton, 1972.
Mason, Michael York. "*Ulysses* the Sequel to *Portrait*? Joyce's Plans for the Two Works." With responses by A. Walton Litz, Robert Scholes, and Richard M. Kain. *English Language Notes* (June 1971): 297–305.
McArthur, Murray. *Stolen Writings: Blake's "Milton," Joyce's* Ulysses *and the Nature of Influence*. Ann Arbor, Mich.: UMI Research Press, 1988.
McCarthy, Patrick A. *The Riddles of* Finnegans Wake. Madison, N.J.: Fairleigh Dickinson University Press, 1980.
McCourt, John. *The Years of Bloom: Joyce in Trieste 1904–1920*. Madison: University of Wisconsin Press, 2000.
McDonald, James L., and Norman G. McKendrick, S. J. "The Telemacheia in *The Odyssey* and *Ulysses*." *International Fiction Review* 16 (winter 1989): 3–10.
McGee, Patrick. *Paperspace: Style as Ideology in Joyce's* Ulysses. Lincoln: University of Nebraska Press, 1988.
McMichael, James. Ulysses *and Justice*. Princeton, N.J.: Princeton University Press, 1991.

Meinecke, Frederick. *Cosmopolitanism and the Nation State*. Trans. Robert B. Kimber. Intro. Felix Gilbert. Princeton, N.J.: Princeton University Press, 1970.

Meyerbeer, Giacomo. *Les Huguenots: Grand Opera in Four Acts*. Text by A. E. Scribe and Deschamps. First produced at the Opera, Paris, February 29, 1836. New York: F. Rullman, 1896.

———. *Les Huguenots: Opera in Five Acts*. Text by A. E. Scribe and Deschamps. First produced at the Opera, Paris, February 29th, 1836. London: Decca Record Company, 1970.

Milbank, John. *The Religious Dimension in the Thought of Giambattista Vico 1668–1744: Part 1, the Early Metaphysics*. Lewiston, N.Y.: E. Mellon Press, 1991.

Milton, John. *The Poetical Works*. Ed. David Masson. 3 vols. London: Macmillan, 1890.

Minogue, K. R. *Nationalism*. London: Batsford, 1967.

Moran, D. P. *The Philosophy of Irish Ireland*. Dublin: James Duffy, 1905.

Moretti, Franco. *Modern Epic: The World System from Goethe to Garcia Marquez*. Trans. Quintin Hoare. London: Verso, 1996.

———. *Signs Taken for Wonders*. Rev. ed. London: Verso, 1983.

Musil, Robert. *The Man without Qualities*. Trans. Eithne Wilkins and Ernst Kaiser. Vol. 1. 1954. London: Picador, 1979.

Nadel, Ira B. *Joyce and the Jews: Culture and Texts*. Iowa City: University of Iowa Press, 1989.

Naipaul, V. S., "The Writer and India." *New York Review of Books*, March 4, 1999, 12–16.

Nairn, Tom. *Faces of Nationalism: Janus Revisited*. London: Verso, 1997.

Newhall, Beaumont. *The History of Photography: From 1839 to the Present*. New York: Museum of Modern Art, 1964.

Nietzsche, Frederick. *The Birth of Tragedy and the Genealogy of Morals*. Trans. Francis Golffing. Garden City, N.J.: Doubleday Anchor, 1956.

Nolan, Emer. *James Joyce and Nationalism*. London: Routledge, 1995.

Noon, William T. *Joyce and Aquinas*. New Haven, Conn.: Yale University Press, 1957.

Norman, Andrew O. "Telling It Like It Was: Historical Narratives on Their Own Terms." In *History and Theory: Contemporary Readings*. Ed. Brian Fay, Philip Pomper, and Richard T. Vann. Oxford: Blackwell, 1998.

Nuttall, A. D. *Openings: Narrative Beginnings from the Epic to the Novel*. Oxford: Clarendon Press, 1992.

Oakeshott, Michael. *On History and Other Essays*. Oxford: Oxford University Press, 1983.

———. *Rationalism in Politics and Other Essays*. London, Methuen, 1962.

O'Brien, Conor Cruise. *States of Ireland*. London: Hutchinson, 1972.

O'Connor, Teresa. "Demythologizing Nationalism: Joyce's Dialogized Grail Myth." In *Joyce in Context*. Ed. Vincent Cheng and Martin Timothy. Cambridge, England: Cambridge University Press, 1992.

O'Donnell, Eliot. *The Irish Abroad: A Record of Achievements of Wanderers from Ireland.* London: Sir Isaac Pitman and Sons, 1915.

O'Grady, Standish. *History of Ireland.* Vol. 1. Ed. N.G.L. Hammond and H. H. Scullard. 1878–80.

Parandowski, Jan. "Meeting with Joyce." In *Portraits of the Artist in Exile: Recollections of James Joyce by Europeans.* Ed. Willard Potts. San Diego, Calif.: Harcourt Brace Jovanovich, 1979.

Parrinder, Patrick. *James Joyce.* Cambridge, England: Cambridge University Press, 1984.

Partner, Nancy F. "Making Up Lost Time: Writing on the Writing of History." In *History and Theory: Contemporary Readings.* Ed. Brian Fay, Philip Pomper, and Richard T. Vann. Oxford: Blackwell, 1998.

Pater, Walter. *Marius the Epicurean.* Intro. Osbert Burdett. London: J. M. Dent and Sons, 1960.

Peake, C. H. *James Joyce: The Citizen and the Artist.* London: Edward Arnold, 1977.

Perl, J. M. *The Tradition of Return: The Implicit History of Modern Literature.* Princeton, N.J.: Princeton University Press, 1984.

Plato. *The Republic.* Trans. G.M.A. Grube and C.D.C. Reeve. Indianapolis: Hackett, 1992.

Platt, L. H. "The Buckeen and the Dogsbody: Aspects of History and Culture in 'Telemachus.'" *James Joyce Quarterly* 27 (fall 1989): 77–86.

———. "The Voice of Esau: Culture and Nationalism in Scylla and Charybdis." *James Joyce Quarterly* 29 (summer 1992): 737–50.

Potts, Willard, ed. *Portraits of the Artist in Exile: Recollections of James Joyce by Europeans.* San Diego, Calif.: Harcourt Brace Jovanovitch, 1979.

Pound, Ezra. *The Cantos of Ezra Pound.* New York: New Directions, 1991.

———. *Literary Essays of Ezra Pound.* New York: New Directions, 1968.

———. "Vorticism." In *Gaudier Brzeska: A Memoir.* New York: New Directions, 1961.

Power, Arthur. *Conversations with James Joyce.* New York: Barnes and Noble, 1974.

Propp, V. *The Morphology of the Folktale.* 1928. Austin: University of Texas Press, 1968.

Rader, Ralph W. "Exodus and Return: Joyce's *Ulysses* and the Fiction of the Actual." *University of Toronto Quarterly* 17 (winter 1978–79): 149–71.

———. "The Logic of *Ulysses*; or Why Molly Had to Live in Gibraltar." *Critical History* 10 (June 1984): 567–79.

Radford, F. L. "King Pope and Hero-Martyr: *Ulysses* and the Nightmare of Irish History." *James Joyce Quarterly* 15 (summer 1978): 275–323.

Ree, Jonathan. "Cosmopolitanism and the Experience of Nationality." In *Cosmopolitics: Thinking and Feeling Beyond the Nation.* Ed. Pheng Chen and Bruce Robins. Minneapolis: University of Minnesota Press, 1998.

Reichert, Klaus. "The European Background of Joyce's Writing." In *The Cambridge*

Companion to James Joyce. Ed. Derek Attridge. Cambridge, England: Cambridge University Press, 1990.
Reizbaum, Marilyn. *James Joyce's Judaic Other.* Stanford, Calif.: Stanford University Press, 1999.
Renan, Ernest. "What Is a Nation?" In *Nation and Narration.* Ed. Homi K. Bhabha. London: Routledge, 1990.
Reynolds, Mary T. *Joyce and Dante: The Shaping Imagination.* Princeton, N.J.: Princeton University Press, 1981.
Rickard, John S. *Joyce's Book of Memory: The Mnemotechnic of* Ulysses. Durham, N.C.: Duke University Press, 1999.
Rilke, Rainer Maria. *The Duino Elegies.* Trans. Stephen Garmey and Jay Wilson. New York: Harper and Row, 1972.
Riquelme, John Paul. *The Teller and Tale in Joyce's Fiction: Oscillating Perspectives.* Baltimore: John Hopkins University Press, 1983.
Rossman, Charles. "Stephen's Villanelle." *James Joyce Quarterly* 15 (summer 1978): 275–323.
Roughley, Alan. *James Joyce and Critical Theory: An Introduction.* New York: Harvester Wheatsheaf, 1991.
Rumbold, Sir Horace. *The Austrian Court in the Nineteenth Century.* London: Methuen, 1909.
Russell, George [AE]. "Nationality and Imperialism." In *Ideals in Ireland.* Ed. Augusta Gregory. London: Unicorn Press, 1983.
"Sabaria Savaria." *The Princeton Encyclopedia of Classical Sites.* Ed. R. Stillwell. Princeton, N.J.: Princeton University Press, 1976.
Said, Edward. *Beginnings: Intention and Method.* Baltimore: Johns Hopkins University Press, 1988.
Schechner, Mark. *Joyce in Nighttown: A Psychoanalytic Inquiry into* Ulysses. Berkeley: University of California Press, 1974.
Schneidau, Herbert N. *Waking Giants: The Presence of the Past in Modernism.* New York: Oxford University Press, 1991.
Schork, R. J. *Greek and Hellenic Culture in Joyce.* Gainesville: University Press of Florida, 1998.
———. "Joyce and Justinian: U 250 and 520." *James Joyce Quarterly* 23 (fall 1985): 77–80.
———. *Latin and Roman Culture in Joyce.* Gainesville: University Press of Florida, 1997.
Schutte, William. *Joyce and Shakespeare: A Study in the Meaning of* Ulysses. New Haven, Conn.: Yale University Press, 1957.
Schwartz, Daniel. *A Reading of Joyce's* Ulysses. London: Macmillan, 1987.
Schwartz, Heinrich. *Art and Photography: Forerunners and Influences.* Ed. William E. Parker. Layton, Utah: Gibbs M. Smith, 1985.
Scott, Bonnie Kime. *Joyce and Feminism.* Bloomington: Indiana University Press, 1984.

Sedgwick, Eve Kosofsky. "Nationalisms and Sexualities in the Age of Wilde." In *Nationalisms and Sexualities*. Ed. Andrew Parker, Mary Russo, Doris Sommer, and Patricia Yaeger. New York: Routledge, 1992.
Segal, Jeffrey. *Joyce in America: Cultural Politics and the Trials of* Ulysses. Berkeley: University of California Press, 1993.
Seidel, Michael. *Epic Geography: James Joyce's* Ulysses. Princeton, N.J.: Princeton University Press, 1976.
———, ed. "*Ulysses'* Black Panther Vampire." *James Joyce Quarterly* 13 (summer 1976): 415–27.
Seidel, Michael, and Edward Mendelson, eds. *Homer to Brecht: European Epic and Dramatic Traditions*. New Haven, Conn.: Yale University Press, 1977.
Senn, Fritz. *Inductive Scrutinies: Focus on Joyce*. Ed. Christine O'Neill. Baltimore: John Hopkins University Press, 1976.
———, ed. *Joyce's* Ulysses: *The Larger Perspective*. Newark: University of Delaware Press, 1987.
Shleifer, Ronald. *The Genres of the Irish Literary Revival*. Norman, Okla.: Pilgrim Books; Dublin: Wolfhound Press, 1980.
Sicari, Stephen. *Pound's Epic Ambition: Dante and the Modern World*. Albany: State University of New York Press, 1991.
Skoller, Eleanor Honig. *The In-Between of Writing: Experience and Experiment in Drabble, Duras and Arendt*. Ann Arbor: University of Michigan Press, 1993.
Smith, Anthony D. *The Ethnic Origins of Nations*. Oxford: Blackwell, 1987.
———. *Nationalism and Modernism: A Critical Survey of Recent Theories of Nations and Nationalism*. London and New York: Routledge, 1998.
Smith, James Penny. "More Allusions in *Ulysses*: A Supplement to Weldon Thornton's List." *James Joyce Quarterly* 12 (spring 1975): 314–7.
Spoo, Robert. *James Joyce and the Language of History: Dedalus's Nightmare*. New York: Oxford University Press, 1994.
———. "'Nestor' and the Nightmare: The Presence of the Great War in *Ulysses*." *Twentieth Century Literature* 32.2 (summer 1986): 137–54.
———. "Usurper; A Word on the Last Word in 'Telemachus.'" *James Joyce Quarterly* 26 (fall 1988): 450–51.
Staten, Henry. "The Decomposing Form of Joyce's *Ulysses*." *PMLA* 112.3 (May 1997): 380–92.
Steed, Henry Wickham. *The Hapsburg Monarchy*. London: Constable, 1914.
Steppe, Wolfhard, with Hans Walter Gabler. *A Handlist to James Joyce's* Ulysses: *A Complete Alphabetical Index to the Critical Reading Text*. New York: Garland, 1986.
Sultan, Stanley. *The Argument of* Ulysses. Columbus: Ohio State University Press, 1964.
"Szombatheley." In *Encyclopedia Britannica*. Vol. 26: 320. Cambridge, England: Cambridge University Press, 1911.

Taylor, Archer. *English Riddles from Oral Tradition*. Berkeley: University of California Press, 1951.
Tennyson, Lord Alfred. *Tennyson's Poetical Works*. Cambridge edition. Boston: Houghton Mifflin, 1898.
Thom, Martin. *Republics, Nations, and Tribes*. London: Verso, 1995.
———. "Tribes within Nations: The Ancient Germans and the History of Modern France." In *Nation and Narration*. Ed. Homi K. Bhabha. London: Routledge, 1990.
Thomas, Brook. *James Joyce's* Ulysses: *A Book of Many Many Returns*. Baton Rouge: Louisiana State University Press, 1982.
Thompson, E. P. *The Making of the English Working Class*. New York: Pantheon, 1963.
Thornton, Weldon. *Allusions in* Ulysses. Chapel Hill: University of North Carolina Press, 1968.
Tillyard, E.M.W. *The English Epic and Its Background*. New York: Oxford University Press, 1954.
Tismaneanu, Vladimir. *Democracy, Nationalism, Myth in Post-Communist Europe*. Princeton, N.J.: Princeton University Press, 1998.
Tracy, Robert. "Leopold Bloom Fourfold: A Hungarian-Hebraic-Hellenic-Hibernian Hero." *Massachusetts Review* 6 (1965): 523–38.
Tucker, Herbert F. *Tennyson and the Doom of Romanticism*. Cambridge, England: Cambridge University Press, 1988.
Twining, Lord. *European Regalia*. London: B. T. Batsford, 1967.
Tysdahl, J. B. *Joyce and Ibsen: A Study in Literary Influence*. Oslo: Norwegian Universities Press; New York, N.Y.: Humanities Universities Press, 1968.
Ungar, Andras. "Among the Hapsburgs: Arthur Griffith, Stephen Dedalus and the Myth of Bloom." *Twentieth Century Literature* 35.4 (winter 1989): 480–501.
———. "Joyce's Hungarian in *Ulysses*." *James Joyce Quarterly* 27 (fall 1990): 648–50.
Unkeless, Elaine. "Bats and Sanguivorous Bugaboos." *James Joyce Quarterly* 15, 2 (winter, 1978): 128–33.
Valente, Joseph. "The Myth of Sovereignty: Gender in the Literature of Irish Nationalism." *English Literary History* 61 (1994) 189–210.
Van Caspel, Paul. *Bloomers on the Liffey: Eisegetical Readings of Joyce's* Ulysses. Baltimore: John Hopkins University Press, 1986.
Verene, Donald Philip. *Vico's Science of the Imagination*. Ithaca, N.Y.: Cornell University Press, 1981.
Vico, Giambattista. *The New Science*. Trans. T. G. Bergin and M. H. Fisch. Ithaca, N.Y.: Cornell University Press, 1968.
Virgil. *The Aeneid*. Trans. John Conington London: Longman, Green, 1866.
———. *The Aeneid*. Trans. W. F. Jackson Knight. London: Penguin, 1956.
———. *The Aeneid*. Trans. Allen Mandelbaum. New York: Bantam, 1981.

Verstraete, Ginette. *Fragments of the Feminine Sublime in Friedrich Schlegel and James Joyce*. Albany: State University of New York Press, 1998.

Voelker, Joseph C. "'Proteus' and the *Vaticinia* of Marsh's Library: Joyce's Subjunctive Selves." *Eire-Ireland* 14 (1979): 133–41.

Watson, G.J.B. "James Joyce *Ulysses*: Epic Novel." In *The Epic: Developments in Criticism*. Ed. R. P. Draper. London: MacMillan, 1990.

———. "The Politics of *Ulysses*." In *Joyce's* Ulysses: *The Larger Perspective*. Ed. Fritz Senn. Newark: University of Delaware Press, 1987.

Weir, David. *James Joyce and the Art of Mediation*. Ann Arbor: University of Michigan Press, 1996.

White, Hayden. *The Content of Form: Narrative Discourse and Historical Representation*. Baltimore: John Hopkins University Press, 1987.

———. *Metahistory: The Historical Imagination in Nineteenth-Century Europe*. Baltimore: John Hopkins University Press, 1973.

Williams, Trevor L. *Reading Joyce Politically*. Gainesville: University Press of Florida, 1997.

Wittreich, Joseph. "From Pastoral to Prophecy: The Genres of 'Lycidas.'" *Milton Studies* 13 (1979): 59–80.

Woodhouse, A.S.P. *The Heavenly Muse: A Preface to Milton*. Toronto: University of Toronto Press, 1972.

Yeats, W. B. *Autobiographies*. London: Macmillan, 1955.

———. *The Variorum Edition of the Poems of W. B. Yeats*. Ed. P. Allt and R. K. Alspach. New York: Macmillan, 1957.

Ziolkowski, Theodore. *Virgil and the Moderns*. Princeton, N.J.: Princeton University Press, 1993.

Index

Abbas, Joachim, 88
Adams, Robert Martin, 127n. 3
Address: rhetoric of anti-ideological affirmation, 16–17, 36; of serial order warped by "Circe," 58–59, 66; of Stephen and the materiality of print, 28, 36–37, 67, 68; of *Ulysses* as epic, 5–7, 9, 16, 18, 29–30, 34. *See also Coactus volui*; Epic fable; Epic temporality
"AE." *See* Russell, George
Aeneid, The. See Virgil
Aldebaran, 69, 91
Alphabet: Gematria, transposition of numbers and letters, 119–20n. 3; and Milly, 68, 69; and Stephen and Bloom in Ithaca, 72, 74
Anderson, Benedict, 13, 16, 33, 76
Annales, 2
Anti-Semitism: Arthur Griffith, anti-Dreyfusard, 121n. 16; Irish chauvinists at Barney Kiernan's, 56, 100, 121n. 16; pogrom in 1904, Limerick, 121n. 16; Richard Wagner and Meyerbeer's Jewishness, 101; Stephen and the "Ballad of Little Hugh of Lincoln", 30, 72–75, 121n. 16, 121n. 17, 121–22n. 18, 122n. 19. *See also* Jewish identity; Nationalism; Nationality
Arendt, Hannah, 77, 93
Aristotle, 37, 77
Arndt, Ernst Moritz, 102
Auden, W. H., 17
Auerbach, Eric, 10
Aurelius, Marcus, 125n. 14
Austria, 20, 22, 28, 53, 83, 85, 112n. 86, 125n. 14. *See also* Austro-Hungarian Empire
Austrian Succession, War of the, 83–86
Austro-Hungarian Empire, 28, 51, 53, 54, 77, 103; in Arthur Griffith, 20; and British politics, 20; Dublin consulate of, 103. *See also* Austria; Griffith, Arthur; Hapsburg dynasty; *Resurrection of Hungary*

Bakhtin, Mikhail M., 93, 96
Barthes, Roland, 9, 11, 14
Beard, Charles, 2
Beckett, Samuel, 34
Beginnings: ALP, as "111," 119–20n. 3; Epic stance, 16–17; Final rhyme, of Milly and Mulligan, 91–93; Milly, and the letter "A," 68–69; nationhood, 76; numerical variations, 70; Stephen, and alphabetic transposition of "11,000," 70. *See also* Alphabet; Birth; Crown symbolism; Epic fable; Nationality
Bell, Robert H., 124n. 1
Bergson, Henri, 115n. 25
Berkeley, Bishop, 37, 89
Bernstein, J. M., 27
Bier, Jakob Liebman Bier, 101. *See also* Meyerbeer, Giacomo
Biography, and history 29; of nation, 77
Birth, 67, 87, 98; of the English language in *Oxen of the Sun*, 12; of Leopold Bloom, 87, 100; of Lucia Joyce, 27; and Maria Theresa's surprise, 125; Martha's, 69; of Milly Bloom, 30, 69, 75, 76, 95; and national identity, 16, 55; of Rudy Bloom, 54,

Birth—*continued*
  87; of Shakespeare, 87; of Stephen, 69, 87;
  and Stephen's fantasy about midwives,
  69–70; Stephen's infernal fantasy, 69–70;
  and the Virgin Mary, 123–24n. 23; and
  role of Mina Purefoy, 124n. 23. *See also*
  Crown symbolism; Fertility; Figures in
  Joyce's fiction; Mother
Black Mass, 80, 124n. 23
Black panther, 41, 64
Blake, William, 116n. 35
Bloch, Marc, 105
Bloody Sunday, 5
Booker, M. Keith, 81
Bowen, Zack, 33, 74, 119n. 2, 122n. 19
Brewer, E. Cobham, 118n. 36, 127n. 1
Brown, Malcolm, 61, 97
Browne, Count von Maxmillian Ulysses, 31, 81–83, 125n. 8
Bull (Taurus), 42–43, 61, 69. *See also* Beginnings; Birth; Figures in Joyce's fiction, Milly; Figures in Joyce's fiction, Stephen; Lessing, Gotthold Ephraim

Caesar, Julius, 22
Caliban, 47–48, 127n. 15. *See also* Renan, Ernest; Shakespeare
Calliope, 44
Calvin, John, 98
Canovan, Margaret, 17
Catherine the Great, 125n. 8
Celtic, 13, 20, 74, 120n. 5
Celtic Revival, 92
Characters. *See* Figures in Joyce's fiction
Chatman, Seymour, 9
Cheng, Victor, 114n. 13
Christ, Jesus, 38, 56, 72, 100, 102, 127n. 4
Coactus volui, 103, 104, 106
Collingwood, R. G., 2
Comedy, 33, 95–96, 106
Connor, Steven, 59
Constellations, 87, 119n. 2. *See also* Birth; Crown symbolism; Epic fable; Shakespeare
Coronation cities: Budapest, 85; Dublin, 31, 84, 85; Florence, 84, 85, 126n. 15; London, 85; Milan, 84, 85; Szekesfehervar (Alba Regia), 53, 71, 120n. 6; Szombathely, 85; 125n. 14; Tara, 71, 103; Vienna, 85. *See also* Crown symbolism; Epic fable; Figures in Joyce's fiction, Virag, Stefan; Meyerbeer, Giacomo
Coronation day (slang, payday), 90; shaven crown (tonsure) and Buck Mulligan, 88, 126n. 27
Croce, Benedetto, 2
Cromwell, Oliver, 49
Crown of St. Leopold, 22, 28, 112n. 85, 112n. 86. *See also* Crown symbolism; Epic fable; *Resurrection of Hungary*
Crown of St. Stephen, 21, 22, 62, 63, 71, 83, 112n. 85, 112n. 86, 118n. 35. *See also* Crown symbolism; Epic fable; *Resurrection of Hungary*
Crown Prince Rudolf, 53, 117n. 19. *See also* Hapsburg dynasty; Mayerling
Crown symbolism, 87; and coronation of Bloom, 118n. 35, 62; of Franz Joseph, 22, 62, 118; in national monarchies, 21, 63, 71, 118n. 36; and ruby ring, 54, 55, 62, 63. *See also* Birth; Constellations; Epic fable; Figures in Joyce's fiction, Bloom, Rudy; Photography; *Resurrection of Hungary*; *Ruby: Pride of the Ring*

Da Gama, Vasco, 8
Daguerre, 77, 124
Daguerreotype, 53, 68, 70–71, 77. *See also* Epic fable; Fertility; Photography
Dante, Alighieri, 65, 107, 118n. 31, 119n. 40
Darkness, 38, 67, 68, 71, 120n. 4. *See also* Photography
Davis, Robert B., 120n. 5
Davison, Neil Randall, 122n. 18
Day, Robert Adams, 114n. 20
Deane, Seamus, 17, 18, 26, 33, 105
Democracy. *See* Nation
De Montfort, Simon, 49
Deuteronomy, 77
Diderot, Denis, 27
Dilthey, Wilhelm, 2
Don Giovanni, 54
Dostoevsky, Fyodor, 96
Dracula. *See* Stoker, Bram
Dreyfus, Alfred, 121n. 16

Druff, James H. Jr., 124n. 23
Dual Monarchy, 52, 112n. 86. *See also* Austro-Hungarian Empire; Epic fable; Griffith, Arthur
Dublin, 3, 5, 9, 10, 12, 19, 21, 29, 31, 33, 46, 53, 77, 82, 84, 85, 89, 106, 107, 112n. 10
Duffy, Enda, 17
Dulceana, 12

Eagleton, Terry, 112n. 10
Easter 1916, 5, 21
Eco, Umberto, 35
Egg, 70, 71, 76, 123n. 20. *See also* Beginnings; Birth; Fertility; Horace
Eleven, 22, 46, 47, 52, 58, 65, 69, 70, 112n. 85, 115n. 33, 116n. 39, 119n. 3, 120n. 6. *See also* Alphabet; Beginnings
Elijah, 57
Eliot, T. S., 2, 35
Elisha, 87
Ellmann, Richard, 17, 105, 117n. 10, 119n. 38, 121n. 16
Emerson, Ralph Waldo, 29
Emmet, Robert. *See under* Figures in Joyce's fiction
Empson, William, 74
Epic fable: as argument of *Ulysses*, 3, 9–13, 24–34; as closure, 13, 30–31; definition of, 1, 9–10, 11, 15; as historiography, 8, 26–34, 67–68, 84, 105; and national identity, 10, 14, 16, 17, 28–29; Sinn Fein and *The Resurrection of Hungary*, 21–22, 28–29, 50–52, 58–59, 112. *See also* Crown symbolism; Epic rhyme; Griffith, Arthur
Epic performance: as communal standard, 11, 13, 31, 34, 92–93; and traditions, 3–4, 83, 93
Epic rhyme, of *Ulysses*, 31, 77, 90–93, 94
Epic temporality: future orientation, 16, 17, 76–77, 78, 79, 92; pastness, 1, 3, 6, 9, 11, 12, 13, 15, 16, 18–19, 30, 35, 36, 49, 51, 56, 58, 83, 103–6; present-mindedness, 1, 8, 11, 13, 15, 16, 19, 28–33, 35–36, 83, 86, 90–91, 92, 103–6
Eve, 76, 123n. 23
Exile, 11, 17, 22, 33, 40, 51, 52, 58, 80, 82, 92, 97, 107

Fabula, 9. *See also* Epic fable
Fairhall, James, 21, 22
Family: disrupted by Stephen's ballad, 72, 121–22; grandfathers in, 56, 83, 105; illegitimacy in, 95; link to historiography, 7, 83; national feeling, analogy with, 52. *See also* Anti-Semitism
Faust, 8
Febvre, Lucien, 105
Fertility: and Milly's first nine-month cycle, in *Ulysses*, 76, 77; and Stephen, ruby eggs, 70, 71
Fevre, Lucien, 105
Figures in Joyce's fiction: ALP, 80; Bloom, Leopold, 3, 6, 7, 9, 12–14, 16, 18, 19, 21, 22, 23, 27, 28, 29, 30, 31, 49–58, 61–67, 69, 70, 72–78, 80–87, 89, 90, 94–97, 99–103, 105, 106, 112n. 10, 115n. 33, 118n. 32, 118n. 35, 119n. 2, 119n. 3, 122n. 19, 123n. 22, 124n. 5, 127n. 3; Bloom, Milly, 9, 30–33, 67–72, 73, 74, 76–80, 89, 90, 92, 95, 119n. 2, 123n. 21, 123n. 22 (as Millicent 67, 68, 70, 73, 94); Bloom, Molly, 54, 63, 74–76, 95, 98, 119n. 3, 122n. 19; Bloom, Rudy, 9, 29, 51, 53–55, 61, 63, 65, 67, 70, 75, 87, 119n. 3, 122n. 19; Bloom, Rudolph, 51, 53, 56, 61, 73, 85, 86, 87; Boylan, Blazes, 54, 63, 119n. 2; Breen, Denis, 54; Breen, Josie Powell, 54, 63; Caffrey, Cissy, 124; Campbell, Foxy, 88; Carr, Private, 63, 134n. 5; Citizen, 21, 51, 55, 56, 100, 101, 122n. 19; Clifford, Martha, 68, 119n. 2; Cohen, Bella, 63, 106; Cohen, Bello, 63; Cohen, Ruby, 63; Conroy, Gabriel, 96; Cunningham, Martin, 9, 21; Deasy, Garrett, 39, 41, 42, 90; Dedalus, Stephen, 3, 4, 6, 7, 9, 12, 13, 14, 16, 18, 19, 20, 21–23, 25–31, 35–48, 49–50, 52, 57, 63–65, 67–76, 78, 80–84, 86–88, 90, 97, 102, 103, 114n. 20, 115n. 29, 116n. 38, 120n. 4, 121n. 16, 122n. 18, 123n. 23, 127n. 15; Dedalus, Simon, 41, 49, 116n. 2, 119n. 2; Dedalus, May Goulding, 64; Donovan, 40; Driscoll, Mary, 123n. 22; Eglinton, John, 70, 116n. 35; Emmet, Robert, 96, 99, 100; Farrell, Cashel Boyle O'Connor Fitzmaurice

Figures in Joyce's fiction—*continued*
Tisdall, 33, 61, 62, 103–6; Hainau, Herr Hauptmann, 95, 127n. 3; Hughes, Harry Little, 73–75; Hugh of Lincoln, 30, 121n. 17; Kiernan, Barney, 55, 56, 82, 83; Lanternjaws, 88; Lenehan, 21; Macdowell, Gerty, 120n. 8, 122n. 19; Moore, George, 12; Mulligan, Buck, 31, 47, 48, 50, 63, 80, 87–90, 92, 118n. 32, 124n. 1; Mulvey, Lieutenant, 95; Nolan, John Wyse, 19, 21, 82, 83; O'Molloy, J. J., 121n. 6, 123n. 22; Power, Jack, 21; Purefoy, Mina, 124n. 23; Russell, George, ("AE"), 70, 120n. 5; Russell, O'Neil, l, 12; Russell, Thomas, 70, 71; Sigerson, Dr. George, 12; Stephens, James, 12; Talbot, 44, 45, 115n. 27; Temple, 88; Virag, Lipoti, 29, 33, 55–57, 60–63, 65, 66, 100, 102–6, 118n. 31, 118n. 32; Virag, Rudolf, 9, 29, 53, 55, 56, 63, 86; Virag, Stefan, 53, 67, 71; Zoe, 106
Flaubert, Gustave, 26, 66
Florence, 16, 84, 85, 126n. 15
Ford, Jane, 123n. 22
Fowler, Alastair, 115n. 33
France, 2, 39, 82, 83
Frederick the Great, 83
French, Marolyn, 66, 122n. 19
Friedman, Lawrence M., 11
Frye, Northrop, 95

Gadamer, Hans Georg, 65, 104, 119, 128
Gaelic League, 49
Genre, 5, 8, 9, 26, 34, 40, 44, 45, 93, 94
Geschichte, 78, 79
Gifford, Don, and Robert J. Seidman, 39, 47, 103, 113n. 11, 118n. 36, 124n. 23, 125n. 5, 125n. 8, 126n. 27, 127n. 3
Gladstone, William Ewart, 20
Gordon, John, 106
Gose, Elliot B., 66
Grant, Ulysses, 125n. 6
Greece, 16, 44
Greek, 41, 43, 44, 69, 88, 106, 114–15n. 22
Greene, Thomas M., 106
Gregory, Lady Augusta, 51
Grenville, J.A.S., 102
Griffith, Arthur, 5, 6, 7, 8, 19, 20, 21, 22, 28, 29, 31, 50–53, 71, 81–83, 85, 86, 109n. 18, 118n. 35, 121n. 16. *See also The Resurrection of Hungary* and under Epic fable; Joyce, James

Handwerke, Gary J., 16, 113n. 5
Hapsburg dynasty, 19, 20, 21, 22, 29, 51, 52, 53, 54, 53, 82, 83, 84, 85, 104, 111n. 72, 117n. 19, 125n. 8, 125n. 14, 126n. 16; Charles VI, 85; Crown Prince Rudolf, 53, 117n. 19; Franz Joseph, 22, 54, 62, 118n. 35; Maria Theresa, 82, 83, 84, 85, 86, 125n. 8. *See also* Mayerling
Hatikvah, 72
Haynau, Baron Julius Jacob, 127n. 3
Hebrew, 57, 69, 72, 74, 80, 118n. 35, 121n. 6
Hegel, Georg Wilhelm Friedrich, 7, 8, 14
Henke, Suzanne, 74
Himmelfarb, Gertrude, 59
Hintze, Otto, 2
Historiography, 1, 2, 17, 18, 28–29; and allegory, 2, 13, 28–29, 53, 29, 53, 59, 76–77, 86, 96, 112n. 86; basic premises of, 2, 12, 28, 51, 57, 58, 59; and "Circe," 58–61; and "Cyclops," 55, 57–58; epic distance as alternative to nationalist values, 6, 7, 8, 9, 12–13, 18, 34; *Geschichte, Historie* distinction, 78–79; and Hegel, 7, 14; of Irish nationalists, 5–6, 10, 17–18; Ranke, 95, 101; Standish O'Grady, 57; Stephen Dedalus, 3, 18–19, 36, 86; as *Ulysses*' distinctive address, 16, 18, 24–25, 58–59, 79, 80, 85, 92. *See also* Address; *Coactus volui*; Epic fable; Epic temporality
History: present-mindedness, 1, 2, 3, 7, 9, 12, 16, 18, 60, 106. *See also* Literature, as history
Hobson, Bulmer, 21
Hofheinz, Thomas C., 107
Hogan, Patrick Holm, 115n. 27
Holy Roman Emperors, 125n. 14
Homer, 10, 28, 36, 43, 76, 125n. 10; and Achilles, 27; and Antiphates, 123; *The Iliad*, 123n. 20; and Odysseus, 83; *The Odyssey*, 3, 10, 30, 95, 125n. 10; and Polyphemus, 83; and Tiresias, 107. *See also Ulysses* chapters; Troy

Home Rule, 20, 98
Hopkins, G. M., 3, 109n. 9
Horace, 76, 92, 123n. 20
Horton, T. W., 114n. 20
Hughes, H. Stuart, 91
Hungarian language, 56, 59, 117, 120. See also Coronation cities; Magyar
Hungary, 19, 20, 21, 22, 28, 52, 53, 63, 71, 83, 84, 85, 112n. 86, 118n. 35, 127n. 4. See also Austro-Hungarian Empire; Crown symbolism; Epic fable; *Resurrection of Hungary*
Hyde, Douglas, 114n. 20

Imitation, 36, 106, 112n. 10
Irish Brigade, 83, 125n. 9
Irish Civil War, 102
Irish Free State, 5, 7, 81
Irish Literary Revival, 49, 57
Irish Nationalism. See Nationalism, in Ireland; Nationality. See also under Epic fable; Joyce, James
Irish Volunteers, 20

Jacobus, Lee A., 115n. 20
Jameson, Frederick, 10, 110n. 30
Jenkins, Keith, 11, 12
Jesus. See Christ, Jesus
Jewish exile in Babylon, 11
Jewish identity: and Bloom, 19, 20, 29, 30, 56, 72, 73, 75, 100; and Milly, 30, 72; and non-Jewish Jews, 100, and Stephen, 122n. 19, 121n. 17. See also Anti-Semitism
Jew's harp, 28
Joyce, James: adaption by, of epic to historiography, 76, 79, 80, 107, 118n. 35, 118–19n. 36; artistry of, 10, 23, 27, 34, 35; concern of, with history in *Dubliners*, 3–5, 16 (in *Portrait*, 3; in *Ulysses*, 3, 16, 27, 85, 92); and epic task of nation-formation, 12, 13, 15, 16, 17, 92, 110n. 30; and Flaubertian irony, 26, 66; and Hapsburg Trieste, 15, 22–23, 52, 53, 112n. 86, 117n. 10.; and ironies in rendering Stephen, 26, 27, 34, 35–47; opinion on Sinn Fein, 5–6, 21, 49, 52, 109–10n. 18. See also Epic fable; Epic temporality; Griffith, Arthur; Historiography; Trieste
—Texts of: *A Portrait of the Artist as a Young Man*, 3, 4, 5, 6, 13, 14, 26, 28, 29, 30, 31, 35, 36, 37, 44, 45, 46, 47, 61, 67, 69, 70, 81, 82, 86, 91, 106, 115n. 29, 122n. 19; "The Dead," 16, 73, 89, 96, 101; "Drama and Life," 15, 62; *Dubliners*, 3–5, 16, 96, 102; *Finnegans Wake*, 80, 91, 107; *Giacomo Joyce*, 121; "Ireland, Isle of Saints and Sages," 49, 127n. 2; *Paris notebook*, 71; *Stephen Hero*, 27, 40; *Ulysses*, 1–19, 21–33, 35, 36, 38, 40, 43–45, 48–53, 67, 70, 74, 76, 78, 80–84, 86, 87, 91–96, 101–4, 106, 107, 110n. 30, 112n. 86, 112n. 10, 113n. 9, 115n. 25, 117n. 18, 122n. 19, 125n. 6, 126n. 27, 127n. 15. See also Figures in Joyce's fiction; *Ulysses* chapters
Joyce, P. W., 46
Joyce, Stanislaus, 5, 52
Judaism: Bloom sings Zionist anthem, 72; Hebrew psalm in translation, as opening of Telemachus, 80; Moses, benediction on Milly, 77
Judas, 72
Judea, 72
Julius Caesar. See Caesar, Julius

Kaczvinsky, Donald P., 116–17n. 39
Kant, Immanuel, 58
Kantoriwicz, Ernst H., 115n. 26
Kearney, Richard, 92
Keats, John, 29
Kenner, Hugh, 3, 46, 80, 84, 115n. 33, 124n. 1
Kettle, Tom, 19
King, Edward, and John Milton, 46
Knight, W. F. Jackson, 42
Kohn, Hans, 128n. 20
Kun, Bela, 63
Kunstlerroman, 14, 19, 26, 35, 74

LaCapra, Dominck, 95
Lamprecht, Karl, 2
Laocoön. See Lessing, Gotthold Ephraim
Latin, 37, 39, 71, 76, 80, 87, 88, 118n. 31, 123n. 20, 126n. 27
Lawrence, Karen, 11, 66, 78

Leaves of Grass, 8
Leda, 76
Lemaire, Joseph Henri, 39
Lessing, Gotthold Ephraim, 38, 40–42
Levin, Jonathan, 79
Lewis, C. S., 16
Lewis, Wyndham, 1
Literature, as history, 3, 78, 79, 91–92. *See also* Address; Epic fable; Epic temporality; Historiography; Joyce, James; Milton, John; Narrative coherence; Pound, Ezra
Little Review, 126n. 27
Lloyd, David, 103
Lombardy, 85, 126n. 15
Louis XIV, 113
Lukacs, George, 13
Lusiads, The, 4, 8, 9
Luther, Martin, 98

Madame Bovary, 26
Madtes, Richard, 126
Maeterlinck, Maurice, 72
Magyar, 20, 21, 117. *See also* Hungary
Mandelbaum, Maurice, 34
Manganiello, Dominique, 17, 118n. 35, 121n. 16
Maria Theresa, 82–86, 125n. 8. *See also* Austria; Austro-Hungarian Empire; Hapsburg dynasty; Spanish Succession, War of the
Martz, Louis, 45
Marx, Karl, 28, 100
Mary, Queen of Heaven, 119n. 2. *See also* Figures in Joyce's fiction, Millicent; Virgin Mary
Mary, Queen of Scots, 118n. 36,
Mayerling, 53, 54, 117n. 19; Crown Prince Rudolf, 53, 54, 117n. 19; Larisch-Wallersee, Countess Marie, 54; Vetsera Maria, 54
McCarthy, Patrick, 116n. 38
McKenna, Stephen, 120n. 5
Meinecke, Frederick, 27
Mendelssohn, Moses, 100–1
Mercadante, Guisseppe, 32, 96, 100, 101; *The Seven Last Words*, 96, 97, 100, 101
Meyerbeer, Giacomo, 32, 96–98, 101; *Les Huguenots*, 97–99; "O beau pays de la Touraine," 98; Raoul de Nangis, 98, St. Bris, 98–99; Tara, Tara, 97, 103; Valentine 98–99. *See also* Crown symbolism
Milbank, John, 32
Miller, Perry, 2
Millicent. *See* Figures in Joyce's fiction, Milly (as Millicent)
Milton, John, 27, 36, 115n. 31, 115n. 32 116n. 35; *Lycidas*, 28, 44–46, 115n. 33; *Paradise Lost*, 28, 116n. 34
Mimesis, 31–32
Minogue, K. R., 23
Mirror, 36, 47, 88–90
Mitchel, John, 109n. 18
Moore, George. *See under* Figures in Joyce's fiction
Moran, D. P., 17
Moretti, Franco, 8, 13
Moses, 8, 71, 77
Mother: Bloom's non-Jewish, 100–1; Stephen's guilt over death of, 39, 41, 46, 64, 89. *See also* Riddle
Mozart, Wolfgang Amadeus, 97

Nadel, Ira, 120n. 3, 121n. 16, 121n. 17, 122n. 18
Nairn, Tom, 5, 36
Napoleon Bonaparte, 63, 102, 125n. 14
Narrative, 9, 10, 11, 12, 14, 67, 75, 76, 77, 78, 112, 115
Narrative coherence: and epic, 1, 81; and historiography, 1, 6, 79, 105; and Milly Bloom, 30, 78; and national vision, 1, 76; and serial order, 76–77, 87, 92
Narrative design. *See* Epic fable
Narrative progression and style: in *Portrait*, 35, 36. *See also Ulysses* chapters
Nation: Bloom's definition of, 55; democracy and, 77, 92, 95; epic rhyme and, 93; and theme of natality, in *Portrait* and in *Ulysses*, 16, 25–26, 30, 76–77
Nationalism: as ideology, 49, 103, 106; in Ireland 5, 6, 10, 15, 16, 17, 18, 49–50; as threat to cosmopolitan states, 53. *See also* Historiography; Nationality
Nationality: as communal identity, 1, 2, 16,

17, 28, 29, 30, 36, 52, 77, 121n. 6; in epic address of *Ulysses*, 5–7, 9, 16, 18, 29–30, 34; as epic fable, 13–14; forgetfulness of, 101–3; as formative myth—William Tell, Alexander Nevsky, Joan of Arc, 11; and internationality, 51–52; as self-expression, 28, 29, 76, 103; as transcendent reality, 15, 16, 18; treatment in Ulysses critically appraised, 17–18. *See also* Renan, Ernest; Yeats, William Butler
Nietzsche, Friedrich, 18, 78
Nighttown, 61, 106, 122n. 19. *See also Ulysses* chapters, Circe
Nolan, Emer, 5–6, 17, 108–9n. 18
Nostos, 31, 122n. 18. *See also Ulysses* chapters

Oakeshott, Michael, 59–60, 86
O'Connell, Daniel, 103
O'Donnell, Leopold, 82
Odyssey, The. See Homer
O'Grady, Standish, 51, 57
Operas, 32, 33; *Martha*, 119n. 2. *See also* Meyerbeer, Giacomo; Mercadante, Guisseppe
Ovid, 115n. 33

Pannonia, 125n. 14
Paradowski, Jan, 107
Parallax, 7, 90, 91
Parnell, Charles Stewart, 19, 92, 106
Parrington, Vernon, 2
Partner, Nancy F., 105
Pastness. *See* Epic temporality
Pater, Walter, 46, 114n. 20
Peake, C. H., 74
Pearse, Padraic, 19, 33
Pentateuch, 9
Perl, J. M., 30, 86, 95
Photography: limitations of, as representational mode, 70–71, 120n. 8; and Milly, as "photo," 67, 89, 120n. 8; and mimesis in *Portrait*, 30; symbol of serial infinity in "Penelope," 30; as symbol of writing with light and Milly, 68, 120n. 4 (and Mulligan, 89–90; and Stephen Dedalus 67–68, 120n. 4). *See also* Daguerreotype

Plato, 89
Plotinus, 120n. 5
Political history, 1, 2, 7, 59. *See also* Griffith, Arthur; *Resurrection of Hungary*
Popov, Nebosja, 92
Popper, Amalia, 121n. 16
Pound, Ezra, 2, 5, 38, 91, 92, 126n. 32
Power, Arthur, 23
Propp, Vladmir, 9

Ranke, Leopold von, 95, 101
Raoul. *See* Meyerbeer, Giacomo
Ree, Jonathan, 52
Reizbaum, Marolyn, 74
Renan, Ernest, 93, 101–2, 127n. 15
Resurrection of Hungary, The: allegorized in *Ulysses*, 22, 28–30, 58–59; attributed to Bloom, 19, 21; contemporary reception of, 19, 20; referred to, in *Portrait*, 29; *Ulysses*, as critical commentary on, 29, 50, 118n. 35, 121n. 16. *See also* Epic fable
Reynolds, Mary, 118n. 31, 119n. 40
Rhyme. *See* Epic rhyme
Rickard, John S., 31, 105, 120n. 3
Riddles, 46, 116n. 38, 116–17n. 39
Rilke, Rainer Maria, 16, 111n. 60
Robinson, James H., 2
Rome, 2, 3, 8, 9, 16, 22, 43, 44, 51, 125n. 14
Romulus, 22
Ruby (color), 69; (gem), 54, 63
Ruby: Pride of the Ring, 54, 63
Russell, George ("AE"). *See* Figures in Joyce's fiction, Russell, George

Saint Bartholomew's Day Massacre, 98–99, 101–3
Saint Leopold. *See* Crown of St. Leopold
Saint Stephen. *See* Crown of St. Stephen
Samuel, Daniel, 115n. 34
Sarsfield, Sir Patrick, 82
Schahriar, Sultan, 77. *See also* Scheherezade
Scheherezade, 77, 78. *See also* Figures in Joyce's fiction, Milly
Schlegel, F. W., 36, 113n. 23
Schmoller, Gustave, 2
Schneidau, Herbert N., 26, 115n. 23
Schork, R. J., 37, 38

Schwartz, Daniel, 122n. 18
Schwartz, Heinrich, 120n. 4
Seidel, Michael, 28, 72, 121n. 18
Septimus, Severus, 125n. 14
Shakespeare: as constellation, 87; and Anne Hathaway, and firedrake, 69; Hamlet and, 27, 50, 54. *See also* Constellations
Sinn Fein. *See under* Epic fable; Joyce, James
Smart, C., 123n. 20
Smith, Anthony, 16, 92
Smith, James Penny, 120n. 5
Socrates, 72, 78, 120n. 4
Sodom, 89
Sophocles, 104
Spinoza, Baruch, 100
Spoo, Robert, 9, 12, 18, 21
State: epic significance of, 4, 6, 10, 14, 97; and historiography, 106
Stephen I, King of Hungary, 71
Stephens, James. *See* Figures in Joyce's fiction, Stephens, James
Stoker, Bram, 114n. 20
Sultan, Stanley, 122n. 19
Synge, John Millington, 105
Szombathely. *See* Coronation cities

Taylor, Archer, 116n. 38
Telemachiad, 4, 36, 44, 45, 81. *See also Ulysses* chapters
Tennyson, Lord, Alfred, 3, 51, 109n. 10
Thom, Martin, 102
Thompson, E. P., 24
Thornton, Weldon, 116n. 38
Tiresias. *See under* Homer
Tonsure, 87
Tracy, Robert, 118n. 35
Trieste, 15, 22, 51, 52, 112n. 86, 119n. 38, 120n. 6
Tristram Shandy, Life and Opinions of, 76
Troy, 3, 38, 43, 44, 115, 123, 128. *See also* Homer
Turner, Frederick Jackson, 2
Tuscany, 84, 126n. 15

Ulysses (Homer). *See* Homer: *The Iliad;* and Odysseus; *The Odyssey*

Ulysses (Joyce character). *See* Browne, Count von Maximillian Ulysses
Ulysses (Joyce) chapters: Aeolus, 119n. 2; Calypso, 90; Circe, 50, 58–63, 66, 70, 75, 91, 95, 103, 106, 116n. 39, 118n. 32, 119n. 40, 123n. 22, 124n. 23, 124n. 25; Cyclops, 50, 51, 55–57, 83, 96, 100, 102, 121n. 16, 123n. 20, 125n. 10; Eumaeus, 23, 75, 97; Ithaca, 28, 53, 72, 75, 77, 78, 90, 95, 121n. 17; Nestor, 28, 36; Oxen of the Sun, 12, 61, 68, 115, 123–24n. 24; Penelope, 26, 30, 31, 75, 80, 89, 125n. 6; Proteus, 28, 36, 37, 40, 67, 69, 88; Scylla and Charybdis, 12, 123n. 20, 127n. 15; Sirens, 119n. 2; Telemachus, 26, 31, 36, 47, 80, 84, 87, 88, 90
Ungar, Andras, 111n. 72, 117n. 18
Unionists, 20
United Irishman, 19

Van Caspel, Paul, 122n. 19
Vico, Giambattista, 25, 32, 33, 34, 104
Villanelle, 122n. 19
Virgil, 2, 3, 6, 8, 9, 16, 38, 41, 42, 43, 50, 65, 114–15n. 22, 119n. 40; Aeneas, 8, 22, 27, 38, 43; *The Aeneid,* 2, 3, 4, 8, 9, 16, 22, 38, 41, 114–15n. 22; Anchises, 3; Laocoön, 40, 41. *See also* Lessing, Gotthold Ephraim
Virgin Mary, 41, 112n. 85, 123–24n. 23. *See also* Mary, Queen of Heaven

Wagner, Richard, 101
Watson, G.J.B., 26, 99, 112n. 10
Weir, David, 6, 10, 66
White, Hayden, 1, 2, 67, 91
Wilde, Oscar, 47
Wild geese, 82
Winckelmann, Johann, 41, 42
Wittelsbach, 54
Wittreich, Joseph, 115n. 29
Wordsworth, William, 27, 46

Yeats, William Butler, 16, 17, 18, 20, 24, 33, 64, 92, 107, 120n. 5

Zamparetti, Anton, 52
Zionism, 72, 121n. 4
Zurich, 117n. 10

Andras Ungar is an assistant professor at the Liberal Arts College of Concordia University in Montreal.

The Florida James Joyce Series
Edited by Zack Bowen

The Autobiographical Novel of Co-Consciousness: Goncharov, Woolf, and Joyce, by Galya Diment (1994)
Bloom's Old Sweet Song: Essays on Joyce and Music, by Zack Bowen (1995)
Joyce's Iritis and the Irritated Text: The Dis-lexic Ulysses, by Roy Gottfried (1995)
Joyce, Milton, and the Theory of Influence, by Patrick Colm Hogan (1995)
Reauthorizing Joyce, by Vicki Mahaffey (paperback edition, 1995)
Shaw and Joyce: "The Last Word in Stolentelling," by Martha Fodaski Black (1995)
Bely, Joyce, Döblin: Peripatetics in the City Novel, by Peter I. Barta (1996)
Jocoserious Joyce: The Fate of Folly in Ulysses, by Robert H. Bell (paperback edition, 1996)
Joyce and Popular Culture, edited by R. B. Kershner (1996)
Joyce and the Jews: Culture and Texts, by Ira B. Nadel (paperback edition, 1996)
Narrative Design in Finnegans Wake: *The Wake Lock Picked,* by Harry Burrell (1996)
Gender in Joyce, edited by Jolanta W. Wawrzycka and Marlena G. Corcoran (1997)
Latin and Roman Culture in Joyce, by R. J. Schork (1997)
Reading Joyce Politically, by Trevor L. Williams (1997)
Advertising and Commodity Culture in Joyce, by Garry Leonard (1998)
Greek and Hellenic Culture in Joyce, by R. J. Schork (1998)
Joyce, Joyceans, and the Rhetoric of Citation, by Eloise Knowlton (1998)
Joyce's Music and Noise: Theme and Variation in His Writings, by Jack W. Weaver (1998)
Reading Derrida Reading Joyce, by Alan Roughley (1999)
Joyce through the Ages: A Nonlinear View, edited by Michael Patrick Gillespie (1999)
Chaos Theory and James Joyce's Everyman, by Peter Francis Mackey (1999)
Joyce's Comic Portrait, by Roy Gottfried (2000)
Joyce and Hagiography: Saints Above! by R. J. Schork (2000)
Voices and Values in Joyce's Ulysses, by Weldon Thornton (2000)
The Dublin Helix: The Life of Language in Joyce's Ulysses, by Sebastian D. G. Knowles (2001)
Joyce Beyond Marx: History and Desire in Ulysses *and* Finnegans Wake, by Patrick McGee (2001)
Joyce's Metamorphosis, by Stanley Sultan (2001)
Joycean Temporalities: Debts, Promises, and Countersignatures, by Tony Thwaites (2001)
Joyce and the Victorians, by Tracey Teets Schwarze (2002)
Joyce's Ulysses *as National Epic: Epic Mimesis and the Political History of the Nation State,* by Andras Ungar (2002)

www.ingramcontent.com/pod-product-compliance
Lightning Source LLC
Chambersburg PA
CBHW020935230426
43666CB00008B/1691